The Future of European Alliance Systems

Also of Interest

**NATO--The Next Thirty Years: The Changing Political, Economic, and Military Setting,* edited by Kenneth A. Myers

Communist Nations' Military Aid, John F. Copper and Daniel S. Papp

**Managing U.S.-Soviet Rivalry: Problems of Crisis Prevention,* Alexander L. George

East Germany and the Warsaw Alliance: The Politics of Détente, N. Edwina Moreton

Arms Control in Transition: Proceedings of the Livermore Arms Control Conference, edited by Warren Heckrotte and George Smith

Soviet Allies: The Warsaw Pact and the Issue of Reliability, edited by Daniel N. Nelson

Brezhnev's Peace Program: A Study of Soviet Domestic Political Process and Power, P.M.E. Volten

Arms Control and Defense Postures in the 1980s, edited by Richard Burt

Communist Armies in Politics: Their Origins and Development, edited by Jonathan R. Adelman

**The Soviet Art of War,* Harriet Fast Scott and William F. Scott

**Foreign Policies of Northern Europe,* edited by Bengt Sundelius

Nuclear Deterrence in U.S.-Soviet Relations, Keith B. Payne

**The Armed Forces of the USSR,* second edition, revised and updated, Harriet Fast Scott and William F. Scott

**Eastern Europe in the 1980s,* edited by Stephen Fischer-Galati

*Available in hardcover and paperback.

Westview Special Studies in International Relations

The Future of European Alliance Systems: NATO and the Warsaw Pact

edited by Arlene Idol Broadhurst

Recent events in Afghanistan and Poland, as well as the Twenty-Sixth Party Congress, have raised questions about the future direction of the Warsaw Treaty Organization. Similarly, pressing issues such as the placement of long-range theater nuclear forces, burden sharing, and threats to the security of Europe from peripheral areas (for instance, the Middle East) call attention to the urgent need for a re-examination of priorities and strategies within the North Atlantic Treaty Organization. This book addresses these military considerations, as well as the political and social dimensions of European security. The distinguished authors discuss four major subjects--European security perspectives, NATO, the Warsaw Pact, and resource allocations for defense--within the framework of comparative alliance approaches. Their detailed descriptions of current problems, diversities, and discussions within the two alliance systems offer insight into the differing ideas of what constitutes security.

Dr. Arlene Idol Broadhurst is engaged in research in Montreal, Canada. From 1978 to 1981 she was assistant professor of international relations in the German Program of the University of Southern California (Munich). She has also been a lecturer in international relations and government in Munich for the University of Maryland and instructor in political theory for the International Communication Agency in Madrid.

To
Garth, Michael and Anna
for whom the world must
be made more secure

The Future of European Alliance Systems: NATO and the Warsaw Pact

edited by Arlene Idol Broadhurst

Westview Press / Boulder, Colorado

Westview Special Studies in International Relations

Published in 1982 in the United States of America by
Westview Press, Inc.
5500 Central Avenue
Boulder, Colorado 80301
Frederick A. Praeger, President and Publisher

Library of Congress Catalog Card Number 82-50954
ISBN 0-86531-413-6

Composition for this book was provided by the editor
Printed and bound in the United States of America

Contents

PART THREE
THE WARSAW TREATY ORGANISATION

PART FOUR
ECONOMICS AND DEFENCE

Tables

Acknowledgements

In May 1981, the University of Southern California, the U.S. Army Russian Institute, and the North Atlantic Treaty Organization sponsored an international symposium on the future of the European alliance systems. In addition to the contributors to this volume, the symposium deliberations were assisted by the following discussants: Dr. Hannes Adomeit (Stiftung Wissenschaft und Politik), Mr. Joseph J. Baritz (U.S. Army Russian Institute) Dr. Dieter Braun (Stiftung Wissenschaft und Politik), Mr. James Brown (Radio Free Europe), Dr. William E. Griffith (Massachusetts Institute of Technology), Professor Dr. Gerhard Schmitt-Rink (Ruhr Universität), and Dr. Douglas T. Stuart (University of Southern California). Mr. Arnold Hottinger (Neue Züricher Zeitung) and Mr. Uwe Nerlich (Stiftung Wissenschaft und Politik) also contributed.

LTC Geoffrey Kleb, Commander of the U.S. Army Russian Institute, and his able staff, particularly Major Andrew Hulze, Director of Education, were instrumental in assuring the success of the symposium.

A dedicated staff at the University of Southern California in Munich endured the travails of symposium organization with graceful fortitude and equanimity. It was a pleasure to be associated with Lois Galpert, Linda Koenig, Judy Martin, Bill Nigh, Mary Sue Packer, Annette Reiserer, and Ray Russell.

Dr. Douglas T. Stuart, Director of the USC Germany Program, faculty colleague, and friend, adopted a policy of non-intervention with regard to the planning and organization of the symposium--a rare gesture of sensible program management. Dr. Lawrence L. Whetten was very helpful in planning the format of the symposium and I am also grateful to Dr. William Tow for many useful suggestions.

Alice Trembour and Kathy Wilson at Westview Press provided invaluable guidance as the book progressed toward completion. Allan Alio of Studio Alio, Montreal, prepared the statistical graphs and Mary Kapadia of MK Word Processing Ltd., Montreal, gave cheerful and much-needed assistance with typing and processing the manuscript.

A special thanks to Major James Reams, U.S. Army Russian Institute, for presenting to the symposium the best student paper on NATO. And vielen Dank to the students in Frankfurt, Munich, Augsburg, and Garmisch for their insightful comments and lively reactions to my theory lectures.

A.I.B.

Editor's Note:

In recognition of the wondrous diversity of the English language, American and British spelling have been retained for this volume. For example, the reader will find 'organization' or 'organisation', 'defense' or 'defence', 'toward' or 'towards', 'Romania' or 'Rumania', 'center' or 'centre', etc., depending upon each author's preference.

Introduction

Part I consists of three chapters which address the question of European security from the perspective of Eastern and Western Europe. These three authors focus on both abstract concepts and concrete realities in the context of shifting European perceptions and attitudes, not only toward miliary defense, but also toward the fundamental political and economic relationships between Western Europe and the United States, between Eastern Europe and the Soviet Union, and between Eastern Europe and Western Europe.

With his usual iconoclastic candor, HEDLEY BULL rejects the idea that there is a body of theory which relates to alliances. In a sweeping and erudite discussion of alliance types, obligations, benefits and drawbacks of alliance membership, the idea of natural allies and the role of alliances in relation to the maintenance of the international order, Professor Bull concludes that while there is nothing very profound in theoretical writings about alliances, these concepts do help define and compare different kinds of alliances. He discusses the distinctive features of NATO and the Warsaw Pact, the reasons for their longevity, the forces of disintegration in NATO, and the future direction for European security. Although threat perceptions of the Soviet Union have remained stable, the core of perceived interests among NATO members has been weakened by European fear of entanglement, neo-isolation in the United States, by a shift in relative power from the United States toward Western Europe, and by collision between American and European public opinion: hence European lack of support for American policies is based not upon anti-Americanism, but rather on "considered rejection of the premises on which American policy rests". Western Europe must become less dependent upon nuclear weapons, particularly those controlled by the United States; it must increase its conventional forces; seek a more prominent role for Europeans in the NATO command structure; and move toward greater unity in foreign policy. In the long run, there is no reason to doubt that Western Europe can balance Soviet power without American power.

MARTIN EDMONDS analyzes the military and economic dimensions of the security situation in Europe in the context of his assertion that security is neither a matter of military provision nor semantics, but requires a much broader definition. He assesses the strengths and weaknesses of NATO, and concludes that the military balance has not shifted significantly, that NATO is as strong as ever in military terms, and that the European option of an all-European security force in military terms fades with each passing year. With clear insight, he describes the dilemma created for the Europeans by the convergence of their difficulty in meeting defense commitments with the simultaneous desire of the United States to expand NATO's role in peripheral areas. In economic terms, the recovery of Europe has led to greater welfare services rather than to increased defense spending, and economic strength is paramount for the Western Europeans; hence the importance of detente. With regard to the political dimension, there has been a profound shift in political attitudes in the younger generation of Europe, expressed in acceptance of European socialist parties which emphasize negotiation, confidence-building measures, arms control agreements, and trade and technical assistance with the Soviet Union and Eastern Europe rather than the military dimension of earlier East-West confrontation. The conclusion, then, is that military means are not sufficient to guarantee security in an interdependent world so the United States must maintain a military role in Europe and it must also accept expanded European political initiatives. What is required is not a new set of institutions for security in Europe, but rather a change in American attitudes.

Chapter 3, written by the editor, examines theoretical concepts developed to explain the formation and disintegration of alliances in relation to the specific cases of NATO and the Warsaw Pact. Common goals; size; external threat; promise of economic, military or political gain; restraint of allies; preservation of the status quo; ideological and cultural similarities; coercion; leadership; and geographical dispersion are discussed as factors, first in the formation of these two alliances and, second, as factors in their potential disintegration. Focus is upon the interests and concerns of the Eastern and Western Europeans rather than upon the interests and concerns of the two superpowers. This perspective stresses the advantages which both sides of Europe have gained from their respective memberships in NATO and the Warsaw Pact. The conclusion suggests that most abstract propositions have limited applicability to NATO and the Warsaw Pact because they were generated from the superpower perspective rather than from intra-alliance and cross-alliance perspectives. The reality behind theoretical abstraction is the need for both alliance leaders to recognize and accept the national and foreign policy independence of their allies.

Part II of the volume focusses directly on the North Atlantic Treaty Organization: the current state of allied relations, the contemporary issues which strain its cohesion, the impact of forces and events beyond its traditional purview, its military and political purposes, and the impact upon it of non-governmental actors. Four chapters, written by an Englishman, a Frenchman, a Canadian, and an American, reflect remarkable variance in perception and emphasis; yet the common and unifying theme of security in Europe and how to ensure it remains salient.

BRIGADIER KENNETH HUNT provides a strong and realistic statement of support for NATO. In bold affirmation of its importance, he writes that there is no alternative to NATO, that its continuation is desired by member governments, that there is an identity of interest within the Alliance, and that there is a need for U.S. forces in Europe. Within the framework of this conviction that European security rests fundamentally on Atlantic unity, Brigadier Hunt argues that in an "alliance of unequals", differing political positions are to be expected. Emphatically rejecting the idea that the survival of the Alliance is currently the issue, Brigadier Hunt discusses various strains within the organization in an attempt to balance European and American perspectives. With regard to the question of sharing the defense burden, he concludes that the United States needs to buy more from Europe and the Europeans need to increase their defense expenditures. Observing that peripheral threats are not really an Alliance issue, the author writes that the Americans have accepted the possibility of military threat in the Middle East while the Europeans have preferred inaction. In this context, then, the European security dilemma becomes one of avoiding the withdrawal of American forces from Europe in order to defend Western interests in the Gulf. A discussion of detente and arms control tends to reflect a balance between European and American perspectives, i.e., just as the United States must accept the domestic pressure in Europe for arms control negotiations, so must the Europeans recognize pressure in the United States against the ratification of SALT II. Problems with the doctrine of flexible response are discussed in equally candid manner as this experienced military specialist concludes that, although the conventional forces of Europe are insufficient and although Soviet superiority in battlefield nuclear weapons has negatively affected NATO strategy, there is no desire in Western Europe to change the basic structure of security.

In an articulate assertion of the need to ensure the development of parallel European cooperation within the Atlantic Alliance, PIERRE LELLOUCHE provides an alternative view of how the European security system can adapt to the new political and strategic realities of the 1980s. These realities--that European security can no longer be geographically limited to the European theater, that there is a fundamental divergence between European and American perceptions of detente, and that parity no longer exists between the United States and the Soviet Union--require a strong commitment by Europe to its own defense. Examining the possibility of increased European defense efforts, Lellouche presents an analysis of French-German relations, intra-European rivalries, and the precariousness of the present German position. Ironically, Lellouche finds that France, despite its ambiguous relationship with NATO, is more supportive of European defense cooperation, more committed to safeguarding its security, and is following defense policies more similar to those of the United States than any other Western European state. He concludes that the need to reconcile the Alliance with a genuine effort toward European defense cooperation must 1) reinforce operational and structural compatability among the forces of France, Britain, and West Germany; 2) rationalize arms procurement policies among these three states; 3) establish a division of labour; and 4) improve British and French conventional forces. The basic plan would give the United Kingdom and France increased responsibility for nuclear defense as well as the task of triggering nuclear escalation in the event of Soviet aggression in Europe by relying on a series of bilateral 'double-key' arrangements between Paris and Bonn, between London and Bonn. It would also deploy French and British intermediate-range systems in West Germany to function in parallel with similar NATO deployment.

MARTEN VAN HEUVEN, an experienced American diplomat, contradicts those who see a crisis in NATO by emphasizing commonalities: contrary to widespread impressions of disarray within the Alliance, he sees a convergence of Western European and American perspectives on dealing with the Soviet Union. To support this view, he cites improvements in military forces, agreement among the allies on the necessity of restraining Soviet behaviour in key regions of the world, and a common recognition that arms control must be used as a vehicle for Soviet restraint rather than as an end in itself. NATO is an association of free nations with common values which has developed a wide variety of fora for consultation, some of which are useful and some of which, such as the Nuclear Planning Group, are not. In a strong statement of support for allied consultation, Mr. van Heuven argues that it not only results in involvement, but in shared responsibility as well. In a cogent attempt to distinguish the perspective of the diplomat from that of the journalist, Mr. van Heuven laments the partial and misleading impressions, the "foul-up factor", speculation, and lack of concern for accuracy which characterize the contemporary press; in particular, the often negative approach of the press has affected the planned deployment of long-range theatre nuclear weapons in Western Europe. A wide-ranging discussion of the public opinion factors which affect deployment includes the role of German and American church groups, public confusion over the function of nuclear weapons, and attempts by the Soviet Union to influence public opinion in Western Europe. The solution to negative public reaction lies in the ability of public officials to maintain close contact with the press and in sustained efforts by allied governments to explain to their publics that deployment will preserve the peace.

DEREK ARNOULD, in a shift away from the European focus of the previous three chapters, invites the reader to consider the question of mechanisms for consultation on Western security beyond the traditional confines of NATO. Mr. Arnould draws attention to the previous NATO experience in consultation on peripheral issues, namely efforts by the Atlantic Policy Advisory Group, the North Atlantic Council, and the Contact Group on Namibia, as well as Western consultation on Zaire. With refreshing clarity, he distinguishes consultation aimed at coordination of policy from consultation aimed at the coordination of the military forces, e.g. coordinating the naval forces of the United States, France, Britain, and West Germany in the Indian Ocean with the interests of Japan, New Zealand and Australia in this region. The problem for NATO then is how to involve non-NATO members in discussions and cooperation for action in non-NATO areas. A variety of alternative schemes which would produce this extended consultation is examined in terms of their effect on small and larger NATO states which do not want to be involved beyond Europe. The conclusion suggests that proposals for change must be approached with great caution and with recognition that, in the past, Western nations have been inventive and adaptable to various problems beyond NATO without implementing major structural change. Mr. Arnould urges Western governments to educate public opinion with regard to the need to preserve NATO as a major component of Western security.

PART III describes and analyzes the Warsaw Treaty Organization (Warsaw Pact) from the perspective of equally dramatic change. Devolution in the Pact, the vulnerabilities and reliability of Eastern Europe as an ally to the Soviet Union, the response of the Soviet Union to events in Poland, the economic, political and social dimensions of security in Eastern Europe, and the question of integration and interdependency among alliance members are issues which form the framework for a thorough and current examination of the Warsaw Pact.

MALCOLM MACKINTOSH, in an essay which reflects his long involvement in Soviet affairs, discusses the factors to be considered in assessing the future direction of the Warsaw Pact. Understanding Soviet attitudes toward military power, toward the buffer zone in Eastern Europe, and toward Soviet planning for the Pact in the context of possible changes in the regimes of Eastern Europe are the three essential ingredients. Mr. Mackintosh asserts that the status of the Soviet Union as a superpower depends on military force and that preservation of the buffer zone is essential, hence, the importance of preserving the Warsaw Pact as a means of organizing the zone. In analyzing and describing the organizational and military command structures of the Warsaw Pact, he demonstrates that Eastern European representatives are given a stronger voice in military matters than was the case before 1968, and that the present structure of the Pact military headquarters reflects a peacetime organization only. Conducting a systematic state-by-state analysis of the Pact members, Mr. Mackintosh concludes that the Eastern European governments would prefer that the Pact's existing structures and Soviet control remain broadly unchanged in the next decade. The Polish crisis, if anything, has strengthened Eastern European resolve to avoid the risks of change. In the end, however, if the Soviet Union were unable to control an ally in the buffer zone, Soviet armed forces would forcibly prevent disintegration of the Warsaw Pact, with or without national opposition.

In a comprehensive review of the Warsaw Pact, IVAN VOLGYES examines the tensions and vulnerabilities which may affect its future stability. This survey begins with a description of those characteristics which distinguish military politics in communist states from those in non-communist states, and moves to a discussion of whether or not the Warsaw Pact constitutes a genuine alliance or one imposed on the participating states. Professor Volgyes concludes that it is the tension between imposed rule and the benefits which accrue to members which provides the dynamics of the alliance. In discussing the evolution of the Pact, the author identifies change in U.S. policy from containment to peaceful accommodation and detente as a major factor which prevented the United States from evaluating the global range of Soviet policy and led to demobilization of NATO, which, in turn, produced the current imbalance between NATO and Warsaw Pact capabilities. Stresses within the alliance are identified as the impact of detente, intra-systemic violence, and the Sino-Soviet split; these stresses are subsequently linked to specific issues of tension over command authority, mobilization of armaments, deployment of WTO forces, and Pact defense expenditures. This assessment is complemented by a thorough examination of the role of the national armies in assessing the strength of the Pact; an effort which concentrates not only on the differences between national armies and parties on the one hand and the Soviet Union on the other, but also on the differences between the Pact as a whole and Soviet policy objectives. In conclusion, the author suggests that U.S. policy should: 1) exploit the differences between various Eastern European states and the Soviet Union; 2) adopt a peace offensive as a propaganda tactic without any substantial concessions; 3) increase U.S. conventional capability; and 4) adopt a global policy of supporting only those states which identify with U.S. policy interests.

Alluding to classical tradition, RICHARD N. LEBOW compares the alliances of Athens and Sparta to NATO and the Warsaw Pact in an attempt to draw appropriate conclusions from historical analogy. He examines the relationship between the Soviet Union and the Warsaw Pact in the context of political change occurring in Eastern Europe and the crisis of legitimacy faced by those governments. The Warsaw Pact is characterized as a necessary instrument for legitimizing Soviet influence in Eastern Europe and for providing an institutional mechanism through which the Soviet Union restrains its allies and prevents domestic changes. The utility of the Pact for the realization of Soviet objectives, however, is increasingly challenged by the dilemma of Eastern European governments, which must establish some modicum of popular support while simultaneously remaining responsive to Moscow. Dr. Lebow argues that the crisis in Poland is indicative of a general trend toward political instability in Eastern Europe, resulting from the failure of Eastern European governments to manage their economies. Identification of this trend leads to an analysis of Eastern European legitimacy, Pact cohesion, and the dilemma posed by the Soviet Union when emphasis on orthodoxy undermines the reliability of its allies and hence the utility of the Warsaw Pact. To cope with this dilemma, Soviet leaders have adopted "defensive avoidance" through which psychological defenses are erected to preserve illusions of unity with Eastern Europe and to ignore critical information which reveals the unwelcome reality of change. Therefore, Poland represents a crisis on two levels: as a challenge to Soviet hegemony in Eastern Europe in the form of a choice between orthodoxy and revisionism, and secondly, as a challenge to the mental health of Soviet leaders. Lebow concludes that the need for Soviet leaders to explain the Polish crisis in acceptable terms (placing the blame on Western agitation) will heighten the Soviet sense of vulnerability and fear for the future.

LAWRENCE L. WHETTEN analyzes the major political and military developments that have influenced Eastern European perspectives of the Pact and of national autonomy. A lucid description of the evolution of the Alliance as a political instrument for bargaining with the West and for implementing Eastern European integration is followed by an examination of East Germany, Rumania, Poland, and Czechoslovakia to determine the degree to which they comply with or deviate from Pact cohesion on specific issues. Professor Whetten reviews the role of the National People's Army in East German legitimization and argues that the DDR substitutes "derived legitimacy" from its role as the forward edge of the Soviet collective security system for "indigenous legitimacy". In the case of Rumania, independent political policies have led to independent military doctrine; hence Rumania is the least integrated of the Warsaw Pact members. While the DDR emphasizes security and Rumania, nationalism, the Polish have concentrated on what Dr. Whetten calls "a national crusade for the restoration of public morality". He suggests that the Polish military should be seen as a political deterrent rather than as military intervention. Discussion of Czechoslovakia centers on the reform of socialism, the split among Czech officers over new Soviet military doctrine, and the significance of the Gottwald Memorandum. The author concludes that the Eastern European states may soon suffer a severe case of *dependencia*, and that the concept of interdependence is not only more relevant for the future, but should be applied to the entire spectrum of regional interactions.

In PART IV, RAINER RUPP examines the economic

implications of defense for both the United States and the Soviet Union. Efficient utilization of resources, the relation of war capability to domestic economic strength, and the constraints imposed on both economies are factors which play a significant role in assessing the relative economic strength of the two alliance leaders, as well as their ability to sustain a renewed arms race. Mr. Rupp provides a series of revealing graphs to compare defense expenditures between the Soviet Union and the United States and between the United States and NATO Europe. He analyzes constraints on the Soviet economy in terms of low productivity, decrease in energy production, infra-structure problems, planning rigidities, and potential labour shortages; and concludes that, despite continued expansion of Soviet military capabilities at least until 1985, these constraints may provide an incentive to seek arms control negotations. In NATO countries, the major constraint lies with increasing social discontent which may prevent NATO countries from giving the necessary political and economic priority to defense. In this analysis, the capacity to make sacrifices, both in the United States and Western Europe, emerges as a critical factor in evaluating East-West capabilities. A thorough discussion of sharing the defense burden demonstrates the myriad ways in which statistics may be presented to defend a particular point of view. The study concludes that NATO must allocate more for defense. Its defense potential depends on its members sharing the same strategic objectives and on assessing defense burdens in a manner which is commensurate with economic wealth. Finally, Mr. Rupp believes that allied cohesiveness, ultimately, depends on the American ability to manage constructive relations with the Soviet Union.

The disparate, varying, and sometimes contradictory conclusions of these twelve chapters are an accurate reflection of the myriad points of view regarding European security which are currently extant on both sides of the Atlantic and on both sides of Europe. Nevertheless, European security continues to be a desirable goal, regardless of the differences of opinion which exist on the methods and approaches most suitable for its realization.

A.I.B.

Montreal, Quebec

Part I

European Security Perspectives

1
European Security Alliances in the 1980s

Hedley Bull

I

I have been asked to provide an overview of European security alliances in the 1980s from the point of view of the theory of alliances. This presupposes, perhaps, that there exists a significant body of theory about alliances in general that can be set forth and applied to particular cases. Is this so?

It might be said that a good deal has been written about alliances by commentators upon international relations, going back to the earliest times. The classical exponents of the law of nations, e.g. classify alliances into offensive and defensive, equal and unequal (in the obligations undertaken by the parties to them), bilateral and multilateral, permanent and temporary, formal and informal. Some writers also classify the parties to an alliance; e.g. Dean Swift distinguishes the 'principal' and 'subordinate' members of an alliance, and another distinction sometimes made is that between 'producers' and 'consumers' of security within an alliance (a distinction made in Canada in the isolationist mood of the 1920s, when it was feared that if Canada entered into obligations to defend European powers, she would figure simply as a producer and not as a consumer). There is a long history of discussion of the obligations of an alliance: e.g. do the obligations of allies to go to war on one another's behalf hold good in a case in which the war to be waged is an unjust one, or does the injustice of the war override these obligations?

There has been much discussion of the conditions that cause alliances to come into being and to dissolve. Are alliances formed essentially because the parties to them share a common antagonism to an outside power or powers, or are there other factors, binding them together, that are sufficient to bring about an alliance even in the absence of any such shared antagonism? The famous 'sandwich' principle of alliance formation, that my neighbour is inevitably my enemy, and my neighbour's neighbour my friend, formulated by the ancient Indian thinker 'Kautilya' exemplifies the former idea. The latter is exemplified by the 'family alliance' among powers ruled by the Habsburg dynasty, most notably Spain and Austria, in the sixteenth and seventeenth centuries, and also by the idea of an informal 'Anglo-Saxon alliance' that will cause the United States, Britain and the so-called 'Old Dominions' always to cooperate, whether they are formally joined in an alliance or not--an idea which had many adherents earlier in this century, and in which General de Gaulle appears to have believed more recently. The idea that NATO expresses the existence of an 'Atlantic Community' similarly invites us to believe that the nations of North America and Western Europe would have reasons for standing together, even if they did not perceive a common external antagonist, which of course they do.

Another perennial topic of debate has been about the benefits or drawback of alliances as vehicles of the national or state interest. Some states at some times have believed themselves to have 'natural allies', just as they have 'natural enemies': in modern Europe up to the time of the Diplomatic Revolution of 1756, it was widely held that France and Austria were natural enemies, and that an alliance between them (such as came about in that year, in response to the rise of Prussia) was in some way contrary to the whole nature of the political system of Europe, which had so long revolved around the polar attractions of France and the Habsburgs. The long history of war and cold war between Christendom and Islam bred a feeling that a Christian power had to choose its allies from among the other Christian powers--a feeling that was outraged when in 1526 Francis I of France concluded an alliance with the Ottoman Sultan against the Habsburg Emperor, and found it necessary to write to the Pope in justification of his action. We may compare this with the sense of outrage generated by Catholic France a little more than a century later, when, under Richelieu's guidance, it allied itself with Protestant Sweden and the Protestant German Princes against the Habsburg Emperor and the Catholic cause in Germany in the latter stages of the Thirty Years' War. As against any such idea of natural alliances, there has been asserted the doctrine, founded in modern ideas of reason of state, that a nation not only does but should conclude or discard allies, or indeed avoid alliances altogether, as its national interest dictates. The stronghold of this idea has been Britain, which as an island great power in the last century enjoyed greater flexibility than any of the continental powers in the choice of allies, and could easily embrace the doctrine Lord Palmerston made famous, that a nation has no permanent friends, only permanent interests.

This debate is linked with another one about the role of alliances in relation to the preservation of the international system or the maintenance of international order. In the tradition of writing about the need for a balance or equilibrium of power in international affairs, alliances are said to play a positive role in restoring a balance that is in danger of being upset when one state develops such great power that it threatens to become preponderant. The successive grand alliances formed to defeat potentially preponderant powers, from sixteenth century Spain to twentieth century Germany, are said to have played this role; and indeed we are sometimes invited to see NATO, dedicated to counteracting the growth of Soviet preponderance in Europe, as standing in this tradition. As against this, there is the idea that alliances play an essentially negative role in world affairs, that they bring about the division of international society into competing groups of states, undermine the working of universal international organisations such as the League of Nations and the United Nations, and impede the ability of particular states to judge international issues on their merits. This was the burden of Woodrow Wilson's disparagement of alliances as obstacles to the solidarity of international society as a whole; it played a large part in Jawarharlal Nehru's conception of 'non-alignment' as the means whereby to create 'a climate of peace' both in Asia and in the world as a whole; and it forms part of the intellectual heritage of the non-aligned movement.

The postwar American alliance system has generated some theoretical inquiry, especially about 'burden-sharing' in alliances (an expression of the constant American feeling that the NATO allies are not carrying a sufficient share of the burdens), about the concept of collective goods in an alliance, the ability of small powers to influence their great power allies (a subject generated, especially by the apparent influence exerted over the United States by Israel), the use of alliances as instruments with which great powers control small powers and intervene in their internal affairs, the impact of nuclear weapons and nuclear strategy on alliances, and the impact of detente or relaxation of tension on alliances.

I do not think that these writings about alliances state anything very profound, nor should I assume that this is because alliances have not been studied enough, rather than because there is nothing very profound to be said about them. Moreover, any particular alliances, like NATO and the Warsaw Pact today, are better studied in their individuality than in terms of models of alliances in general. But at least the latter supply us with some concepts that help to define alliances and compare different kinds of them, and on these I shall draw in brief considering the following questions:

1. What are some of the distinctive features of NATO and the Warsaw Pact as security alliances?

2. Why have they lasted so long--for their long duration is one of their most striking features?

3. How strong today are the forces making for disintegration within NATO as opposed to those making for continued cohesion?

4. What is the most promising way forward in the current crisis of European security?

II

If an alliance is a combination of states to make or threaten war against an outside state or states, then NATO and the Warsaw Pact are genuine alliances. Being alliances they differ from collective security organisations such as the U.N. (which is a collective security organisation among other things) and the O.A.S. (which is both a collective security organisation and an alliance), which are directed not against specific external target states but against any state that breaks specified rules (such as the rule prohibiting 'aggression'). They also differ from mere arrangements by which one state guarantees the security of another, without the latter's making any contribution of its own to a common effort; an alliance implies reciprocity of contribution to a common cause, and cannot take the form of unilateral or one-sided assistance by one state to another. Many arrangemets in the present world that have the appearance of defensive alliances--I am thinking especially of bilateral treaties between a superpower and a weak Third World state--should best be regarded as guarantees rather than as alliances.

NATO and the Warsaw Pact have more specific features in common. They are both formal, defensive and multilateral alliances, concluded and maintained in peacetime. In both cases the treaties of alliance on which they are based have given rise to international political organisations and joint military command structures. They are both unequal alliances; in each case a group of

European states (and in the case of NATO, Canada), facing adversaries they do not feel that they can cope with on their own, look to a superpower protector. In both cases, the superpower protector assumes a disproportionately high share of the common burdens of defence, and in return exerts a disproportionately large influence in the international political organisation and joint military command.

There are also some striking differences. The inequality within the Warsaw Pact is much greater than that within NATO. The European allies of the United States, collectively, match it in population and wealth, even if not in political unity or military power; moreover, they include countries such as West Germany, France, Britain and Italy that are very substantial factors in world affairs, even singly. The European allies of the Soviet Union--despite the substantial size and potential influence of Poland, the economic vigour of the German Democratic Republic, the industrial importance of Czechoslovakia--are small powers by comparison. None of them possesses nuclear weapons or permanent membership of the U.N. Security Council, as France and Britain do, nor do they have the position in world industry and trade occupied by even the smaller members of NATO, let alone that of an economic giant like Western Germany.

There is also a difference in the extent to which the two alliances can be said to rest on the consent of their populations or even their governments. We in the West are prone to make facile judgements about the restiveness of eastern European peoples under Soviet dominance. It would be wrong to assume that Eastern European peoples have no deep attachment to socialism and, but for Soviet policy, would be ready to embrace Western principles of economic and political organisation at the first opportunity. It would be wrong also to imagine that the governments and peoples of eastern European countries perceive no military threats from the West, or need for Soviet support against them; in East Germany, Poland, and Czechoslovakia there is a fear of West German discontent with the political status quo in Europe that would drive them towards alliance with the Soviet Union, even if their governments were not tied to Moscow by party or ideological bonds--although it is fair to say that since Germany's formal acceptance of the territorial status quo on its eastern borders, brought about by the Brandt government's *Ostpolitik* and confirmed in the Helsinki Final Act, this fear of West Germany has abated in eastern Europe.

Yet we cannot ignore the fact that underlying the unity of the Warsaw Pact countries at the state to state level, there is the unity of ruling communist parties, and that the position of these ruling parties is reinforced, even if it is not wholly created, by Soviet military power. In the experience of Western Europe since 1945, there is no equivalent of the Soviet military interventions in Hungary in 1956 and Czechoslovakia in 1968, or of the prolonged threat of Soviet intervention that has accompanied the present, protracted crisis in Poland, just as it has exerted its effect upon all eastern European governments throughout the postwar period.

It is true that American influence in Western Europe has been consistently exerted against communist parties; that in France and Italy in the early postwar period, as in Spain and Portugal more recently, this influence has been important; that British troops, with American support, helped to crush the communist rebellion in Greece immediately after the war, that the Marshall Plan was intended, among other things, to undermine the prospects of communism in Western Europe, and succeeded in this aim. But the North Atlantic alliance could not have survived a United States military intervention in the affairs of one of its European members, such as the Soviet Union has several times carried out in the affairs of its Warsaw Pact allies. The United States in NATO enjoys a primacy based on the consent of the other allies, whereas the position of the Soviet Union in eastern Europe is one not of primacy merely but of hegemony, maintained by military coercion.

Another striking difference between the two alliances is a geopolitical one. The Soviet Union is physically a European power; the United States is not. A governing belief in the West, and perhaps also in the Soviet Union in the postwar period has been that if the United States were to withdraw from Europe, the Soviet Union would be bound to dominate it. It is time that this belief were subjected to criticism and debate, about which I shall say more below. But it has been the prevailing view, and until recently, it has seemed obviously true. From acceptance of it, there has followed the persistent Soviet attempt to detach the United States from Western Europe, by the advocacy of plans for withdrawal of military bases, nuclear-free zones, a European security system that would replace NATO and the Warsaw Pact--defined in such a way as to weaken or exclude the American military presence in Europe, while the Soviet Union inevitably remains part of it. There has also followed the West's suspicion towards all these proposals and also its concern about the maintenance of naval supremacy in the Atlantic and elsewhere, which is essential to a maritime coalition of states, and which is now apparently threatened by the growth of Soviet naval power.

III

The European security alliances have displayed a remarkable capacity for endurance: the North Atlantic alliance since 1949, the Warsaw Pact since 1955. In other parts of the world, alliances have not been so long lasting. The Sino-Soviet alliance of 1950 was breaking down by the end of the 1950s, and by the end of the 1960s had lost all meaning. Western alliances such as the Baghdad Pact, SEATO, CENTO, the series of British-sponsored agreements for Commonwealth defence cooperation in south east Asia, the U.S. defense treaty with Taiwan have either disappeared or lost what substance they originally had. NATO and the Warsaw Pact, indeed, are symbols of the continuity and immobility of international politics in Europe since the end of the Second World War, in a world which elsewhere has been characterised by change and turmoil.

NATO has survived the prolonged crisis over German rearmament and entry into the alliance that preoccupied it in the early 1950s; the clash between U.S. and Anglo-French policies in the Middle East, culminating in open rupture in the Suez crisis of 1956; the clash between American 'Atlanticism' and Gaullist Europeanism that split the alliance for much of the 1960s; and the crisis of October 1973, when America and Western European countries adopted contrasting policies in relation to the Middle East war and access to oil. The Warsaw Pact survived the Hungarian and Polish crises of 1956, the split in the world communist movement following the emergence of the Sino-Soviet dispute into the open during the Cuban missile and Himalayan crises of 1962, the Czech crisis, and the defection of Romania in 1968.

The emergence of the strategic nuclear balance between the superpowers and the progress of nuclear proliferation led some to argue that alliances in general, and NATO in particular, were not compatible with the requirements of the nuclear age; given the all-or-nothing nature of nuclear war, it was said, an alliance must either federate and become a single nuclear power, or disintegrate into many nuclear powers. But in fact NATO has proved, so far at least, to be able to adapt itself to the era of nuclear weapons. The emergence of the Soviet strategic nuclear threat to United States' cities has not in fact destroyed either the willingness of the

United States to afford strategic protection to Western Europe, or the belief of Western Europeans that this protection is the best available to them. NATO did not 'federate' along the lines favoured by advocates of Atlantic nuclear singularity, nor did it disintegrate into a series of self-reliant nuclear weapon states; by the late 1960s, it had found practical solutions to the problem of the control of nuclear weapons, and the stark alternatives posed by nuclear theoreticians were shown to have been misguided.

The emergence of detente in the late 1960s and early 1970s--between the two superpowers, between West Germany and its eastern neighbours, and between the two alliances--was also said to be fatal in its implications for NATO and the Warsaw Pact. Each, it was said, presupposed a belief among its members in a common external threat; to the extent that the relaxation of tension undermined that belief, it would deprive the two alliances of their rationale. In face, however, detente between the superpowers has come and gone, while leaving the two alliances in place. Detente between West Germany and its neighbours, it is true, remains, as does a strong sense in West European countries as a whole that whatever has happened to Soviet-American detente, their own detente with the Soviet Union is still in place. But this, too, has not proved fatal to the alliances. The Conference on European Security and Cooperation, consummated in the 1975 Helsinki Final Act, did not advance the goal long sought by the Soviet Unionn (and proclaimed even in the 1955 Warsaw Pact itself) of a European security treaty that would replace NATO and the Warsaw Pact, but by confirming the existing division of Europe, assured the two alliances of a continuing role.

How, then, do we account for this extraordinary record of persistence? Some would say that the longevity of NATO and the Warsaw Pact reflects the fact that each represents not merely an alliance in the classical sense but also a community transcending state frontiers. NATO from its inception has given rise to claims that there is, or should be, 'an Atlantic Community'. Nor are these claims without substance. The governments and peoples of NATO's fifteen nations are indeed involved in close economic cooperation--as part of the wider cooperation of the Western world as a whole, expressed, for example, in the OECD, or in the case of its European members, in the EEC. If we except the Portuguese dictatorship, the rule of the colonels in Greece and the present military government of Turkey, we may say that their governments have indeed embraced certain common values. The peoples of the NATO countries, moreover--although they share this with other Western countries--

do have a sense of sharing a kind of economic, social and political life that is distinct from that which prevails in the non-Western world.

The Warsaw Pact governments likewise see themselves as more than a mere alliance in the old-fashioned sense; they are part of a 'Socialist Commonwealth' that qualifies their sovereignty <u>inter-se</u>, and they are guided by principles of 'proletarian internationalism' that do not affect relations among non-socialist states. Like NATO, the Warsaw Pact also is an expression of wider forms of cooperation among its constituent governments and peoples: the bonds among ruling Communist parties, the economic links expressed in CEMA, the consciousness of Soviet and east European peoples that they experience a way of life that is in some measure common and distinct from the rest of the world. The Warsaw Pact countries also have sources of unity aside from the perceived need to combine against an external threat.

But these communities, quasi-communities or nascent communities, in West and East, may be less the cause than they are the result of the persistence of the two alliances; at all events, the sense of security against external threats, which each alliance provides, has supplied a vital condition for the development of these other forms of cooperation. The persistence of the two alliances rather has its roots in the strategic interests which the member states of NATO and the Warsaw Pact have believed themselves to have. The governments of Western Europe and North America have perceived a need to contain a possible Soviet threat to Western Europe, and to provide the countries of Western Europe with a sense of security against such a threat; the Western European countries have felt unable to achieve these objectives without the support of the United States, and for its part, the United States has felt it to be a vital interest to provide this support. The Soviet leadership has felt threatened both in its domestic political position and in its control of eastern Europe by Western European and American power, and the leadership of some of the eastern European countries have felt that their domestic position and national aims are similarly threatened from the West and require Soviet protection. Despite defections or partial defections from the alliances, as certain European countries have judged it possible to move into quasi-neutral, quasi-aligned positions (France; Romania), despite the splits that developed within the alliances in the 1960s, the impact of the superpower strategic nuclear stalemate, the emergence of European detente and other changes, these perceptions have remained basically stable.

IV

There is good reason, then, to be sceptical about suggestions that the crisis of the alliance in the 1980s is about to tear it apart. On the other hand, the present tensions within NATO are of a serious nature, for they concern the core of common perceived interests that has held the alliance together throughout its previous trials. In Western Europe, especially in northern Europe, there is a powerful body of opinion which maintains that the threat to West European countries from the Soviet Union has diminished, even if it has not in relation to eastern European countries, or to parts of the Third World where the Soviet Union is following a more adventurist policy. There is also a body of opinion, reflected in the peace movements in Germany, Britain, the Low Countries, Norway and Denmark especially, which sees alliance with the United States as a source more of insecurity than of security to Western European countries. Those who take this view, even if they accept that there is a Soviet threat to Western Europe, believe that the United States' policies may involve the European members of the alliance in a conflict with the Soviet Union in the pursuit of objectives that are more American than European. The deployment of further United States nuclear weapons systems in Europe--the proposed Pershing II and cruise missile systems--is thought to heighten these dangers, and there have been allegations that United States plans carry the risk of a war in which the destruction would be confined to Europe and the superpowers themselves would be immune. Western European members of NATO have always had two opposite fears about the United States: that it will fail to come to their assistance (or fail to maintain in the Soviet mind the belief that it will), and that it will provide a kind of assistance that is not wanted, by embroiling them in a war that is not their own, or that is conducted in such a way as to subordinate their own particular interests. In the late 1970s and early 1980s these fears have been growing in response to the achievement of nuclear parity by the Soviet Union, the reaction against detente in the United States, and the growth of economic ties between Western Europe and the Soviet Union.

The core of common interests has also been questioned in the United States, where a new mood of exasperation with the European allies because of their failure to give sufficient support to United States policies (as over Iran, Afghanistan and Poland), their longstanding failure to assume a greater share of the defence burdens of the alliance, the opposition expressed in Europe to acceptance of the theatre nuclear force deployments and new manifestations of anti-American feeling, has led to a questioning of the old assumption that the defence of Western Europe is a vital interest of the United States. Ever since the creation of NATO, European governments have been inclined to take it for granted that the security of Western Europe is such a paramount interest for the United States that Washington's contribution to the alliance would be maintained, whatever policies were adopted in Europe. John Foster Dulles' threat in the 1950s of an "agonising reappraisal" of the American commitment to Europe, should Europe not accept German rearmament, was perhaps a bluff. Neither the Suez crisis, nor the crisis arising over the policies of General de Gaulle, which were always posited upon the assumption of continuing American protection for Europe, nor the 1973 crisis in the alliance arising out of events in the Middle East, ever led to a calling in question of the American commitment. If neo-isolationism with regard to Western Europe were to grow in the United States, alongside neutralism and anti-Americanism in Europe, the one feeding off the other, it is not difficult to imagine that the alliance could face divisions more serious than it has ever encountered before.

A basic cause of the present crisis in the alliance is the shift in relative power that has taken place from the United States towards the Western European allies in the last decade and a half. In the 1950s and early 1960s the United States had overwhelming predominance in world politics in economic, military and political terms. NATO, as it developed in these years, was a very unequal alliance, the United States shouldering a disproportionately high share of the burdens, and enjoying in return a position of unquestioned leadership. But in the years since 1956, the position of the United States has declined not only in relation to Western Europe, but also in relation to other centres of power in the world. In the late 1960s the United States lost ground economically in relation to Western Europe and Japan; in the 1970s it declined militarily in relation to the Soviet Union, while also experiencing a series of reversals and humiliations at the hands of Third World countries (1971 the entry of China into the U.N.; 1973 the oil crisis; 1975 the Communist victory in Indochina; 1979 the Iran hostage crisis). Western Europe, on the other hand, has grown in stature. The European Economic Community looms larger than the United States in world trading affairs. France, now that it has acquired political stability as well as a strong economy, a credible nuclear force and a distinct line of its own in foreign policy, has become once again a significant power. Western Germany draws strength not only from its position as an economic giant and as the principal contributor to the conventional defence of Western Europe, but also from its newly-established freedom of manouvre in foreign policy, which is the fruit of the series of agreements with its eastern neighbours brought about by Brandt's Ostpolitik.

It is not merely that the intrinsic power of Western European countries has grown in relation to the United States; it is also that the position of the Western European countries is made stronger by the decline of the United States in relation ot other major centres of power. The ties that now exist between Western European countries and the Soviet Union--not merely the economic ties, but also the common interests recognised on both sides in working for detente in Europe, establishing the possibility of collaboration against the United States for some purposes--strengthen the hand of West European countries, and especially of West Germany, in relation to Washington. It is also relevant that while, in recent years, there has been a deterioration in the relationship of the United States to many Third World countries, the Western European countries have been building up a special relationship with these same countries. While United States policy has moved closer to Israel, the West European countries have sought to embrace the Arab world by recognising the right of Palestinian self-determination and calling for the participation of the Palestine Liberation Organisation in a political settlement. While the Reagan Administration has alienated much of black Africa by moving closer to the Republic of South Africa, European policy seeks to develop a special relationship with black Africa, solemnised in the Lomé II agreement between the EEC and African, Pacific and Caribbean countries. The support given by France to the forces of change in Central America is one of a number of signs that here also Western European countries may seek to fill the vacuum created by the alienation of local opinion from United States policy.

For the United States the setback of the last fifteen years have been traumatic in its effects. American public opinion is in the grip of a resolute and self-assertive mood, and under the Reagan Administration, it may be argued, has committed itself to a stance in foreign policy that is designed more to gratify this mood than it is to take account of the complexities of the world outside. At all events, the directions in which American public opinion has been pushing United States foreign policy, in the latter years of the Carter Administration and under the Reagan Administration, have brought it into collision with the mainstream of opinion in West European countries. The policy of breaking off detente with the Soviet Union and subordinating arms control negotiations to a military build up to restore a favourable balance of power, has induced in West Europe a fear that the United States is losing sight of its responsibility at all costs to avoid a nuclear war. The pursuit of these policies in the European theatre, especially by means of new theatre nuclear force deployments and economic sanctions against the east, has spread alarm in Western European countries at the effect this will have upon the more peaceful relationship, cemented by growing trade ties and the much vaunted natural gas pipeline, that were believed to be growing up with the Soviet Union. The signs that the United States may contemplate a primary reliance on military means in securing access to Middle East oil have been met by scepticism about the effectiveness of such a policy. The centrality, in United States policy in the Third World, of support for those forces most willing to oppose the Soviet Union, has also alienated those large sections of West European opinion which hold that radical change in many Third World countries is inevitable and desirable, that Western countries can best protect their interests by coming to terms with it, and that the influence of the Soviet Union is not the major source of the problem.

It is now sometimes said in the United States that Western European countries, because of the economic problems they face of inflation, unemployment, capital outflows and industrial decline in relation to east Asian competitors, are in the grip of a spiritual malaise, and it is this which is causing them to fail to stand up for American policies and to drift towards accommodation with the Soviet Union. I believe that this appreciation is mistaken. The failure of West European countries to support much of recent American foreign policy proceeds not from any lack of willingness to face the problems of foreign policy, but from a considered rejection of the premises on which American policy rests. Western European countries have different interests from the United States in relation to superpower detente, East-West relations in Europe and policy in the Third World; in addition, there are deep differences of perception as to the nature of the problems and the solutions to them. In the West European countries, moreover, far from there being a sense of malaise, there is a burgeoning sense of a need for them to take positive action in advancing their own solutions.

V

The decline of inequality between the United States and its West European partners calls for radical thinking about the alliance in future. The West Europeans, now that they are richer and more powerful, should recognise that they must carry a larger share of the burdens of the defence of Western Europe, as the United States has long maintained. The Americans, on the other hand, have to recognise that in these new circumstances they cannot expect the same loyal and unquestioning support for their policies that they were able to count on in the past: the more the West Europeans mobilise their potential for defence and foreign policy, the more they are likely to insist on following their own judgements as to what their interests are and how they can be protected.

The West European countries, I believe, should take steps to make themselves less dependent on the United States. They need to spend more on defence and to make greater efforts to collaborate with one another. It is true that there are great political obstacles to increased defence expenditure in European countries, but these obstacles would be less formidable if the policies of West European governments were less visibly tied to unpopular United States policies than they are at present.

In the long run, it is not inconceivable that West European countries could provide a counter-balance to the Soviet Union, even without alliance with the United States. The countries of the European Community are superior to the Soviet Union in population, wealth and technological capacity. They are, of course, inferior in political unity and in the political will to mobilise their defence potential, and for the foreseeable future such an idea is purely visionary, but there is no inherent reason why the Soviet Union cannot be balanced without the engagement of American power.

In the short run, the continuation of the alliance remains vital to Western Europe. But if it is to retain its support in Western European opinion, certain changes are necessary. First, the security of Western Europe should be made less dependent on nuclear weapons, and especially on nuclear weapons that are American controlled. My own view is that the French and British nuclear forces should be developed <u>in tandem</u> to provide the basis of a European nuclear deterrent, the exact form of which we cannot yet define; it was in my view unfortunate that the British government, in opting for the Trident system, failed to explore the possibilities of cooperation with France. American nuclear weapons based in Europe should be subject to increased European control: a major objection to the proposed Pershing II and GLCM deployments, little noticed in the public discussion, is that they will be American weapons under wholly American control.

Secondly, the West European countries should make greater efforts to increase the size and quality of their conventional forces in Europe. The presence of the American component of NATO forces in Europe, complicating the problem of separating an attack of West Europe from one on the United States, will remain important for a long time. The proportionate increase in the European components of NATO forces in Europe, however, will need to be recognised in changes in the command structure that will give Europeans a more prominent role. Moves towards greater defence self-sufficiency in Europe will, I believe, make defence expenditure more acceptable to the public in West European countries, while also providing some measure of credibility to the idea that a European Community is in process of development. One of the conspicuous features of a community is that it provides for its own defence, and for so long as Western Europe remains parasitic upon the United States in this respect, it will lack this feature.

Thirdly, greater unity in defence policy is inseparable from greater unity in foreign policy. Some progress has already been made in the latter field: foreign policy coordination among the Ten--the process known as European Political Cooperation--has already proceeded a certain distance. We cannot yet speak of a common foreign policy, because there is no single political entity whose policy that could be. We have rather to speak of the coordination of policy among a close concert of powers; this is what has been developing, but there is a need to take it further.

These new policies for Europe involve difficulties and dangers. West European public opinion is deeply divided over the issue of nuclear weapons, and among those who do support nuclear weapons, few are yet ready to exchange the American for an Anglo-French nuclear umbrella. A militarily less dependent Western Europe cannot be achieved unless a leading role in it is played by West Germany; yet if the Federal Republic is to assume that role, it will have first to overcome some of its inhibitions about returning to a more 'normal' position in world affairs, whilst also allaying the anxieties both of its allies and of its eastern neighbours. The unity achieved by Western Europe since 1945 has been achieved against the background of a U.S. presence; we do not yet know whether, if that presence were to be withdrawn or reduced, the unity of West Europe would survive it. If West European unity is to be increased, some appropriate form of institutional expression will have to be found for it: the Community of Ten, which includes neutral Ireland but not allied Norway, does not seem adequate, and is handicapped by the need for unanimity; on the other hand, suggestions of a directorate of the major powers are very naturally greeted with the opposition of the smaller countries. Above all, perhaps, moves to create a more independent and militarily more self-sufficient Western Europe will have effects on the United States that are difficult to predict. Will the United States be gratified that its European allies are at last shouldering the burden of the common defence, or provoked into a premature withdrawal from the alliance that might be ruinous for all its members?

2
European Security: New Wine in Old Bottles

Martin Edmonds

There is a temptation with many institutions to pull them out by the roots in order to see that they are still growing. NATO has not escaped close attention, and even if it has not exactly been torn out by the roots, it has had little opportunity to enjoy periods of uninterrupted, sustained growth. Perhaps it is the inevitable outcome of any voluntary international institution which is made up of independent, sovereign states, each of which has the right to investigate whether or not the institution continues to serve its separate, national interests. Fifteen such members, with the largest to the smallest having equal right and opportunity to demand and conduct these self-analytical exercises, is a recipe, if not a guarantee, that NATO as an international institution is likely either to atrophy through lack of attention or become abhorrent from its agreed objectives.

It has been argued that the strength of NATO derives from its essential nature as an alliance of independent states and its flexible structure. Assuming this to be an accurate assessment NATO must also adapt and move to maintain its relevance in respect of both the changing priorities, objectives and attitudes of the member states and the international environment within which it has to operate. The point at issue is whether or not the assumption that the process of continual review and reappraisal made possible by NATO's loose structure and

---

This chapter is a modified version of two earlier papers: one was presented to the 22nd Annual Convention of the International Studies Association, Philadelphia, March 16th 1981; the other was given at a political science seminar, St. Andrews University, Scotland, April, 1981.

conditions of membership is either sufficient or employed enough to ensure that its relevance is fully sustained. Paradoxically, as the pace of change in the international environment increases, and the attitudes and preferences of each of the NATO members become more volatile, the very strength of NATO--its flexibility and adaptability--may well have become a source of weakness in that recently it has been denied sufficient time for consolidation of military operational capability or continuity of strategic planning.

When NATO was first established in the early 1950s as a development from the agreement between the United States (US), Canada and ten western European states to pledge assistance collectively should any one be attacked, the perception of threat was well, if simply, defined: the source was the Soviet Union and the dimension was military. The clarity with which the nature and type of threat was identified in the 1950s, and the consensus among the NATO members on the means with which that threat should be met, no longer prevails. Although the source of the threat may have changed little, the emphasis it has been given in the calculations of the NATO members has. The nature of the threat has likewise changed; it is now perceived to be multi-dimensional, and not confined only to military attack. But, most especially, the conclusions as to what are the most appropriate responses have changed, along with the criteria by which they are analysed and judged.

All complex organisations and institutions must, if they are to survive, have the capacity both to adjust to changing circumstances, internal and external, and retain a clear definition or appreciation of the purposes and ends for which they exist. NATO is no exception, except in its special category as an international organisation; but, even so, the principles still apply. Any organisation which has survived over thirty years has proved itself to be exceptional under any set of circumstances, and for this NATO stands out when compared with most other modern international organizations; but it should not automatically be assumed that a demonstrable capacity to survive through thrity years of change is guarantee either of a further thirty years meaningful existence, or, even, of contemporary relevance.

Much of NATO's past success in surviving so long can be attributed to a clear consensus among its members of what its overriding purpose should be. Few would take issue that this success has been the military security of the North Atlantic region from external attack by force of arms. Though originally unspecified in the

Treaty, it was also agreed that the most likely source of military threat came initially from the Soviet Union and later with the support of its Warsaw Treaty Organisation allies. Although the emphasis given to the intentions of the Soviet Union may have been perceived differently by the NATO members over time, the stark realities presented by the size, range, and scope of Soviet military capabilities, both tactically and strategically, have served to prevent NATO from becoming anachronistic and to keep its members reminded of their common purpose. For as long as the Soviet Union continues to modernise and expand its armed forces, little in this respect, is likely to change among the NATO allies.

Or is it? Even if the threat to the West were assumed to be only on a military dimension, the scope and range of Soviet capability has now become so extensive that it is not unreasonable to ask the question whether or not the old pattern of institutional arrangements within NATO, which was laid down in the early 1950s both in relation to the NATO integrated commond structure and to the system of national forces operating under internatonal command, is any longer adequate. From a purely military standpoint, might not the question today be to consider the appropriateness of a totally new organisational framework and set of operational arrangements constructed with an awareness of the contemporary military environment? With the hindsight and experience of NATO, such a proposition may be a preferred alternative to the present NATO structure which has been adapted, modified and adjusted to a point where further change might either be difficult to accommodate or incorporate in a time frame sufficient to be relevant.

Such a challenging and, perhaps, radical question is not posed either out of self-indulgent perversity or with post-trigesimal celebration analysis, but out of a firm conviction that circumstances have changed so radically in Western Europe, in the relationships between the members of the Western alliance, and between them separately and collectively with the Eastern bloc, that NATO faces not only the real danger of becoming peripheral to the central issues but also counter-productive in the search for new international arrangements and agreements. This assessment is not to say that on a purely traditional military dimension, NATO does not still have pertinence and relevance; but it does lay down the challenge whether or not the time has come seriously to consider finding a new bottle for the 1980s vintage wine.

SECURITY: PURE SEMANTICS?

One pressing reason why NATO warrants close attention is the insistence today that it is in a state of 'crisis', faces impending collapse, and manifests chaos and disarray. Although these descriptions have been used many times in the past and from each situation of, apparently imminent demise, the alliance has emerged intact, stronger and wiser. There seems today among many of NATO's analysts a conviction that the present problems are more serious, more fundamental and more intractable than any preceding. As one writer has graphically put it, "this time the wolf is really at the door", (or did he mean the bear?).[1]

It is really of little consequence whether NATO's current crisis is perceived through a maximalist or a minimalist perspective if NATO per se no longer is addressed to the central concerns of the Western Alliance members. Since NATO is first and foremost an organisation designed principally to deter military attack from the Soviet Union and to defend the North Atlantic region should that deterrence strategy fail, any crisis within it, by definition, should be concerned with military strategic or structural problems. But NATO's problems do not originate at the military level and do not concern serious shortcomings within the integrated military command; they are not internal and specific to NATO as an international organisation. Rather, NATO faces a crisis because the member nations have to exist in an international environment in which economic and political considerations have increasingly to be taken into account. Political and economic threats to the West and to the members of the Western Alliance are now perceived to be significant factors in national policy, and these do not necessarily require military solutions. NATO's crisis, in other words, is a crisis of exclusivity; it, alone is no longer perceived as the guarantor of the security of its members. Can therefore NATO broaden its scope? Should it? And if it did, what consequences would follow?

In 1966, the US Secretary of Defense, Robert McNamara, expressed the view that the concept of 'security' had become grossly oversimplified. He challenged the "almost universal tendency to think of the security problem as being an exclusively military problem and to think of the military problem as being exclusively a weapons system or hardware problem"; and concluded that force alone does not guarantee security.[2] At the time, Mr. McNamara was concerned to emphasise his approach to defence planning, i.e. that it was amenable to basic economic principles and, therefore, a point could be reached where diminishing marginal returns on military and defence spending would begin to operate. But the thrust of his argument still applies: in providing for defence and security against a Soviet threat, the NATO partners must recognise that merely to spend more, or to deploy new categories of weapons, does not necessarily enhance perceptions of security. The more that security is perceived to be a multi-dimensional concern, the more likely that over-commitment to purely military solutions will cause confusion and create opposition. Thereupon the threshold of diminishing marginal returns to the alliance as a whole, and to most of its individual members, will lower.

This, indeed, is what has been happening over the past two decades. Stimulated on the one hand by economic and political developments in the West, particularly in Western Europe where economic growth has developed rapidly and simultaneously with new political institutional arrangements, and on the other by Soviet strategic and foreign policy within which the dual and related aspects of massive technical military development, expansion and political detente with the West have featured prominently, the NATO members have increasingly moved away from early perceptions and definitions of 'security'. The old perceptions of a form of impenetrable barrier raised between the West and the Soviet bloc behind which each could pursue its separate development, as if the other never existed--a variant of international intra-European apartheid--ceased to prevail. First, the means of securing the barrier by which the Soviet Union was 'contained' became open to challenge once the Soviet Union acquired the strategic capability to threaten the U.S.; therefore, the security 'guarantee' to Western Europe became more dependent on U.S. leadership and powers of persuasion than on military superiority. And, second, the vulnerability of Western security as a whole to economic disruption became evident to all after the 'energy crisis' of 1973 when fossil fuel supplies were curtailed, tripled in price over a short period, and caused massive dislocation to the advanced industrial states.

'Security' as a concept is neither a matter of military provision nor semantics. It is concerned with the provision by governments of states alone, or in alliance, to provide, as a matter of singular and paramount responsibility to their populations, for the protection of society's internal values.[3] Though ambiguous and open to wide interpretation, the concept of 'security' encompasses not only the protection of the institutions of the state, the population, and economic interests against external physical interference, but also the creation and maintenance of those sets of circumstances which are most advantageous to the population to live their lives according to agreed sets of values and priorities and to aid in the growth of general material and spiritual well being. Emphasis and too much resource allocation on the former can be prejudicial to the objectives of the latter; nor is the former necessarily capable of defending the society against all threats on every dimension.[4]

When considering European security, it is fundamental to recognise that there has been a marked shift in perception among the Western allies since the early days of the alliance. NATO's 'crisis' per se is not a security crisis in the sense it would have been thirty, or even twenty, years ago, i.e. that Soviet military power cannot be stopped either by deterrence or defence. The 'crisis' is one of confidence and relevance: confidence in NATO itself, its objectives, and its capabilities; and its relevance in relation to, and in contrast with, the demands of the individual members of the alliance for economic growth, political stability, and expanded welfare. Moreover, the issue is not simply one of guns or butter; all aspects of security are closely interrelated. "If the member countries (of NATO) are slack, uncertain of their direction and questioning their basic institutions, this sooner or later will translate itself into weakened will and weakened capacity to maintain military security".[5]

It is apposite therefore to re-examine NATO within the broader definition of security and to recognise the immutable link between the military and all other dimensions. To encompass this broadened perspective it becomes necessary to analyse the military, political and economic dimensions relevant to the current situation within Europe. This is done not through the perceptions of the European members of the Western alliance, but from a distance; as might be expected. The particular views of individual governments sometimes vary quite widely, and in no way are representative of all.

EUROPEAN MILITARY SECURITY: NATO STRENGTH

On a purely military dimension, there is evidence enough to support the proposition that NATO today is as strong, prepared and well equipped as it has ever been in purely absolute terms. In comparative terms, when seen against the forces of the Soviet Union and the Warsaw Treaty Organisation, there is no evidence to lead to the conclusion that the military balance of power has shifted adversely or that it has moved significantly against the NATO allies.[6] This assertion is in contrast with the plethora of reports and analyses which convey a pessimistic view of NATO's current status; it differs from them, however, more in its being confined to the purely military dimension than in respect of political considerations. Indeed, it has, as confirmation, no less a supporter than the NATO Secretary-General, Dr. Luns, who found occasion in 1980 to state boldly that NATO was stronger than the members tended to think and that provided they remained (politically) united was able to "exert great influence on global developments".[7] It was, however, a military strength based on the U.S. nuclear commitment and conventional armed presence in Europe. That commitment has recently been reaffirmed and strengthened by the new Reagan administration through the declared intention to replace existing, but increasingly obsolete, U.S. theatre nuclear weapons with modern and more effective substitutes.

Assuming, in purely military capability and operational terms, NATO is as strong as it has ever been, it is even stronger in organisation, policy planning and infrastructure. Despite periodic expressions of concern at the states of readiness of different national force contributions, levels of morale among NATO manpower, unreliable and obsolete equipment, and the difficulties of reinforcement, this strength is evident. Here, the very age of the organisation becomes a valuable asset and an important factor when deciding the prospects or likelihood of radical change. For thirty years the organisation has survived numerous crises and overcome purportedly insurmountable problems, and during that time its permanent staffs, both national and international, have amassed an impressive amount of experience, conventional wisdom and basic 'nous'--intelligent perception--not merely to see what problems lie ahead and from what quarter, but more especially to know the probabilities of certain outcomes given specific courses of action (or inaction). All organisations work to survive, and NATO has a reservoir of experience upon which to call in this respect.

Whatever is the value attached to the NATO staffs, it must also be recognised that the professional civilian and military personnel of the member states who are in positions of influence over national defence policy-making have never lived in a world where they have enjoyed authority and also when NATO has not existed or been a dominant influence. For the Western allies, NATO is a point of reference, a <u>conditio sine qua non</u>, of Western European military security, and a premise upon which purely national defence and security provisions are made. To change, NATO would demand an entirely new way of thinking and a complete reversal of traditional attitudes among those officiers and civil servants who also see NATO as an important posting in their personal career structures.

But the real strength of NATO depends less on endogenous factors, and more on the Soviet Union and the extent of the military threat it poses. Whatever the range of interpretation of Soviet military capability and intention, one inescapable fact with which all European states have to come to terms is the formidable military force that Soviet leaders could summon if they were so disposed. There is little that any single European NATO member can do against the forces arraigned against them in Eastern Europe and only the NATO regional security alliance, including the U.S. contribution within Europe, amounts to any practical and meaningful military response. Not all European leaders are wholly convinced of this and seem constantly in need of reassurance, or of stern reminders, to maintain alliance cohesion. So immediate is the presence of massive numbers of Soviet divisions and so aware are NATO members that their collective security is greater than the sum of separate parts, there is little time, or occasion, to think seriously of military alternatives to NATO. Little time or no, Dr. Luns goes further to liken any alternative to NATO as an obsolete _fata morgana_, implying that NATO is not merely unique, but an essential prerequisite for European security.[8] As such, NATO's strength would appear to lie in its military indispensibility. So long as European security is a military concern, NATO is likely to continue to be seen in those terms. Certainly the only remotely realistic option--an all European security force allied to North America in a form of bilateral trans-atlantic military alliance--received a fatal setback with the demise of the EDC in 1954. In military terms the European option moves further away with each successive year; but that is only in military terms.

Finally, the military strength of NATO is enhanced by the continuing tangible and psychological returns to each member, particularly the smaller states. Alliance and political coalition theory postulate that no participant will accept the terms, and therefore the costs and constraints, of membership of an alliance if the returns are not commensurate. These returns can take many forms, many of which are difficult, if not impossible, to quantify: for example, there is the reassurance of being part of an enterprise with others who share similar values and who seek common objectives; there is the access through membership to an organisation whose range and scope is greater than any member could ever aspire alone; and there are the material advantages and gains which membership brings. This last category would include, in the case of NATO, the information which NATO provides on a range of technical subjects both military and non-military, access to the alliance infrastructure, including air, ground and sea facilities, warning systems and communication networks, and availability of assistance and advice. But the most valuable return to the members is the opportunity NATO constantly provides for meeting, consultation and discussion on all manner of domestic and international issues. Part of NATO's survival technique has, significantly, not been to confine these returns to military matters and issues concerning the integrated military command, but to broaden members' interests in political, economic and social questions.

EUROPEAN MILITARY SECURITY: NATO WEAKNESS

Paradoxically, NATO's military strength is also its principal source of weakness. The explanation is not complex: the more that the NATO allies maintain their levels of military capability and operational flexibility sufficient to achieve the military security objectives of deterrence and defence of Western Europe, the more that military decisions both at the strategic policy planning and at the tactical operational levels impinge on the political dimension. What is determined as necessary for purposes of collective regional military security need not also be necessary for the security interests of the individual states. With recent Soviet military developments at both the tactical nuclear and the conventional levels, the agreed NATO responses have given cause for domestic political opposition, thereby raising the security dilemma mentioned above that when all factors are taken into consideration there comes a point when, for each state, the principle of diminishing marginal returns begins to operate. For some of the population of western Europe, some political parties and, even, some office-holders, this point has been reached, even passed. It does not necessarily mean, however, that European security is being undermined by such a realignment of forces; what it does mean is that NATO has to find new approaches to the European military security problem. These may not be easy to find under the current NATO arrangements, and certainly will hinge on U.S. attitudes and leadership.

Taking, first, the problems arising from current NATO strength at the tactical nuclear level, it can be seen that the NATO decision to deploy modern long range theatre nuclear weapons, committed to Europe by the U.S. in response to the Soviet introduction of medium-range Backfire bombers and mobile surface launched medium range SS20 missiles with MIRVed warheads, has prompted and stimulated an outburst of political opposition within Western Europe. Part of the irony of their situation lies in the fact that these new weapons, the Tomahawk cruise and the Pershing II missiles, do not represent a significant departure from earlier U.S. tactical nuclear capabilities deployed in Europe, reaching as far back as the late 1950s. But that is not the point; the new weapons have acted as a catalyst to (latent) opposition to nuclear weapons in Europe; an opposition which has been growing in popularity and which has marshalled reasoned and sophisticated, as distinct from purely emotional, counter arguments to NATO policy statements.

The explanation why resistance to the idea of modernising NATO's tactical nuclear weapons has arisen in the past two years can be found in its coincidence with other concerns which are more political and economic in nature. But the combination of a number of issues emerging simultaneously meant that they contributed to each other. Under normal circumstances each might have passed unnoticed, or with only limited public outcry; together they have heightened public consciousness. The issue of tactical nuclear weapons, however, has aroused public concern on its own, mainly because of the technical novelty of the weapons systems proposed. Innovation and technical ingenuity almost inevitably attract attention.

The problem with NATO's new generation of theatre nuclear weapons was less their immediate military appropriateness and more one of their broader political and strategic implications. The objective of introducing the cruise missile and the longer range Pershing II missile into Europe by 1983 was to offset Soviet introduction of the 'Backfire' bomber and the SS20 missiles. The significance of these two Soviet tactical nuclear delivery systems was that they added a new dimension to Soviet theatre capability: in sum, they represent increased range and enhanced accuracy. They effectively brought the whole of the European NATO area within what was defined as 'tactical' range, and confronted those NATO nations on the periphery of the European central front with the same predicament with which West Germany and Denmark had been faced for twenty years. This in itself was not an entirely new situation, since earlier Soviet missiles and aircraft exceed the required range, but these were classified as being strategic, and applied to a totally different set of circumstances and relationships.

The concern among the Western European leaders about the NATO response lies in the extended range of their new tactical nuclear weapons (TNW), because it brought a nuclear capability to their tactical options which could deliver nuclear warheads on Russian soil. The important distinction between tactical and strategic weapons for European security suddenly became blurred. And from the situation that emerged it was immediately assumed, first, that the Soviet Union would view NATO tactical nuclear weapons as a strategic threat and, therefore, an important target for preemptive attack; and, second, that since the Soviet Union, according to a definition of Europe from "the Atlantic to the Urals", was a European state, the United States would be in a position to contemplate a strategic war against the Soviet Union from Europe without the North American continent being affected. Both situations have led to a conclusion that TNW modernisation has served to make Europe a prime nuclear target, and therefore more vulnerable. The doubts first expressed by the French about the reliability of the U.S. nuclear strategic guarantee to Europe therefore still continues, but with increased poignancy.

In any event, West Germany is the state likely to be most affected in the event of a war on the central front; it is hardly surprising, therefore, that within that country the most vociferous opposition to NATO long-range theatre nuclear weapons (LRTNW) is to be found. Although Chancellor Schmidt has accepted U.S. TNW's on German soil, it has not been without considerable opposition from within his own party, nor without stipulating a number of conditions. Similar opposition to cruise missiles being stationed in Europe has been recorded in Britain and Italy, but both states have, finally, agreed to accept them. Even then, the policy is not irrevocable, especially since the cruise missile remains an unproved and unreliable weapon up to the present time and tests recently have given cause for concern.

The necessity of placing tactical nuclear weapons in Europe is a consequence of, first, the existence of similar Soviet weapons and declared Soviet policy to be prepared to use such weapons in the event of war; and, second, of the persistent inability of NATO members to meet the force levels both in manpower and equipment, which the NATO integrated command considers the minimum necessary to defend Western Europe for a limited period by conventional military means. To compensate for the NATO shortfall, the relatively early use of tactical nuclear weapons has been assured. It is a prospect few cherish, but until NATO's conventional forces are improved both in kind and number, commitment to TNW must continue.

Looking to improve NATO's conventional force levels and states of readiness, the U.S. leadership has for some time been putting pressure on the NATO European partners to increase their financial contributions to the alliance, modernize their forces, and assume more of the burden of their own defence and security. Under the Reagan administration this repetitive exhortation has on occasion assumed a different tone, with disparaging comments, made perhaps in frustration, about the European's lack of commitment. This form of U.S. pressure, however, has not come at a propitious time, since each of the NATO states, on political grounds, can barely afford to maintain the levels of expectation of its population let alone propose substantial increases in contributions to NATO as well.

To ameliorate the effects of the low contributions to NATO forces by the member states, the idea of collaboration and cooperation in weapons development and production has been actively canvassed by NATO advisers and military commanders. The principal objective has been to reduce unit costs and further the standardization of NATO military equipment. Longer term interest would include the rationalisation of the defence industrial base of the western alliance which, as a by-product, would further the interests of political, economic and military cohesion. In military terms the multiple objective of rationalisation, standardisation and interoperability of NATO equipment is both practical and logical. In political and economic terms, sectional and national interests have prevailed in the face of the imbalances of market size and structure and technical expertise between the United States and Western Europe. The military imperatives of standardisation only make practical sense, as the failure of the "two-way street" concept has demonstrated, if U.S. hegemony extends extensively over the Western Europe defence industrial base. This is a prospect which the European states have not only recognised but have also strongly resisted; furthermore their separate industrial interests have also stood in the way of defence industrial rationalisation to an extensive degree among themselves.[9] As a consequence, NATO continues to be equipped with a disparate range of weapons from several national sources with some, but far from extensive, commality.

It is not so much the priority of the NATO members to protect their national defence industrial base which is a source of NATO weakness, but the increasing reluctance of the European members to devote scarce resources to weapons development and procurement.* In the early years of NATO, the problem paradoxically was less one of conventional equipment and more of available manpower. Today the situation is reversed in degree, and the shortfall is more in equipment. In some areas NATO weapons systems are a match qualitatively for those of the WTO (Warsaw Treaty Organisation); in others, there is qualitative and quantitative inferiority. The Europeans have the option either to purchase, or co-produce, U.S. equipment with the penalties such a course of action incurs, or attempt to develop advanced equipment on their own. The latter course is politically preferable to them, but the costs involved in trying to participate in what is essentially a super-power conventional arms race is both expensive and an impossible burden on their individual resources. As the West Germans have recently discovered with the Tornado and as the French and British discovered earlier with the AFVG (Anglo-French Variable Geometry) Aircraft, modern advanced weapons technology is only for the wealthy. The prospect for the future, in the absence of industrial rationalisation and a high injection of resources into research and development, is for the material contributions of the West European states to NATO to decline steadily. To a degree the deterioration has already started as states freeze defence spending, stretch out procurement schedules, and limit further their range of programmes. The paliative of arms exports is not sufficient to arrest this trend.

Whilst on the one hand the Western European states are finding it increasingly difficult to sustain their levels of contribution to the alliance, on the other they are being put under additional pressure from the U.S. to broaden their frame of reference beyond purely the security of Europe and the North Atlantic region. The Soviet invasion of Afghanistan and military presence in the Indian Ocean, Africa and the Middle East has raised the perception of threat to sources of western strategic materials and industrial raw materials. The U.S. has responded with the concept of the Rapid Deployment Force (RDF), and considers that the NATO partners should recognise a common strategic interest and give the concept material support. The proposal not only

---

* Any discussion of NATO weakness should also include recognition that the absence of France from the integrated command structure is a handicap, the IEPG (Independent Equipment Programme Group) notwithstanding.

raises the prospect of extending, further, Europe's already restricted resources, but also conjures up in the perception of several leaders the possibilities of 1914 in reverse. They do not welcome the prospect of being drawn into a conflict between the U.S. and the Soviet Union through NATO entanglements and have viewed the U.S. proposal with caution. Nonetheless, the 1973 oil crisis demonstrated that they are vulnerable to interference in energy supplies outside Europe, and some policy should be formulated to afford an element of protection; as yet, none other than a declaratory gesture by Britain has been forthcoming, thus causing further military strain between the two sides of the Atlantic.

EUROPEAN SECURITY: THE ECONOMIC DIMENSION

Much of NATO's military weakness stems both from a lack of political conviction as to the appropriate strategy and from economic constraints which impinge on the capacity of the European states to provide an adequate contribution to NATO's military conventional capability. To make an adequate military contribution presupposes either a strong political commitment which accepts sacrifices in living standards and income levels, or a healthy, expanding and advanced economy. Throughout the 1960s and 1970s the national economies of West European states returned impressive results: levels of investment were high; standards of living rose; per capital income increased dramatically; industrial output doubled. West Germany, France and the Benelux countries headed the list. These impressive results were not paralleled with corresponding increases in defence spending or any serious attempt to assume greater responsibility for national and regional collective security from the U.S. Instead, the pattern of resource allocation was directed towards the provision of welfare services and facilities, thus meeting, and moreover, encouraging, the rising expectations of the population. Now that this period of rapid economic growth has ended and the states concerned face both increasing domestic unemployment and the current international recession, the arguments in support of expanded military spending to improve security attract little sympathy or support. From the perspective of a broader interpretation of security, the attitude is an urgent need to arrest the economic decline, restore levels of full employment and generate new life in the economy; it is not to add to what many feel is already a high, and economically counter-productive, military budget.

The tendency to focus inwards on national economies rather than outwards on military threats from the Soviet

Union has given rise to the perception that many Europeans would rather be 'red than dead'.[10] Such a simplistic view distorts the situation which is better reflected in the approach that the economic health and strength of the European economies are paramount and to this end they should be looking to ways of furthering detente with the Eastern bloc, broadening trade links to the East and working towards further economic cooperation and integration within the European Economic Community. Nowhere is the dichotomy between the pressure for expanded military effort and policies of detente and confidence-building measures with the Soviet Union more evident than in West Germany. Since West Germany is considered the second most important member of NATO after the U.S., these domestic debates are becoming a critical factor for the future direction of European security.

The imperatives of economic security have assumed many levels for the Western European states. In some areas, states have attempted to look to their economic future through their own endeavours as, for example, in the competition for energy sources. France and Germany compete against each other, and indeed with the U.S. for oil supplies; it is quite compatible with this competitive approach that Germany should rely for almost one-third of its oil and 14% of its natural gas on supplies from the Soviet Union. In other respects, members of the EEC are looking and working towards extended collective economic integration, and continue to be wary of further U.S. economic encroachment and hegemony. In the technical and advanced industrial fields, for example aerospace, there is growing resistance to U.S. market penetration which has led to a situation in which future European economic security is increasingly seen as separate from, and in competition with, the U.S. Already it has been suggested that the U.S. has been replaced by West Germany as the economic strong man of Europe and that the other European members of NATO should, both within and outside the EEC, adjust their own economic strategies accordingly. The EMS (European Monetary System) sponsored largely by the West Germans, is just one manifestation of this new orientation.

EUROPEAN SECURITY: THE POLITICAL DIMENSION

It is almost invidious to delineate between political, economic and even, military dimensions of security for each overlaps the other. Nevertheless, it is possible to stipulate that there have been distinctly political developments within Europe which have tended to influence European attitudes towards the most effective means to ensure their collective and individual security. These developments can be broadly categorized as either external or internal.

Perhaps one of the more significant political trends within Europe over the past twenty years has been a combination of a more 'dirigiste' approach of states to economic, industrial and welfare planning, and a wide acceptance of the European socialist parties not merely as establishment, 'system' parties but also as less radical in their policies, and able to gain support in the political centre. The effect has been for the socialist parties within Europe not just to constitute the largest single coherent political group in Europe, and in the European Parliament, but also to form the governments of the majority of states. This political development both influences public opinion and is a consequence of it, one aspect of which is a less sceptical amd manichean view of the Soviet Union and Soviet intentions. This is not to suggest that the fundamental differences which divide the Western allies from the Eastern bloc have been broken down; nothing could be farther from the truth. But what it does mean is, in part, a civil-military division between political leaders and military advisers as well as readiness by the former to seek non-military alternatives to security and Soviet threats through negotiation, confidence-building measures, arms control agreements, trading relationships, and technical assistance.

Emerging as the dominant economic force in Europe, West Germany, through its initiatives, had an impact on European political attitudes to the Soviet Union. Ostpolitik and detente have brought rapproachement between the two Germanies and established extensive West German economic ties with the Eastern bloc as a whole. Moreover, West German trade with the East now amounts to a significant proportion of its total exports, and the experience cannot but impact on public attitudes. Germany is not alone in this regard; France also has significant political agreement with the Soviet Union, and Britain, for all the Conservative administrations "iron lady" rhetoric, has the Soviet Union and the Eastern Europeans as major trading partners. A shift in political attitude to the East is especially evident among the younger generation and within the moderate centre and centre-left ranks, and is likely to continue to gain strength.

The situation, however, is not one of either/or: either rapproachement with the Soviet Union or with the United States. Economic and political ties with the U.S. remain strong, especially between the U.S. and

Britain. No irreparable political rift is likely within the basic political ranks of the Western alliance, but the terms of the alliance have changed. The old, military security orientation of the North Atlantic alliance in which the attitude 'if you are not for us, you are against us' no longer applies. It is not incompatible for Western European states to have closer ties with the Soviet Union, and still play a full part in the western alliance. Indeed, many feel that the political opportunity for Europe to play the role of "honest broker" between the super-powers, and bring the two to the conference table to stabilise the security situation in Europe is one that should be developed. To some extent the initiative has been already taken, as the Europeans' decision to recognise the PLO (Palestine Liberation Organisation) contrary to U.S. preferences demonstrated.

The internal political shifts in Europe have been in part the consequence of a strengthened economic position which has brought with it a new confidence, and in part the result of a gradual disaffection, if not disillusion, with the United States. The latter has to some degree been a failure of U.S. leaders to set an example and a direction for the Europeans to follow, and also an effect of the crisis of confidence the U.S. itself experienced after the war in South East Asia and the domestic scandals surrounding its major institutions of government in the early 1970s. If the U.S. wants to lead the West, and its political institutions were to be representative of, if not epitomise, the democratic principle for which they all stand, the succession of crises of the early 1970s gave the Europeans ample reason to question the inviolability and permanency of the Atlantic relationship.

Of the shift in political attitudes towards security which challenge 'not NATO itself, but its priority', arguably the most significant cause is a new regionalism. Essentially external, this new regionalism is a feeling of 'joint identity' as Europeans in contrast with the sense of isolation and impotence each felt during the 1973 oil crisis, the SALT talks and in face of the international economic recession. The European movement, stronger on the continent than in Britain, is not just supportive of this nascent sense of European collective identity, but actively works to promote it. The creation and operation of the political institutions of the European Community have moved this sense of political 'separateness' and uniqueness a stage further, even though the media coverage of European affairs tends to concentrate on areas of national differences of policy and interest rather than on commonalities and agreement.

The political realignment of the European Community externally has moved significantly away from the all-embracing paramountcy of the East-West conflict. The European states have adopted a much more pragmatic attitude towards, for example, the Mediterranean members of NATO, the Middle East and the North-South dialogue. Indeed, the East-West issue no longer dominates domestic politics, or for that matter, government priorities. Critics of this development feel that if NATO and the Western alliance are to survive, a political offensive has to be instituted to reassert the essential threat to Western values posed by the Soviet Union as a political philosophy as well as a military force. This, it is felt, is only possible by the United States' constantly taking the initiative to emphasise and strengthen the linkage between members of the alliance; thus blocking the gradual 'finlandisation' of the region. But for this to be successful, and to stem the domestic political tide, not only must the United States recognise the greater influence which Europe currently exercises throughout the world, but it must also work towards regenerating the Western economies to ameliorate and neutralise the nationalist and socialist political tendencies of their populations. First, however, the U.S. needs to find a resolution to its own domestic problems.

EUROPEAN SECURITY PERSPECTIVES: A CONCLUDING OVERVIEW

Europe's security dilemma stems immediately from the realisation that in an interdependent world it is not sufficient merely to look to military means to guarantee and protect core values, especially since those means themselves become a source of political vulnerability, a target for Soviet strategic forces, and a contributory cause of economic instability and weakness. A changing international environment, coupled with domestic problems and new political attitudes, have raised a challenge to the premises, structures and policies of the old institutional arrangements. Core values are equally well seen as being protected by the success of the Western economies to sustain growth and their political systems to retain legitimacy. The latter may well depend on the former. The critical question is whether or not the time has come for a change in present international alignments, or for a reassertion and a strengthening of past assumptions and definitions.

Whatever the answer, however practical or impractical it might be, the one question which advocates for change have to answer is: What if the Soviet Union were to march West? It is not sufficient to be ostrich-like and pretend such an eventuality could or would never happen; to do so would be an abdication of authority and responsibility in government. Some form of collective security agreement is a prerequisite and there are arguments in favour of the current NATO arrangements with or without modification, since it has experience. The United States needs the alliance for political and legal domestic reasons to give its support legitimacy. Alternatives would have to run the gamut of the domestic American political process, the outcome of which is not as predictable as was once assumed. Indeed, the desirability of the European commitment has been challenged as an essential ingredient of American security interests.[11]

Changed perspectives on security have changed attitudes towards the Atlantic Alliance, to the East-West conflict, and to internal European political ties. Europe has found both a new sense of power and identity, and arising from the strain and uncertainties of the super-power relationship, greater regional independence is an attractive direction in which to develop. But the likely outcome is neither NATO, the Western alliance and the U.S. on the one hand, nor the European Community on the other. The outcome is more likely to be adjustment to intra-alliance political, economic and military relationships, with expanded European political initiatives which leave the U.S. to shoulder more of the fall-back military security burden. To a degree, the United States is faced with the classic 'Catch 22' situation in which it cannot improve it's situation: either it accepts the military role for Europe, and pays the cost, or it backs away and runs the risk of weakening, or even permanently damaging, the political cohesion of the Western alliance. This prospect may well be sufficient to persuade U.S. leadership to seek new arrangements to accommodate these new, and challenging, developments in European security.

FOOTNOTES

1. Pierre Hassner, "Intra-Alliance Diversities and Challenges: NATO in an Age of Hot Peace" in Kenneth Myers, ed., NATO: The Next Thirty Years (Boulder, Colo.: Westview Press, 1980) p. 373.

2. Robert S. McNamara, "Population and International Security", International Security 2:2 (Fall, 1977): 25.

3. Arnold Wolfers, "National Security as an Ambiguous Symbol," in Wolfers, ed., Discord and Collaboration (Baltimore, Md.: Johns Hopkins Press, 1962), pp. 147-165.

4. Martin Edmonds, "Function of Armed Forces" European Military Institutions, USSG (Edinburgh 1971):10.

5. Martin J. Hillenbrand, "NATO and Western Security" International Security 2:2 (Fall 1977):21-22.

6. Martin Edmonds, "European Attitudes Towards NATO: Quot hommines tot sententiae". Unpublished paper presented at the panel on the Future of NATO 22nd ISA Convention, Philadelphia March 16th 1981.

7. Joseph Luns, "Political Problems in the Future of NATO," in K. Myers, ed., NATO, The Next 30 Years (Boulder: Westview Press, 1980), pp. 37-8.

8. Joseph Luns, "NATO: The Next Ten Years," R.U.S.I. Journal (December 1977):7.

9. M. Edmonds, ed., International Arms Procurement: New Directives (New York: Pergamon, 1981).

10. Pierre Hassner, "Intra-Alliance Diversities and Challenges," pp. 384-5.

11. For example, see A. Ned Sabrosky, "America in NATO: The Conventional Illusion". Paper delivered at the Annual Meeting of the International Studies Association, Philadelphia, Pennsylvania, March 18-21, 1981.

3
Speculation on Abstract Perspectives: NATO and the Warsaw Pact

Arlene Idol Broadhurst

ALLIANCES AND THE MEANING OF THEORY

To ally or not to ally? That is the question which has provoked controversy among scholars, international lawyers, and politicians (albeit for different reasons) throughout ancient and modern history. What alliances are, how and why they are formed, and why they either endure or disappear are abstractions which reflect the current tension within both the North Atlantic Treaty Organization and the Warsaw Pact. It is fashionable in some academic and military circles to eschew the relevance of theoretical perspectives to the so-called 'real' world. Without delving too deeply into the sterile realm of debates between theory and practice, or the utility of theory, perhaps clarification of the use of the word 'theory' will prove beneficial. If one accepts a scientific definition of theory (or pseudo-scientific, as the case may be), one presumably is limited to the empirical meaning of theory as initially utilized in the natural sciences where observation leads to the construction of theorems which, in turn, become the basis for testing, explanation and prediction.[1]

A second approach is to view theory as simply abstract thinking through which scholars, practitioners, and even journalists describe, explain, and generalize about the development of human events. It is precisely in the process of trying to explain what is happening at any given time that we are led to speculation (abstract thinking) about the nature and significance of what has occurred and what we think may occur. In this sense, theory almost always follows fact; that is to say, without some basic knowledge of events, even if viewed in the abstract form of trends and aggregates, it is irrelevant to speculate. Modern scholarship is replete with debates on interpretation and reinterpretation of history; with awareness of the relativity of perspective; with the self-serving nature of most apologia of national policy; and with the equally self-serving nature of most opposition to national policies. These efforts, however riven with controversy, are a reflection of the struggle to identify change and to explain its meaning.

Such attempts to explain the changing political world provided the starting point for thinking abstractly about alliances. Thucydides' study of Sparta and Athens, Vattel's doctrine of equality of states, Grotius' concern for the dangers of restraining aggressors, Polybius' analysis of Rome and Carthage, and Machiavelli's strategy for controlling allies are examples.[2] Modern attempts to explain, and sometimes to justify, the creation and extension of the two large alliance systems of Europe in the post-World War II period have also resulted in generalizations about the particular experiences of states in alliance with other states. Whether these generalizations are 'theories' or simply abstracted explanation is really a moot point.

How meaningful are these abstract propositions to the study of the European alliances? <u>All</u> analysis and explanation of NATO and the Warsaw Pact <u>is</u> based on some form of abstracted presupposition, explicit or otherwise, about the nature of these two alliances, the conditions under which they were created, their success or failure in maintaining cohesion, and the likelihood of their collapse.* Perhaps examining those abstract propositions which are common to alliance studies in the specific context of NATO and the Warsaw Pact will contribute to our understanding of the problems which beset them. If not, perhaps it will be least demonstrate the degree of our failure to comprehend.

ALLIANCE FORMATION

A wide variety of scholars (and dilettantes) have discussed and attempted to identify the conditions or factors which result in the formation of alliances.[3] There has been no attempt, perhaps because the task is impossible, to place these conditions in order of priority; therefore, researchers are free to select or preclude, depending on predetermined conclusions or on what best applies to the research information collected.

---

* The astute reader will find those presuppositions in this chapter as well as in the other chapters of this volume.

Although the following factors may not be inclusive, they are representative of the breadth of possibilities. Alliances are said to be formed: 1) to realize common goals; 2) to increase resources (power); 3) to counter external threat; 4) to restrain allies; 5) to respond to the outbreak of war; 6) to preserve the status quo; 7) to preserve ideological and cultural similarity; 8) to maximize payoffs; and 9) in response to coercion by a more powerful state.

Realizing Common Goals

Most of the above-named conditions could be subsumed under the general rubric of identifying common needs or a common goal, but that is not a very useful idea since it could apply to any form of alliance, cooperation, cohesion or integration. More importantly, it obscures the possibility that alliances may form to create a vehicle for the safe pursuit of uncommon goals. Perhaps the definition of a security alliance should be a group of states which agree to cooperate in defense for the purpose of pursuing divergent political goals and objectives.

In the case of NATO, it is precisely such bland assumption that the interests and goals of the United States are parallel to those of the Western European states which has created so much tension. In the past, tension in NATO has been ascribed to the failure of American leaders to consult their European allies. The issue is much more serious than mere communication and goes well beyond the cosmetic solution of more consultation. Precisely because the goals do not converge, consultation with the European allies will not solve the problem. In fact, consultation is only useful to the Western Europeans if they can persuade the United States to change its course in accordance with European policy. If not, prior consultation takes on the appearance of collusion and approval of U.S. policy which the Europeans have been taking great pains to avoid.[4]

On the other hand, it is commonly assumed that the goals of the Soviet Union do not converge with those of the Eastern European states and that the continued existence of the Warsaw Pact can be attributed to Soviet use of force. This assumption ignores the fear in Eastern Europe that the United States and its Western European allies would forcibly overthrow the communist governments of that region. It was not clear until the 1956 Hungarian crisis that neither the United States nor the other NATO states would intervene in Eastern Europe, particularly in Eastern Germany.

Emphasis on common goals, then, has perpetuated the tendency to view NATO as a democratic alliance in which the goals of its members are similar, thereby ignoring the difficult question of conflicting purposes; and it has perpetuated the opposite view of the Warsaw Pact which obscures the possibility that shared goals, such as the preservation of communist party authority, could exist.

The Desire to Increase Resources

The immediate problem of explaining the formation of alliances by referring to the desire of states to increase resources is a definitional one. This conveniently innocuous word, 'resources', may refer to joining an alliance in order to gain access to economic resources such as minerals, hydrocarbon fuels or to aid, trade, and production/marketing opportunities. It could also, and often does, refer to increased power through the gain of additional military capability, or it could refer to increased diplomatic influence.[5]

Thus, the desire for increased resources could describe the creation of NATO in terms of reduced defense costs for the Western Europeans and/or their desire to add U.S. military strength to their defense capability; the same point can be made with regard to the Eastern Europeans, the Soviet Union and the Warsaw Pact. If one assumes that increased resources refers to political influence, then the formation of the alliance may be viewed in terms of the greater influence Europeans could exert over the direction of U.S. security policy through NATO than they could if the organization didn't exist. The contrary argument would be that the United States, through NATO, is able to force the Western Europeans into supporting policies which they would otherwise oppose.

What seems most plausible is that relations between the United States and the Western Europeans in NATO do not constitute a zero-sum game, and that both sides increased resources in forming an alliance, depending on whether a political, economic or military definition prevails. Lack of precision in the concept not only creates confusion with regard to which of these intepretations is dominant, but it also fails to distinguish the motives of individual states in forming alliances from the collective purpose of the alliance as a whole.

Likewise, the application of desire for increased resources to the Warsaw Pact grouping is ambiguous. Earlier studies of this alliance system demonstrated that the Soviet Union was draining resources from the

Eastern European states by forcing them to bear a disproportionate share of the defense burden. This interpretation is offset by those who argue today that the Warsaw Pact has been the vehicle by which the Soviet Union has modernized the Eastern European conventional forces, and through which the officers of Eastern Europe have received advanced training.[6] More recent studies of the Warsaw Pact members suggest that since the early 1970s the Eastern European states have become an economic burden to the Soviet Union, and that the relationship is increasingly characterized by interdependency rather than dependency.[7]

The desire to increase resources, then, is an amorphous concept which has meaning only in context of specific time periods, specific issues, and specific alliances.

Countering External Threat

The intention of both NATO and the Warsaw Pact to counter an external threat has been submerged in a morass of doubts about whether the threat was as real as it was perceived in 1949 and in 1955, respectively. Countering an external threat implies assumptions about deterrence, balancing power, and the preservation of peace which cannot possibly be proved or disproved. If the alliance specialist makes the assumption that the threat was real, then the argument follows that NATO or the Warsaw Pact was instrumental in countering its adversary with effective deterrence strategies. If the assumption, on the other hand, is that the threat was exaggerated, then both NATO and the Warsaw Pact were unnecessary. If they were unnecessary, then the most unlikely conclusion is drawn that the United States and the Soviet Union simply created these two alliances in order to suppress the sovereignty and independence of the Eastern and Western European states.

Historical assessment of the conditions under which NATO and the Warsaw Treaty Organization were created has fluctuated wildly between traditionalists and revisionists who periodically comb the historical record seeking evidence to support conflicting points of view. With regard to the formation of NATO, two schools of thought contend: that NATO was established in response to the threat of Soviet-supported communism or that it was formed to further the hegemonic and expansionist designs of the United States.[8] Hence there is substantial disagreement on a fundamental condition of alliance: was the United States seeking to protect Western Europe or to transform it subtly into a semi-satellite?

As is nearly always the case, the way in which the questions are posed will determine the outcome of research.[9] For example, exclusive focus on U.S.-Soviet relations has tended to blur the role of the Western Europeans in the creation of an Atlantic alliance. It is useful to recall that the creation of NATO in 1949 was preceded by several European actions which reflected concern for Western European security, but were not necessarily directed at the Soviet Union. The Dunkirk Treaty signed in 1947 between France and Great Britain was specifically aimed at the threat of renewed German aggression as was the Treaty of Brussels (1948) signed between France, Britain and the Benelux countries.[10] Despite Churchill's 'iron curtain' speech in 1946, the proclamation of the Truman Doctrine in 1947, and the emergence of communist regimes in Eastern Europe from 1945 to 1948, the Western Europeans did not mention the Soviet Union or communism in either of these treaties, except to refer to the wartime alliance with the U.S.S.R. Instead, their agreement to cooperate "in case of armed attack in Europe" was couched in vague language, while they clearly expressed in the treaties their fear of a resurgent Germany. Equally clear was their determination to assure that Western European security efforts would be supported by the United States. Article 9 of the Brussels Treaty provides that the signatories "may invite any other state to accede to the present Treaty". Vague language provides ample opportunity for subsequent generations of scholars to debate the question of who was perceived as the potential aggressor and who the Western Europeans were intending to include in future alliance arrangements.

A similar controversy surrounds the formation of the Warsaw Pact. Was it formed as a defensive reaction to the creation of NATO, as an expression of traditional Russian imperialism, or as a reflection of fears in the Soviet Union and Eastern Europe of a re-armed and aggressive Germany? The Treaty of Friendship, Cooperation and Mutual Assistance which stipulated the formation of the Warsaw Pact cites a "remilitarized West Germany and its inclusion in the North Atlantic bloc" as the present danger. Once again, the interpretative focus on antagonistic superpowers obscures the interests of other states; in this case, the Eastern European states. If the Eastern European governments were fearful of a rearmed and strengthened Germany, and if, as the preamble to the Pact suggests, they feared Western attempts to overthrow their governments, then certainly one can assume that the Pact was organized, at least in part, to counter a perceived external threat, and not solely because the Soviet Union forced these states into military cooperation.

The concept of perceived external threat is essential in considering the formation of defensive alliances, but it needs to be refined in order to reflect both the uncertainty of identifying aggression and, more importantly, the possibility that once the alliance is established, the object of perceived threat may change.

If resurgent Germany is no longer seen as a threat to European security, is it possible that threat perceptions of the Soviet Union have also changed; that detente, however much it is seen by the superpowers as a failure, continues to hold the promise of normal relations for the Eastern and Western Europeans? Increasingly, the Western Europeans see the United States as an aggressive force which needs to be restrained and Eastern Europeans see the Soviet Union in similar terms.

Restraining Allies

The fourth proposition, that states join alliances in order to restrain their own allies is an interesting reversal of Machiavelli's dictum that it is inherently dangerous for small states to ally with larger powers.[11] Emphasis on the restraint of allies is fairly recent, rising out of theoretical assumptions about the multipolarity of the international system. While earlier alliance studies tended to focus on bipolar rigidity and on monolithic bloc structures, the recent trend is to emphasize decentralization and diversity; consequently, alliances are viewed as a forum through which smaller states can restrain and influence larger states.[12]

Certainly the Western Europeans have emphasized a need to restrain the Americans and to force more moderate reactions to events, not only in Eastern Europe, but to events outside the treaty obligations of the Atlantic alliance as well. Allied reaction to the 1973 oil crisis, to the invasion of Afghanistan, to detente, and to sanctions in the Polish crisis provide ample evidence of such attempted restraint. By the same token, Rumania, Hungary, and Czechoslovakia have been seen, at varying times, as exerting restraining influence on unilateral Soviet action. It is, of course, unclear whether the Europeans were aware of these opportunities for influence over superpower action in 1949 and 1955 respectively, or whether those were opportunities for influence which emerged later as conditions in Europe changed. The fact that neither Eastern nor Western Europe has been completely successful in restraining the superpowers does not negate these efforts. In both instances, the superpowers have interpreted efforts of restraint as evidence of disloyalty which threatened the cohesion of the alliances.

The idea of restraining allies may also be related to the shift in perceived threat discussed previously. If Eastern Europe's fear of Western aggression and Western Europe's fear of Eastern aggression has shifted to a belief that both superpowers are contributing to world instability, the tendency will be towards greater effort at restraint of the United States and the Soviet Union within each alliance rather than withdrawal. Such developments suggest a profound change in Eastern and Western Europe from cross-alliance perspectives to intra-alliance perspectives.

Responding to the Outbreak of War

The fifth condition under which states form alliances is in response to the outbreak of war; it reflects the distinction between wartime alliances and alliances formed in times of peace.[13] This condition does not apply to either NATO or the Warsaw Pact, unless one is prepared to argue that the outbreak of war includes the cold war, or what Pierre Hassner calls, the "hot peace".[14] Such application is clearly not the intention of those who employ this concept to study the outbreak of hostilities manifested in direct military confrontation. Indeed, these two alliances in Europe were formed upon the cessation of hostilities.

Preserving the Status Quo

Preservation of the status quo as a reason for forming an alliance is a concept so conveniently vague as to be applicable under any and all circumstances, by any and all protagonists. The status quo, logically, could be either war or peace, but it is usually invoked to draw a distinction between the purposes of NATO (to preserve the peace) and the purposes of the Warsaw Pact (to invade Western Europe). Description of states as either following a status quo or revisionist foreign policy reflects the distinction accepted by many alliance specialists between offensive and defensive alliances.[15] Since the Warsaw Pact has never attacked Western Europe and since NATO has never attacked Eastern Europe, it becomes increasingly difficult to characterize either alliance as offensive. It is rather a prejorative classification which ignores the difficulties of establishing aggression before the fact, and its only value seems to lie in its effectiveness as propaganda. The current dispute over the Soviet build-up of forces and the American decision to increase defense spending, in which first the Americans, and then the Russians, issue official versions of force levels to demonstrate that the adversary is expanding military capability in preparation for offensive action is illustrative.

If State A has the dominant position in a military situation in which external threat is perceived, it would be foolish to adopt any policy that is not oriented toward preserving the status quo. Likewise, if State B were in an inferior position, with the same perception of threat, it would be foolish to follow a policy which accepted the status quo. This kind of dichotomous distinction inevitably leads to dichotomous thinking in which nuance is sacrificed to what Robert Jervis calls "spirals of misperception".

It may well be more useful to consider that both the Warsaw Pact and the North Atlantic Treaty Organization are status quo, defensive alliances--that each is committed to preserving a certain way of life for its members; neither treaty makes any reference to intentions to change the status quo. Perhaps some of this confusion may be explained by the tendency of analysts to confuse military planning documents and military contingency plans with foreign policy objectives.

Preserving Ideological and Cultural Similarities

The sixth condition, to preserve ideological and cultural similarity, could only have been proposed in reference to NATO and the Warsaw Pact by someone completely ignorant of the exaggerated lengths to which most Western and Eastern Europeans are prepared to go to demonstrate the uniqueness of their national cultures and ideologies. It is fashionable at the moment to pretend that the current anti-Americanism in Europe, particularly in Germany, is a recent development related only to the unpopularity of theater nuclear weapons. In fact, Western Europeans, particularly the British, have been resisting the onslaught of American values, in all aspects, since the 19th century. That resistance waned in the immediate post-World War II period as American influence was reinforced by much-needed American military and economic assistance. Since the 1960s it has been reinforced again by the growing strength and confidence of Western Europe.

Similarly, no one familiar with the extraordinary diversity of Eastern European cultures, languages, religions, national traditions, and even political ideologies could possibly assert that the Warsaw Pact grouping was created in response to a common desire to preserve ideological and cultural similarity.[16] It is widely recognized that the Eastern European states have resisted--sometimes with the lives of their populace--the expansion of Soviet control and Soviet influence in their domestic affairs. What has not been so obvious is that they have also resisted Russian attempts to dominate their economic, religious, and cultural institutions.

It is only in the distorted and simplistic atmosphere of the superpower focus that preservation of common ideologies and cultures is even remotely acceptable as a condition for forming a security alliance.

Alliances by Coercion

The concept of coercion has often been applied to the formation of the Warsaw Pact, thus implying that the Eastern Europeans had no fear of attack from the West and that they became allies of the Soviet Union only in response to the threat of invasion by Soviet armed forces. As observed earlier, giving emphasis to the coercive aspects of alliance formation tends to obscure East European fears of a rearmed and resurgent Germany as well as the fears of their governments that the Western European states, in cooperation with the United States, might attempt to break the domination of the communist parties. We must be careful to distinguish the formation of the Warsaw Pact from use of military force by the Soviet Union to preserve internal communist party authority in the Eastern European states. However reprehensible the Soviet invasions have been, they are not the sole reason for the existence of the Warsaw Pact.

Regardless of how absurd these fears of Western intervention in Eastern Europe appear today, they must certainly form part of any understanding of the motives of the Eastern European governments in participating in the formation of the Warsaw Pact. An identifiable common interest reinforced by the perception of external threat led to the formation of the Warsaw Pact; in other words, the dichotomous distinction between voluntary and non-voluntary alliances is meaningless because it is so difficult to assess those multiple interests which the act of joining an alliance represents, and because the conditions under which threat is perceived may change.[17]

Maximizing Benefits

The final condition for the formation of alliances to be discussed in this essay is the idea that states form coalitions in response to the calculation of perceived costs and benefits, and that the ultimate goal is to maximize benefits or payoffs. Arguing that states seek to 'maximize payoffs' is similar to arguing that states form alliances because they have identified a common interet. It may be true, but it doesn't tell us very much, and it certainly does not provide a systematic basis from which one alliance could be compared with another. Maximizing payoff is a theoretical construct which can be used to explain anything, even events which are directly antithetical. If we accept that the Soviet Union and the United States formed the two European alliance systems to maximize payoffs and then we accept that France, Great Britain, Rumania, East and West Germany, etc. joined these alliances to maximize payoffs, what is the significance of the construct? This ambiguity is especially noticeable when we can also assert that Sweden, Switzerland, Yugoslavia, and Austria remained outside the coalitions in order to maximize payoffs. Payoff is an idea which has meaning only in terms of carefully constructed games in which rewards are clearly and easily identified, known to all the players, and form the object of the game.

Application of these simple game theory concepts to the formation of alliances has provided a convenient framework for addressing the complicated question of sharing defense costs in both alliances, but it is limited by the difficulty of accurately estimating tangible and intangible contributions of alliance members, by its zero-sum assumptions, and, ultimately, by the difficulty of assessing intentions, particularly in hindsight.

ALLIANCE DISINTEGRATION

Many attempts have been made, in a variety of alliance studies, to identify the conditions and attributes which threaten cohesion. A sample follows: 1) failure of the alliance to achieve its goals; 2) absence of external threat; 3) lack of shared ideology; 4) failure to limit the size of the alliance; 5) failure to assure that rewards exceed costs; 6) decline in alliance leadership; and 7) failure to limit the geographical disperson of alliance members.[18] Identification of the conditions which may lead to the formation of alliances obviously implies that the absence of the same factors may lead to disintegration. Hence, the list above partially constitutes a negative expression of the factors leading to formation; however, there are a few exceptions, such as the restraint of allies and the role of alliance leaders, which are particularly important for NATO and the Warsaw Pact.

The question of cohesion within alliances has also been approached from the perspective of the attributes of the member states and from the attributes of the alliance itself. The latter approach tends to focus on purpose, ideology, size, structure, decision-making processes, capabilities, and the quality of alliance leadership; the former on dichotomous variables such as democratic and authoritarian states (or open and closed policies as contemporary international relations theory would have it), developed-underdeveloped status and large or small states.[19] Since the attributes of the member states of NATO and the Warsaw Pact differ so dramatically, even within the two alliances, this analysis will be concerned only with alliance attributes and not those of individual member states.

Alliance Goals and Disintegration

Perhaps the most confused area of abstract thinking with regard to alliances lies with the question of purpose and scope. Some theoreticians have suggested that alliances which are too broad and general in purpose are likely to fail, while others have concluded that alliances which are too limited in scope will fail. The contradictory nature of these findings has more to do with the number of 'broad' alliances which have failed in the last 200 years and the number of 'limited' alliances which have also collapsed than it does with establishing purpose and scope as a suitable variable upon which to predict either continuation or collapse of any specific alliance. NATO and the Warsaw Pact are two examples of enduring alliances--one is based on a treaty which states its purpose in very broad terms of cultural, political, economic, social, and security objectives; the other is more limited and refers primarily, although not exclusively, to security objectives.

It is difficult to understand how an alliance can be said to have failed in achieving its goals if the goals themselves are numerous, broadly defined, and constantly changing in response to contemporary political interests and issues.

Close examination of the North Atlantic treaty provides a good example of numerous and broadly defined goals. The Preamble of the Treaty states that its members:

> "are determined to safeguard the freedom, common heritage and civilisation of their people, founded on the principles of democracy, individual liberty, and the rule of law".[20]

Article 2 stipulates that NATO members will further peaceful and friendly international relations by

> "strenghtening their free institutions..promoting conditions of stability and well-being (and to) seek to eliminate conflict in their international economic policies and will encourage economic collabora-

> tion between any or all of them."

Article 4 requires the members to consult "whenever, in the opinion of any of them, the territorial integrity, political independence or security of any of the Parties is threatened". Most importantly, for this discussion of NATO goals, even the central purpose of NATO is stated in ambiguous terms. Article 5, often described as the core of the treaty, states:

> "The Parties agree that an armed attack against one or more of them in Europe or North America shall be considered an attack against them all; and consequently they agree that, if such an armed attack occurs, each of them...will assist the Party of Parties so attacked by taking forthwith, individually and in concert with the other Parties, such action as it deems necessary, including the use of armed force to restore and maintain the security of the North Atlantic area." (Emphasis mine)

The underlined portions of Article 5 clearly provide that the United States or any European state could respond to attack without action by NATO and it makes equally clear that the nature of such action is to be determined by individual signatories.[20] With goals expressed in these broad terms, NATO could only fail to meet them if democracy, individual liberty, and the rule of law collapsed in Western Europe and North America, or if it failed to take any action, individually or collectively, in the event of armed attack, and if there were no economic collaboration between its members. On the contrary, it very often seems an alliance in search of purposes that are relevant to a world in which the European Community and OECD have usurped its economic functions, in which the Western European Union has preempted its commitment to democracy and the rule of law, and in which armed attack on Western Europe is increasingly less likely. Indeed, one might argue that the current controversy over extending NATO's reach to include the Persian Gulf is another manifestation of NATO's search for relevance.

Similar arguments may be set forth with regard to the Warsaw Pact and its goals. The Treaty of Friendship, Cooperation, and Mutual Assistance (Warsaw Pact) is not quite as sweeping in expressing its goals, but they are as vaguely defined as those of the North Atlantic Treaty. In the Preamble, the members express a desire "to create a system of collective security in Europe based on the participation of all European states, irrespective of their social and political structure...".[21] The Treaty signatories pledge themselves to "friendship, cooperation and mutual assistance in accordance with the principles of respect for the independence and sovereignty of States and of non-intervention in their domestic affairs". The Warsaw Pact has clearly not been successful in creating an all-European security system, and, of course, no one would argue that the Soviet Union has shown respect for independence and non-intervention in the domestic affairs of its neighbors.

Article 2 of the Warsaw Pact pledges the members to cooperate in general reduction of armaments and the prohibition of atomic, hydrogen and other weapons of mass destruction. In Article 5 the States agreed to "take concerted action" to "defend the peaceful labour of their people, guarantee the inviolability of their frontiers and territories and afford protection against possible aggression".

The core clause of the Warsaw Treaty, Article 4, is as ambiguously stated as its mirror image, Artcle 5 of the North Atlantic Treaty:

> "In the event of an armed attack in Europe on one more of the States parties to the Treaty by any Sate or group of States, each State party to the Treaty shall...<u>individually</u> and in agreement with the other States parties to the Treaty, by all means <u>it considers necessary</u>, including the use of armed force." [22] (Emphasis mine)

Indeed, the Warsaw Pact even sets forth the specific conditions under which it would be dissolved. Article 11 states in this regard:

> "In the event of the establishment of a system of collective security in Europe and the conclusion for that purpose of a General European Treaty concerning collective security, a goal which the Contracting Parties shall steadfastly strive to achieve, the present Treaty shall cease to have effect as from that date on which the General European Treaty comes into force."

The Warsaw Pact has been in existence for twenty-seven years; the fact that it has not realized its goals has had no impact on its longevity. The same may be said for NATO's thirty-three years. Neither alliance has been challenged with regard to its central purpose--to resist armed attack in Europe--and, therefore, neither can be said to have failed or succeeded in this respect.

It is of no use whatsoever to say that an alliance which is broad in purpose will endure at the same time we observe that most of its purposes have been rendered inoperative. It is equally illogical to argue that an alliance limited in scope and which stipulates the specific conditions under which the alliance would cease to exist will endure, despite any change in its external environment.

Absence of External Threat

Linking external threat to internal cohesion and its opposite, external peace to internal dissention, are ancient and familiar concepts in political theory which were developed originally in reference to the governance of individual states and later applied to alliances. With regard to the demise of alliances, it is argued that in the absence of external threat, dissension among the signatories will increase, eventually destroying the minimal cohesion necessary for continuation of the alliance itself. It would be challenging indeed to find a period in the history of NATO during which there was an absence of dissent among the members; dissent occurs for many reason other than the presence or absence of an external threat. Perhaps it would be useful to distinguish wartime coalitions from other alliances, but it hardly seems applicable to NATO and the Warsaw Pact since on both sides there seems to be growing public conviction that the original threat has probably subsided, and an equally strong determination on the part of signatory governments today to continue their commitment to the two alliances.

In the case of NATO, the emphasis on threat has shifted from armed attack as expressed in Article 5 to the threat of political dependence reflected in Article 4. Concepts such as Euro-neutralism, Finlandization, fears that detente would lead to the subversion of Western European political independence, even recent American objections to the Soviet-Western European agreement on natural gas are strong testimony that the threat to Western Europe now expressed in the form of Soviet influence and dependency upon the Soviet Union rather than Soviet military action, is regarded as very real indeed by the Americans. On the other hand, the Western Europeans appear to have few fears of any subtle threat of Soviet influence and remain committed to the benefits of detente. They are also sufficiently prudent not to urge withdrawal from NATO, just in case peace in Europe has, in fact, been a function of the deterrent effect of NATO. Alliance membership, similar to deterrence itself, is dependent upon uncertainty about the opponent's motives and intentions. Despite a genuine desire for independence from the United States and many of its policies, the Western European governments are clearly not ready to commit themselves to an all-European security arrangement which does not include the United States and Canada.[23] It remains to be seen what impact, if any, growing pacifist movements in Western Europe will have on these perceptions.

Uncertainty also characterizes attitudes in Eastern Europe, not only towards the Soviet Union itself, but towards Western Europe and the United States. While the fear of a resurgent Germany has diminished, if not disappeared, there is still sufficient uncertainty about the motives of the United States and its allies to warrant caution in Eastern European governments. A recent example of this caution was Rumanian's warning to the United States that it should not impose sanctions on Poland.[24]

The idea that absence of an external threat to security alliances will lead to their demise may be an accurate observation; the problem is that it ignores the ability of alliance leaders as well as other members to perpetuate an atmosphere in which the appearance of threat seems plausible. Uncertainty not only guarantees the success of this strategy, but also provides a margin of safety in case the absence of threat has been miscalculated.

Lack of Shared Ideology

Lack of shared ideology has often been suggested as a possible source of disintegration of alliances in the past.[25] Today, in response to the influence of psychologists, it is fashionable to talk of different political 'perceptions' rather than ideologies--it is less judgemental and appears more neutral. In fact, what we appear to be talking about is the political orientation of governments to varying forms of socialism, communism, and capitalism. It should be obvious, even to the most biased observer, that none of these forms exist today in pure form, if indeed, they ever did. Theoretically, what distinguishes these concepts is the role of the state in the economic order. To wit, there is more central planning and control in the Soviet Union and the Eastern European states than in Western Europe, and there is more centralization in Western Europe than in the United States. This simplistic ideological approach has obscured the competitive interests of the states involved, and it really has nothing at all to do with the disintegration of cohesion. The Eastern Europeans are increasingly viewed as having challenged the centralized authority of the

Soviet Union and also of their own governments in economic planning and yet the Warsaw Pact shows no sign of collapse.[26] Many Eastern European analysts agree that these signs of resistance to central authority, of rejection of the Soviet model, and the emphasis on pluralistic socialism are inspired not by pure ideological concerns, but rather by the practicalities of economic development, resource and capital scarcity, and the patterns of world trade.

Differences in ideological emphasis can also be found among the NATO states. There is a conservative government currently in Britain, a socialist government with communist Cabinet members in France, a social democratic government in Western Germany, a socialist government in Greece, a liberal government in Canada, a military regime in Turkey, and a conservative Republican government in the United States. Surely these governments do not represent a 'shared ideology'; in fact, there hasn't been a shared ideology since the creation of NATO so lack of the same therein is hardly a credible factor in its potential disintegration. It has even been suggested that Turkey and Greece pay a disproportionately large portion of NATO costs in per capita terms precisely because they lack social, economic, and cultural bonds with the other member states and, therefore, suffer from greater uncertainty with regard to the willingness of their allies to assist in the case of attack.[27]

Other analysts have argued that the commitment to democracy and the rule of law constitutes a shared ideology in NATO and that commitment to a Socialist Commonwealth and to the principles of proletarian internationalism is the shared ideology of the Warsaw Pact. Even if this judgment--which ignores the multiplicity of forms in which democracy and socialism appear in the various states--is correct, its linkage to alliance collapse is not at all persuasive.

Size Principle

Firstly, the application of William Riker's size principle to the continuation of alliances suggests that the size of any given alliance is determined by the minimum number of members which are necessary to meet the purpose of the alliance; therefore the winning strategy is to reduce the number of members.[28] In other words, the smaller the alliance, the larger the benefits which accrue to each member. Application of this principle to international alliances has greatly distorted Riker's initial proposition in which he states the precise conditions under which the size principle is operative:

> "In social situations <u>similar to n-person, zero-sum games</u> with side payments, participants create coalitions just as large as they believe will ensure winning and no larger."[29] (Emphasis mine)

Neither the Warsaw Pact nor NATO is a zero-sum game in which the gain of one player is an automatic loss to the other; indeed, this theoretical construct could use a dose of 'spill over', a concept developed with regard to integration theory and the European Community.[30] To be sure, there are side payments in NATO and in the Warsaw Pact, and differences in benefits as well, but if any state withdraws from either alliance, it is likely to be for reasons of national and foreign policy independence rather than to protest inequitable benefits or costs.

Secondly, Riker's assumption that dissatisfied members react by joining the opponent coalition stretches the credibility of the theory to the breaking point. He argues that "the West" (presumably NATO) will lose members through a tendency to miscalculate side payments resulting in a gain to the Soviet Union of disaffected allies from NATO "until the two great coalitions are roughly equal in size". Riker does not reveal what hidden hand of homeostasis would insure that when the two great coalitions reach equal size, the size principle will automatically cease operating. Of the fifteen members of NATO, which one is likely to leave NATO and join the Warsaw Pact? France left NATO, at least in principle, but there has never been a suggestion that its intention was to join the Warsaw Pact. Indeed, is any Eastern European state likely to leave the Warsaw Pact to join NATO?

One could argue that proposals for a purely Western European defense system, comprised primarily of Britain, West Germany and France represent a tendency in the direction predicted by the size principle, but not many would agree that they represent a winning coalition. Other proposals, for an expanded security arrangement to include Japan or an all-European security arrangement directly contradict the assumptions of the size principle. Comparing the two alliances suggests that the size principle has no relevance at all to the continuation of either. The Warsaw Pact had eight members and one has withdrawn in twenty-seven years; NATO had fifteen members and one has become semi-attached in thirty-three years. (Albania formally withdrew from the Warsaw Pact in 1968. France still participates in some NATO activities despite French forces having been removed from NATO's consolidated command.)

An assumption which is more likely with regard to the size of alliances is that the larger alliances are, the larger the bureaucracy they spawn; perhaps these large bureaucratic structures, more than any single factor, will ensure the continuation rather than the decline of the alliances. The organizational and command structures of both the Warsaw Pact and NATO have increased in size, complexity, and expenditures since their incipience and the costs of dismantling either would be staggering. While the cost of such an operation may not be determining, depending upon the conditions under which such dismantling were to occur, the paring down effects of the size principle are not apparent in either alliance.

Coalition theory has also raised the question of the distribution of reward (benefits) and the allocation of costs in relationship to the maintenance of alliances. The fundamental proposition holds that cohesion will diminish if members' costs exceed rewards or if public benefits are not supplemented with private benefits.[31] The continuing controversy within NATO over the issue of burden sharing and the Rumanian refusal to support expenditure increases within the Warsaw Pact are primary examples of cost/benefit calculation. The extent to which these equity issues are present is the degree to which they create tension within the European alliances. Making decisions is more complex and more difficult in an atmosphere of perceived inequity than otherwise. Whether or not this dissatisfaction leads to the collapse of alliances, or to greater expenditures, remains open to question.

The United States, which has historically borne the greater costs of NATO, has been willing to accept that burden, not only in exchange for leadership and preponderant influence, but also as a function of its relative wealth. There is nothing to indicate that it has abandoned this willingness, despite periodical objection to the inequity of defense expenditures; indeed, the recent and dramatic increase in American defense spending would suggest exactly the contrary.

Rewards of NATO membership (if anyone except scholars calculate security in these terms) continue to outweigh its costs not only for the United States, but presumably for the Western European governments as well. The latter have increased their contribution to NATO in the past few years, despite the simultaneous development of more independent positions in relation to the United States. Given that the Western European states still spend a relatively small percentage of their national budgets on defense, one of the attractions of NATO may well be the savings it has made possible. For the United States and its allies, cost/benefit calculations have been a source of tension, but they are not sufficiently salient to force withdrawal of member governments. On the contrary, the high cost of defense may well force some states to remain in the alliance, despite their preference for alternate arrangements.

Decline in the Strength of Leadership and Monolithic Alliances

Since the defeat of American forces in Viet Nam, the Watergate scandal, and the rapid reversals of policy during the Carter administration, it has become popular both in Europe and in the United States to argue that cohesion in the NATO alliance has diminished due to the weakness of American leadership. In a similar vein, analysts of Eastern European and Soviet affairs concentrate on the 1956 Hungarian crisis, the 1968 Czechoslovakian crisis, Rumanian resistance to increased defense expenditures, the current crisis in Poland, and the beleagured position of the Soviet Union in Afghanistan to illustrate a weakened alliance leader, able to maintain alliance cohesion only through the use of force. In both cases, it is not at all clear to what degree these events have actually affected alliance leadership and to what degree they have been used by smaller allies to curtail the preponderance of superpower states like the United States and the Soviet Union. Since 1945 no American president has been popular in Europe while in office, and the same applies to Soviet leaders Eastern Europe. Leader popularity is not a particularly sound basis on which to assess leadership success; perhaps the longevity of these two alliances is a more appropriate measure. Whatever the mistakes and miscalculations of the governments of the Soviet Union and the United States, the alliances which they guaranteed to support in 1949 and in 1955 show no signs of imminent collapse.

Alliance theoreticians have often attempted to distinguish between monolithic and pluralistic alliances in a manner which implies the question of alliance leadership. Logically, a monolithic alliance, one completely dominated by a single state, would weaken if the leader is weakened. But first of all, what is a monolithic alliance? The Warsaw Pact is often cited as an example, but even a cursory reading of the literature on the Pact indicates that a considerable amount of bargaining and negotiation occurs among its members. On the other hand, a pluralistic alliance has been defined as one:

> "marked by recognition that the ultimate locus of decision-making authority resides with the nation--rather than in the alliance as a whole or with its leading member(s)--and with acceptance of diversity in ideology, institutions, and other salient attributes."[32]

This definition could apply to the Warsaw Pact: Rumania did refuse to contribute troops to the invasion of Czechoslovakia, Poland does have a government controlled not by the communist party but by the Polish military, and both Hungary and Czechoslovakia have implemented economic reforms which are at considerable variance with Soviet economic orthodoxy. On the other hand, many Western Europeans would argue that NATO has been so dominated by the United States that it does not fit the description of a pluralistic alliance; hence the distinction between principle and subordinate members.

What should be obvious is that within any grouping of states or individuals, some sort of bargaining will result from diversity of interests and perceived needs--a process which denies any single state the opportunity for complete control of outcomes.[33] There are no monolithic alliances, neither as an existing type nor as an 'ideal' type that defines the end of a continuum. 'Ideal types' do not assist efforts to undertand how alliances actually work; in fact, they obscure the similarities between alliances and the differences among allies within one alliance.

Geographic Dispersion

The final point to be addressed with regard to the conditions under which alliance cohesion may diminish is the proposition that if geographical distance between members of an alliance is too great, cohesion will evaporate. Presumably the theoretical progenitor of this idea is the classical dictum that far-flung empires will encounter problems trying to control peripheral areas.[34] It is difficult to establish any direct basis for application of this principle to the North Atlantic Treaty Organization or to the Warsaw Pact. Most analysts would agree that cohesion (or acceptance of superpower leadership) in NATO and the Warsaw Pact was very strong during the 1950s and 1960s, and that it appeared to wane in the 1970s and 1980s; however, the reason for that shift may lie in the gradually increasing strength and confidence of the Western and Eastern Europeans rather than in the geographical distance between the member states. The principle was apparently developed in reference to the United States and the collapse of CENTO; it does not seem relevant to the

European security alliances. If the point of this proposition is that regional clusters of states are more likely to be homogeneous than widely dispersed areas, it may be applicable, but then the dependent variable shifts from geography to cultural factors.[35]

CONCLUSION

Many of the abstract propositions which have been developed in connection with the study of alliances were derived from the systemic or macro-level perspective of international relations and they provide a useful framework for analysis in that context. They are limited, but certainly not useless, when applied to the study of specific alliances. Attempts to classify alliances into dichotomous types is problematical as it tends to lead researchers into either-or judgments which are laden with prejorative overtones.

There has been a tendency to view and study the European alliance systems from the perspective of U.S.-Soviet relations and the balance of power rather than from the interaction of allies within each alliance.[36] The superpower perspective produced abstract generalizations about the nature of alliances which are different from the abstractions which emerge from the perspective of the alliance itself. Regional integration studies have yielded a wealth of information on the interaction of nation states within a community which may also be applicable *mutatis mutandis* to alliance studies. Foci on conflicting interests, bargaining, mutual concessions, the role of interest groups, protective devices such as weighted voting and graduated cost assessments which benefit smaller and weaker states are a reflection of the fundamental assumption that regional economic communities are composed of states with equal rights, if not with equal obligations. The tendency to treat both NATO and the Warsaw Pact simply as an extension of superpower relations and superpower leadership hampers the ability of all member states within both alliances to find areas of compromise and conciliation. Too often, the issues which confront the members of these alliances are cast in terms of a zero-sum game in which American victories are interpreted as Western European defeats and Eastern European successes as a loss in prestige for the Soviet Union. Unfortunately, the theoretical propositions of alliance studies tend also to reflect NATO-Warsaw Pact differentiation rather than commonalities combined with interaction patterns and behavior within each alliance.

The European states, because of their unique historical experiences since World War II, have developed a healthy, if belated, respect for the independent sovereignty of other states; their regional institutions reflect this respect in a very concrete way. The Americans and the Russians, also because of unique historical experiences since World War II, have tended to assume that size and military capability make some states more equal than others; their diplomacy often reflects this perspective. It should not be surprising, then, that when these two radically different perspectives are brought to a single alliance, dissension, frustration, and conflict will arise. It would certainly be wrong to conclude that the presence of such conflict is a harbinger of alliance collapse.[37] As this essay has attempted to demonstrate, there is a paucity of theoretical or abstract propositions which apply to comparative approaches to the study of NATO and the Warsaw Pact, and there is pressing need to supplement those few propositions which focus on the relationships among equal and sovereign states within security alliances.

Equality within alliances does not have to be defined solely in terms of weapons production, number of tanks, troops, missiles, and percentage of GNP devoted to defense expenditures; it could also be defined in terms of sovereign independence. It is ironic indeed that the United States and the Soviet Union, whose revolutions in 1776 and 1917 respectively were based in part on this principle, seem to have lost sight of its validity. It may seem idealistic to insist upon first principles, but this sense of equality and respect for sovereign states lies at the heart of alliance and community cohesion. What is missing in both of these alliances is not strength of leadership, but rather leadership which regards its partners as sovereign equals, with a right to national independence in the case of the Warsaw Pact and with a right to foreign policy independence in the case of NATO.

FOOTNOTES

1. Ted Robert Gurr, Politimetrics: An Introduction to Quantitative Macropolitics. (Englewood Cliffs, N.J.: Prentice-Hall, 1972), Chp. 1.

2. Thucydides, History of the Peloponnesian War, ed. Richard Livingstone (Oxford University Press, 1960); Emmerich de Vattel, The Law of nations (New York: AMS Press, repr. 1863 ed.); Hugo Grotius, The Rights of War and Peace, Including the Law of Nature and Nations (Westport, Ct.: Hyperion Conn., repr. 1901 ed.); Polybius, Discoursing of the Warres Betwixt the Romans and Carthaginenses, trans. Christopher Watson (Norwood, N.J.: Walter J. Johnson, repr. 1568 ed.); Niccolo Machiavelli, The Prince, trans. George Bull (London: Penguin Books Ltd., 1961).

3. The following references are arranged in chronological order:

   Arnold Wolfers, Alliance Policy in the Cold War (Westport, Ct.: Greenwood 1976); Hans J. Morgenthau, Politics Among Nations: The Struggle for Power and Peace (New York: Alfred A. Knopf), 5th ed. rev., 1978, Chp. 12; George Liska, Nations in Alliance: The Limits of Interdependence (Baltimore: Johns Hopkins University Press, 1962); Joseph Frankel, International Relations (New York: Oxford University Press, 1964), pp. 166-170; Charles O. Lerche and Abdul A. Said, Concepts of International Politics (Englewood Cliffs, N.J.: Prentice-Hall, 1963): 116-117; Mancur J. Olson Jr. and Richard Zeckhauser, "An Economic Theory of Alliances," Review of Economics and Statistics 48 (1966): 266-279; W.H. Riker The Theory of Political Coalitions (New Haven: Yale University Press, 1967); Robert E. Osgood, Alliances and American Foreign Policy (Baltimore, Md.: Johns Hopkins University Press, 1968), Chp. II; Bruce M. Russett, "Components of an Operational Theory of Alliance Formation," Journal of Conflict Resolution 12 (September 1968): 286-301; Philip M. Burgess and James A. Robinson, "Alliances and the Theory of Collective Action: A Simulation of Coalition Processes," in International Politics and Foreign Policy, ed. James N. Rosenau (New York: The Free Press, 1969), pp. 640-653; Francis A. Beer, Integration and Disintegration in NATO: Processes of Alliance Cohesion and Prospects for Atlantic Community (Columbus: Ohio State University Press, 1969); Idem, Alliances: Latent War Communities in the Contemporary World (New York:

Holt, Rinehart & Winston, Inc., 1970); James E. Dougherty and Robert L. Pfaltzgraff, Jr., *Contending Theories of International Relations* (New York: J.B. Lippincott Company, 1971), pp. 301-304; Louis Rene Beres, *The Management of World Power: A Theoretical Analysis* (Monograph Series in World Affairs, University of Denver, 1973); John D. Sullivan, "International Alliances" in *International Systems: A Behavioral Approach,* ed. Michael Haas (New York: Chandler Publishing Co., 1974), pp. 100-122; Patrick M. Morgan, *Theories and Approaches to International Politics: What Are We To Think?* (New Brunswick, N.J.: Transaction Books, 1975), pp. 201-205; Michael P. Sullivan, *International Relations: Theories and Evidence* (Englewood Cliffs, N.J.: Prentice-Hall, Inc., 1976), pp. 173-176, 189-199; Ole R. Holsti, "Alliance and Coalition Diplomacy," in *World Politics*, eds. James N. Rosenau, Kenneth W. Thompson, and Gavin Boyd (New York: The Free Press, 1976), pp. 337-372; Charles Ostrom and Francis W. Hoole, "Alliances and Wars Revisited: A Research Note," *International Studies Quarterly* 22 (June 1978); Walter F. Hahn and Robert L. Pfaltzgraff, Jr., eds., *Atlantic Community in Crisis: A Redefinition of the Transatlantic Relationship* (Elmsford, N.Y.: Pergamon, 1979).

4. See David Calleo, *The Atlantic Fantasy; The U.S., NATO, and Europe* (Baltimore: Johns Hopkins University Press, 1970): David Watt, "The European Initiative," *Foreign Affairs* 57:3, Special Ed. (America and the World, 1978); Christoph Bertram, "European Security and the German Problem," *International Security* (Winter 1979/1980): 105-116.

5. See Trevor Taylor, "Power Politics," in *Approaches and Theory in International Relations*, ed. Trevor Taylor (London: Longman, 1978):122-140, for a competent description and critique of power-politics thinking; and Michael P. Sullivan, *International Relations: Theories and Evidence*, pp. 155-176 for a cogent discussion of power, power theory, and balance of power.

6. Dale R. Herspring, "The Warsaw Pact at 25," *Problems of Communism* (September-October 1980):6-8 and Malcolm Mackintosh, "The Warsaw Pact Today," *Survival* (May - June 1974):124.

7. Paul Marer, "Has Eastern Europe Become a Liability to the Soviet Union: III--The Economic Aspect," in *The International Politics of Eastern Europe*, ed. Charles Gati (New York: Praeger, 1976), p. 79;

Sarah Meiklejohn Terry, "The Implications of Interdependence for Soviet-East European Relations: A Preliminary Analysis of the Polish Case," in <u>The Foreign Policies of East Europe: New Approaches</u>, ed. Ronald H. Linden (New York: Praeger, 1980), pp. 186-266. See Archie Brown, "Eastern Europe: 1968, 1978, 1988," <u>Daedalus</u> (Winter 1979) for a persuasive argument that the gradual pull of Eastern Europe is away from the Soviet model.

8. See, for example, the contrasts between Robert Osgood's assertion that NATO was created by the United States to deter Soviet expansion; Walter LeFeber's argument that the Truman administration's fanatic anti-communism was a veil to obscure an American drive for prepronderance; Alfred Grosser's judgment that NATO reflected the prime concern of the Europeans to secure an American guarantee of European security; and John Lukacs' suggestion that the mistrust between the Soviet Union and the U.S. which led to the creation of NATO and the Warsaw Pact was all due to a misunderstanding. It is sobering to realize that all four authors are discussing the same two-year period (1947-1949). Robert Osgood, <u>Alliances and American Foreign Policy</u>, Chp. III; Walter L. LeFeber, <u>America, Russia and the Cold War, 1945-1975</u> (New York: John Wiley and Sons, Inc., 1976, 3rd ed.), Chp. IV; Alfred Grosser, <u>The Western Alliance: European-American Relations Since 1945</u> (New York: Continuum Publishing Co., 1980), pp. 82-95; and John Lukacs, <u>A History of the Cold War</u> (New York: Anchor Books, 1962, rev. ed.), p.77.

9. This insight comes from James N. Rosenau during a lecture on the level of analysis problem at the Amerika Haus, Munich, West Germany, 1978.

10. <u>Treaty of Alliance and Mutual Assistance between Britain and France</u> (Treaty of Dunkirk), 4 March 1947, Articles I, II, III; and <u>Treaty Between Belgium, France, Luxembourg, the Netherlands and Britain</u> (Brussels Treaty), Brussels, 17 March 1948, Preamble and Article VII. Both treaties reprinted in J.A.S. Grenville, <u>The Major International Treaties 1914-1973</u>. (London: Methuen & Co. Ltd., 1974), pp. 365-367.

11. Niccolo Machiavelli, <u>The Prince</u>, Chp. XXI.

12. Robert L. Rothstein, <u>Alliances and Small Powers</u> (New York: Columbia University Press, 1968); Patrick J. McGowan and Klaus-Peter Gottwald, "Small State

Foreign Policies", International Studies Quarterly (December 1975) 19:4.

13. See J. David Singer and Melvin Small, "Alliance Aggregation and the Onset of War, 1815-1945," in Quantitative International Politics, ed. J. David Singer (New York: The Free Press, 1968), pp. 247-286. An excellent discussion of war and alliances may also be found in Randolph M. Siverson, "War and Change in the International System," in Change in the International System, ed. Ole R. Holsti, Randolph M. Siverson, and Alexander L. George (Boulder: Westview Press, 1980), pp. 211-229.

14. Pierre Hassner, "Intra-Alliance Diversities and Challenges: NATO in an Age of Hot Peace" in NATO: The Next Thirty Years, ed. Kenneth A. Myers (Boulder, Colo.: Westview Press and London: Croom Helm, 1980), pp. 373-395.

15. Osgood, Alliances and American Foreign Policy, p. 25.

16. Peter F. Sugar, ed., Ethnic Diversity and Conflict in Eastern Europe (Santa Barbara, Ca: ABC-Clio, 1980); and Bernard L. Faber, ed., The Social Structure of Eastern Europe: Transition and Process in Czecho- slovakia, Hungary, Poland, Romania, and Yugoslavia (New York: Praeger, 1976).

17. For example, Bruce Russett uses this distinction to explain why the larger nations of NATO assume the burden of defense expenditures for the alliance, but in the Warsaw Pact for the two years studied (1965 and 1967), the smaller nations paid a disproportionate share of the defense burden, i.e. the Soviet Union was forcing them to bear defense expenditures which were not a function of their GNP levels. Cited in John Sullivan, "International Alliances", pp. 111-113. Sullivan then suggests that reversal of the pattern may indicate that the Warsaw Pact is "becoming more voluntary" and that the smaller nations of Eastern Europe are increasingly confident of the Soviet Union's deterrent ability. (See fn. 27 for further elaboration).

18. See fn. 3 for sources.

19. Ole R. Holsti, "Alliances and Coalition Diplomacy," pp. 344-345.

20. North Atlantic Treaty between Belgium, Canada, Denmark, France, Iceland, Italy, Luxembourg, the Netherlands, Norway, Portugal, Britain, and the

United States, Washington, 4 April 1949. Reprinted in Grenville, Major International Treaties, pp. 335-337.

21. Treaty of Friendship, Cooperation and Mutual Assistance (Warsaw Pact), in Grenville, p. 365.

22. Ibid, p. 366.

23. For a particularly sensitive description of the problems faced by Canada in the Alliance, see Charles Pentland, "The Canadian Dilemma," in Dilemmas of the Atlantic Alliance, ed. Peter Christian Ludz, H. Peter Dreyer, Charles Pentland and Lothar Ruehl (New York: Praeger Publishers, 1975), pp. 159-175.

24. New York Times (Sunday, February 14, 1982), p. 14.

25. See George Liska, Nations in Alliance, for the idea that an alliance ideology is the primary prerequisite for alliances; Hans J. Morgenthau, Politics Among Nations, for a discussion of alliances serving identical, complementary and ideological interests. For a more recent statement of ideologies in Europe, see Raymond Aron, In Defense of Decadent Europe, trans. Stephen Cox (South Bend: Regnery/Gateway, Inc., 1977), Chp. X.

26. Dale R. Herspring, "The Warsaw Pact at 25", passim.

27. Bruce Russett, cited in Sullivan, "International Alliances," p. 113. Russett also speculates that Greece, Turkey, and Norway bear a larger defense burden because they share a common border with a Warsaw Pact country. So does the Federal Republic of Germany. Other analysts argue that some states contribute more to the alliance because they "value" it more. What is demonstrated here and in fn. 17 is that some states pay more for common defense than others, but we have no clear idea why.

28. William H. Riker, The Theory of Political Coalitions, 1962.

29. Ibid.

30. Ernst B. Haas, The Uniting of Europe: Political, Social and Economic Forces, 1950-1957 (Stanford University Press, 1958).

31. Philip M. Burgess and James A. Robinson, "Alliances and the Theory of Collective Action" cited in fn. 4 and Harvey Starr, "A Collective Goods Analysis of

the Warsaw Pact after Czechoslovakia," International Organization (Summer 1974) 28:5.

32. Ole R. Holsti, "Alliance and Coalition Diplomacy," p. 350.

33. See Robert S. Jordan, Political Leadership in NATO: A Study in Multilateral Diplomacy (Boulder: Westview Press, 1979).

34. Edward Gibbon, The Decline and Fall of the Roman Empire, ed. J.B. Bury (New York: The Heritage Press, 1946), Vols. I, II, III.

35. Establishing a clear understanding of what constitutes a region, other than geographical location, is an exceedingly complex task which is the subject of much controversy in international relations. See Bruce M. Russett, International Regions and the International System (Chicago: Rand McNally, 1967) and Werner J. Feld and Gavin Boyd, eds., Comparative Regional Systems (New York: Pergamon Press, 1980).

36. Exceptions to the general superpower focus are Richard E. Neustadt, Alliance Politics (New York: Columbia University Press, 1970); Alvin J. Cottrell and James E. Dougherty, The Politics of the Atlantic Alliance (New York: Praeger, 1964); N. Edwina Moreton, East Germany and the Warsaw Alliance: The Politics of Detente (Boulder, Colo: Westview Press, 1978) and Robin Remington, "The Warsaw Pact: Communist Coalition Politics in Action," Yearbook of World Affairs, 1971.

37. For a well-written analysis of Atlantic relations which concludes that the present balance in Europe is not only stable, but will continue to be so, see Anton W. DePorte, Europe Between the Superpowers: The Enduring Balance (New Haven: Yale University Press, 1979).

Part II

The North Atlantic Treaty Organisation

4
Atlantic Unity and European Defence

Kenneth Hunt

A FEW FACTS FIRST

The defence of Western Europe rests squarely on the North Atlantic Alliance. The underlying rationale of the Alliance is the American commitment to Europe. U.S. forces in Europe are the physical expression of this commitment. NATO is the mechanism for the presence of U.S. forces in Europe.

These are the political and military facts around which the security of Europe--a wider notion than just its defence--is built. Europeans want to identify the United States with their security, want any threat to them to be at once a threat to the United States as well. The United States is the only power that can match the Soviet Union; hence Europeans judge that the men in Moscow will be more powerfully deterred from launching an attack on Europe if it involves attacking Americans at the same time. The link between Western Europe and the United States is thus the basis of allied deterrence.

There is no disposition among NATO governments to seek any other security arrangements; these are considered the best and strongest obtainable. They offer great advantage not only for Europe, but also for the United States, for whom NATO provides allies to help keep a political and military balance with the Soviet Union, and permits defence at a distance from American shores.

IDENTITY OF INTEREST

Identity of interest has made the Alliance durable and continues to suit both sides of the Atlantic. But the Alliance depends nonetheless on the health of the relationship between Western Europe and the United

States, which, not infrequently, gives cause for concern. Fifteen years ago Henry Kissinger titled his book on the Alliance, The Troubled Partnership.[1] Just recently, four institutes of international affairs have jointly talked of 'the current transatlantic crisis' and of "differences between Europeans and Americans ... on a whole spectrum of issues, ranging from defence to economics and basic foreign policy". Because of this perceived magnitude of disagreement, the authors wrote a joint report calling for action.[2]

Though the difficulties are by no means new, they have come sharply to the fore again following a period of uncertain leadership from Washington and assertive policies from Moscow. Some of the problems faced are inherent in the nature of an alliance between a superpower and a number of small states, between a global power and what are now largely regional ones. But circumstances have also changed since the NATO Treaty was signed. In 1949 the European members were weak and some of their economies were in ruins: the willingness of the United States to bring its great military and economic strength to their aid gave the Alliance its essential basis. Now the Europeans are rich, so Washington can reasonably look to them to do a great deal for their own security. And the United States can no longer extend protection to them as easily as it once did; the growth of Soviet power has been such that U.S. forces are now severely stretched.

If, however, Europeans have largely outgrown their former political and economic dependence on the United States and often follow the direction of perceived interests of their own, they have not outgrown their security dependence. They still look to American protection, still need U.S. forces in Europe--both conventional and nuclear. The latter is particularly important because, as a result of U.S. policy and European politics, no European nuclear force has emerged, only the national nuclear deterents of Britain and France. Indeed, faced with possible threats to vital economic resources outside the NATO area, Europeans depend on the United States, as a global power, more than ever. Since the United States also needs allies to help compete with Soviet forces around the world, the reason for Atlantic unity remains constant. Alliances, however, need nourishment through constant, close consultation, and through political cooperation which has not always taken place. Unreconciled differences of view have strained the cohesion on which European security depends. They need attention.

STRAINS ON ALLIANCE COHESION

Burden Sharing

One of the recurring differences among allies centres around an American view, periodically articulated, that the burden of defence is not fairly shared. Foreign exchange costs can also be brought into the argument. The issue has not recently caused as much trouble as in the past, a surprising absence given the long period during which the U.S. economy and the dollar have weakened. But it can be reiterated as it was recently in a plaintive sub-heading in NATO Review: "European Contribution Not Fully Appreciated".[3] The problem, though, is not simple because there is no agreement on how the burden should be measured; therefore, disagreements over the resources each ally should, can and will provide are not unnatural.

The normative question of what should be is inherent in any alliance: while it is possible to assess what military forces the alliance as a whole may need to meet an enemy threat, it is rarely easy to say precisely what portion of those forces should be provided by each ally, unless it is merely a matter of manning a discrete national frontier. The apportionment has, therefore, tended to be rather arbitrary, based partly on military requirements and partly on the national capacity which may vary, to secure these forces. The simplest test of national effort may be the size of defence expenditure in relation to GNP (gross national product) or GDP (gross domestic product), but nations for whom such a comparison is unflattering will point to other yardsticks, such as the trend of spending over a period of years, or perhaps manpower in the armed forces or the quality of forces. In truth, no single indicator is wholly satisfactory, but equally no combination of indicators can disguise the fact that some allies do not carry their fair share, however measured.

Occasionally an incapacity to pay any more is quite evident: Turkey plainly cannot, at the moment, increase its contribution and it needs economic assistance from others just to maintain equilibrium as an ally. All member countries are suffering from the effects of economic recession and from low growth rates combined with high inflation and high unemployment; hence there are serious constraints on the ability to devote more resources to defence.

Even if the economic situation improves, the ability to provide more resources will still vary; some countries have greater resources and perhaps a stronger social fabric than others. Political choice or political will is usually involved, and the force of domestic factors has to be recognised. A weak coalition government may be much less able than a firmly supported one to defer pressing social claims for resources in favour of defence, however strongly urged by allies to do so. Survival in office may be at stake; governments do not invite their own demise if they can help it. (Survival in the Alliance is not an issue since no member will be ejected and, if necessary, other allies can be left to pick up any tab, and a potential successor government may be even worse, e.g. leftward-looking ones which might want to cut defence anyway.)

It is not always the same allies which lag in defence spending; each nation's position may depend on the administration in office at a particular time. In 1977, NATO members pledged themselves to aim at a real increase in defence expenditure of 3% per annum. Some states have achieved this, othere have not. At one time it looked as though the United States might not reach the target, but spending has now increased sharply in the wake of events in Afghanistan and U.S. allies are expected to follow suit. The obvious danger for the Alliance is potential resentment among Americans if Europeans are thought to be backsliding. Such attitudes create strains akin to those which, in the early 1970s, led to pressure in the United States Congress for withdrawal of some of the forces from Europe--a move only narrowly averted.* Reduction of U.S. troops in Europe is not a desired objective of the Europeans, particularly at a time when U.S. forces need to be available in the Gulf area and elsewhere. So Europeans will have to demonstrate that they are willing to contribute fully to defence. For want of a better measurement, the annual increase of 3% in real terms is the standard by which their contribution will generally be judged. For the sake of continued harmony within the Alliance, one hopes the European members will meet the projected percentage.

The argument can be aggravated by the problem of arms sales, which show a steady imbalance in favour of the United States which sells far more to Europe than it buys. It is very difficult to persuade some U.S. Congressmen that weapons should be bought other than from their own districts, and so despite the 'two-way street'

---

* Refers to the Mansfield Amendment to reduce the level of U.S. troops stationed in the Federal Republic of Germany. (Ed.)

concept--the purchase of weapon systems on both sides of the Atlantic--the traffic has remained mostly in one direction. Occasionally European purchase of American arms helps to offset U.S. foreign exchange expenditure on its forces in Europe, but the result is fewer jobs in Europe. At a time of recession not only is employment politically important to governments, but spending money on the domestic economy may also help to underpin the defence budgets themselves. It is much easier to secure defence budget approval in national parliaments if some of the resulting expenditures create employment. Certainly an adequate armaments base in Europe is important for European security; American readiness to buy arms from Europe is another facet of burden-sharing.

Threats Outside the NATO Area

A problem which has recently tested the machinery of the Alliance and its ability to provide for European security is that of responding to threats that arise outside the Treaty boundaries. The question of whether or not these boundaries should be extended is irrelevant; there is general acceptance that such extension is neither politically possible nor desirable for a variety of reasons. Rather it is a matter of reaching agreement on what individual allies--those who are willing and able--should try to do, and what the implications are for the rest of the Alliance and for European defence.[4]

Just as some allies are reluctant to spend more on defence, so some are not willing to be drawn into security problems outside Europe. Reluctance to be involved in the periphery may stem simply from a desire not to reduce limited resources in Europe where they can be most effective; or from a desire not to get involved in the often emotive politics of the Middle East or Africa; or, to put it bluntly, from the feeling that it is all better left to the United States, which has more power. It is also possible, however, that distaste for peripheral involvement will be tempered by reluctance to accept and support American ideas and policies.

It is, perhaps, worth digressing at this point to observe that NATO allies are often under considerable pressure from Washington to see events as Americans see them; with the inference that this American view is, of course, the correct one, and to disagree with it is to show lack of cohesion. Europeans may perhaps be forgiven a certain wry cynicism. It is not only that each fresh American administration comes bounding in with fine new ideas and acts as if history were starting from this point forward, it is also that the record of U.S.

foreign policy over the years has been an uneven one. For many years, the United States acted as though Taiwan were China and the 900 million Chinese across the straits did not exist. Until the October War of 1973, American policy in the Middle East was almost completely one-sided, in effect enhancing Soviet potential for influence in the Arab states. The more even-handed policy that Henry Kissinger very sensibly embarked upon still has constraints which arise from American domestic rather than strategic considerations. And U.S. policy in the Gulf has not been noticeably successful. This is not, I hasten to add, to suggest that Europeans have a monopoly of foreign policy wisdom, far from it. It is just that it is in the nature of an alliance of unequals that American policy should usually be pressed upon Europeans, accompanied now and again by some tendency to preach or exhort.

The Europeans are, therefore, justified in some questioning of U.S. foreign policy if, indeed, it has yet been formulated. An example which appears pertinent is the underlying premise that East-West causes lie at the root of problems in the Middle East. Patently the reasons for the Arab-Israeli dispute, for the Iran-Iraq war, for the rise of militant Islam or new nationalisms lie elsewhere and so may their solutions. While the Soviet Union will exploit events to its own advantage, it does not always engineer them. The strong military emphasis in current American attitudes towards Middle East problems should also be questioned, particularly when it is arguable that good relations with Arab states would deter Soviet expansionism as well or better.

Europeans, however, should be ready to admit that there is a military problem in the area which can be compared briefly with the situation in Europe. Here, security has been maintained by drawing, in effect, a line across the continent and manning it with military forces. Among these forces are Americans, thus identifying the United States with the defence of Europe. Expressed more colourfully, we have laid an American across the road, so that no Soviet advance can be made without running over him, and in that fact lies the strength of deterrence. The same objective was what President Carter intended to accomplish in the wake of the invasion of Afghanistan. He declared a vital Western interest in the integrity of the Gulf area and drew a notional line around it. He made clear that the United States would resist Soviet military expansion across that line, in effect proposing to lay an American across the road as in Europe. There was, of course, a problem: there were no American forces in the Gulf area, it was difficult to know quite where the road might be, and the inevitable slowness with which troops could be gotten there was likely to reduce the effectiveness of military action.

Nonetheless, the United States did accept the possibility of a military threat to Middle Eastern oil resources, on which Europe depends even more than does the United States, and was prepared to take action. Many in Europe--with the notable exceptions of France and Britain--have preferred inaction and dependence on an American response. That way could spell disaster for continued alliance: American public opinion will simply not understand or accept European unwillingness to help defend resources vital to Europe itself.

The point is that the issue of peripheral threat needs careful treatment. Deterrence of any Soviet ambitions in the Gulf requires, of course, political action as well as military. All the allies can play a part politically; indeed the very diversity of some of their views may be helpful in exercising influence in different countries. The American position in the Gulf, and thus the Western one, is not made easy by a prevailing Arab view that the United States is unwilling or unready to press Israel hard enough to bring about a settlement of the Palestinian problem which is acceptable to the Arab states. Europeans have a discernibly different approach--a collective one reached through consultation among the Ten of the EEC--which many Americans find unwelcome. If the allies are to reach a unified position, there will have to be some reconciliation of the different perspectives. Despite the fact that it bears the weight of responsibility in practice, if the United States insists on following its own policy, it can strain the cohesion of the allies, regardless of whether it presses them to conform or even to do nothing.

The Allied military aspect is simple by comparison, though it, too, may be affected by American disatisfaction with European contributions. Direct military assistance for American efforts in the Gulf is likely to come only from France and Britain, although there are airfields in eastern Turkey which, under certain circumstances, the United States might be allowed to use. But generally, for Europeans, the task will be to fill gaps left by American units withdrawn from Europe or by American reinforcements due here but diverted to the Gulf. The security dilemma for the Europeans is painfully clear: on the one hand, if these force gaps are not filled, the defence of Europe will be weaker; on the other, if U.S. forces are not earmarked for the Gulf, European economies could be at the mercy of Soviet military threat in that region.[4]

DETENTE AND DIVISIBILITY

As has been suggested above, many Europeans have not found it easy to agree with some strands of American policy outside the NATO area. There was a general reluctance to comply with the request for sanctions against Iran, partly because it was thought they would not work very well and partly because they risked cutting Iran off from the West altogether. Likewise, there was difficulty over the response to events in Afghanistan. That some action was eventually taken in both cases was due to the necessity of maintaining alliance cohesion, even though Washington sometimes acted without consulting Europe. It was a question of supporting the Americans--'they are, after all, the best Americans we've got, the only ones we've got'. The last two years of the Carter administration were difficult for the Alliance because it was not easy to agree upon common policies to deal with urgent events outside the area in which the Alliance was designed to operate.

Perhaps, a certain divergence of alliance views on Iran was to be expected, but the invasion of Afghanistan should have united allies. Here was a hostile Soviet action, effectively opening up a new front in a vital area where the West had little or no strength. In fact, while there was universal condemnation of the invasion, the steps that Washington requested did create gaps between the United States and some allies. The most notable example was West Germany which did not want to take action against the Soviet Union quite as readily as the United States was prepared to do, and did not want to give up the benefits of detente. A strand of public opinion in Germany saw Europe as a relatively stable region into which instabilities from the external world should not be imported: they wanted Europe to be a sort of island of detente. Such a concept of detente may be extreme, but it is shared by many other Europeans and by some Americans as well.

West Germany is certain to view political events from a perspective that is different from that of the United States. Its foreign policy is, to be sure, firmly based on the Atlantic link--the *Ostpolitik* is securely rooted in an over-riding *Westpolitik*. Given its geographical location, the Federal Republic needs good relations with Eastern Europe, and with East Germany notably, and thus to be on reasonable terms with the Soviet Union, since the foreign policies of Eastern Europe are clearly subject to Soviet direction. In the era of detente, West Germany developed close trading links with the East and particularly East Germany, and a large number of German jobs now depend on this trade.

Sanctions against the Soviet Union were thus not an easy step for West Germany to take. Ironically, President Reagan has now lifted the grain embargo, not because some other allies continued trading with the East, but for purely internal reasons. Domestic considerations were allowed primacy over foreign policy, whereas Germany's actions sprang from a mixture of the two. Poland could provide a more difficult test of European security. If Soviet divisions should intervene in Poland, it is probable that all the NATO allies will abandon detente. Whether West Germany would sever its trading links with East Germany is a more difficult question. Merely to pose it is a reminder that on some issues there may not be a completely unified view, free of special interests, despite the fact that the conflict arises, not in a peripheral area, but in Europe itself.

Attitudes to Moscow that differ at least in degree from those held by Americans will continue to be the European tendency. The Soviet Union is in Europe and cannot be wished away; Europeans must find some way in which they can live with such a difficult state. It is not surprising that they hope Washington will manage its own links with Moscow in such a way as will enable a working relationship to emerge. Different attitudes to arms control negotiations bring our fairly clearly what the Europeans desire.

ARMS CONTROL

Perhaps Europeans tend to give arms control a more political interpretation than do Americans; arms control negotiations are seen as part of the political process in Europe. Americans tend to look at the military balance and the numbers more carefully since these can have ample domestic political resonance, even if they do not impact so immediately upon foreign policy. Europeans look at numbers too, but in a more general way, because they want to ensure both reasonable parity and an American sense of being secure, on which their own protection depends. They also see arms control negotiations as a vehicle for achieving political stability. Even conservative European governments wanted SALT II ratified, because a failure to do so would damage relations with the Soviet Union which they want Washington to manage.

As a recent study has observed, failure to pursue

arms control would also "seriously undermine the legitimacy and political support of Western defence policy, especially in Europe, where the idea has taken strong roots".[5] Stated bluntly, it will be difficult for European governments to gain parliamentary approval for defence budgets unless some commitment is made to their reduction. The NATO decision to deploy Long Range Theatre Nuclear Weapons (LRTNF) taken in December 1979 was, therefore, accompanied by proposals for arms control negotiations without which the deployment decision would not have been possible. Even a new administration in Washington, reluctant to be involved in arms control until its increased defence programme was approved and until a carefully constructed negotiating position was realized, was forced to accept that LRTNF arms control negotiations would have to go forward; otherwise the consensus behind the deployment decision would evaporate. The United States has thus had to recognise the reality of domestic pressures in Europe, just as Europe had to recognise American domestic pressure against the ratification of SALT II. The differences of perspective are familiar, even if they are of emphasis and priority rather than substance. Though the United States may like to let arms control lie fallow for a while, it is likely to return to acceptance of its importance as part of the machinery for maintaining a military balance and avoiding instabilities. However, arms control negotiations are not likely to bring much relief to the military problem in Europe. Where strategic nuclear systems are concerned, the United States--by a combination of increased military spending and complementary arms control measures--may be able to retain or restore parity. Since parity is the context for European security and the cornerstone of NATO strategy, it will provide solace to Europe as well.

Arms control related to the European theatre is a different issue in all respects. The Soviet Union has built up a substantial superiority in theatre nuclear forces (TNF). As with strategic systems, NATO wants parity, at least, but it is difficult to believe that the Soviet Union can be persuaded to negotiate away its advantage. If NATO merely seeks parity in missiles, for example, the Soviet Union would have to stop building now and let NATO catch up--not a particularly welcome idea in Moscow, one supposes. If other theatre systems besides missiles are introduced, as the Soviet Union may want, then the analysis not only becomes complex but difficult to manage, e.g. dual-purpose systems are involved which risk giving Moscow leverage over weapons NATO needs for conventional defence. There could be advantages analytically in combining TNF with renewed SALT negotiations aiming, perhaps, to allow each side a mix of nuclear systems within agreed limits. Washington, however, will not want to be hurried into such a complicated negotiation, or even into SALT, until its own defence plans are more firmly established.

It is in the interest of the Soviet Union to play on the particular nerve of European keenness for LRTNF arms control and an American wariness about the same; to prevent Soviet propaganda from undermining the political support for LRTNF deployment, the alliance members will, therefore, have to develop a consensus. If European political support for LRTNF begins to falter, would the United States apply pressure or lose patience with Europeans who, after all, asked for the weapons in the first place? The issue needs sensitive treatment which will not be fostered by occasional American asides about neutron weapons at the same time; the Soviet Union fully understands this political reality, but some Americans seem slow to comprehend its implications.

Efforts aimed at mutual and balanced force reduction (MBFR) have been equally thwarted: seven years of negotiating has produced no agreement. As with TNF, the negotiating problem is that the Soviet Union enjoys superiority and NATO wants parity so the Soviet Union must be persuaded to surrender its advantage. It is possible that no progress will be achieved until a SALT agreement, perhaps one on LRTNF too, is in place. Certainly security in Europe has to be seen as a whole; MBFR is not and cannot be divorced from the balance of nuclear weapons. Despite American and European divergence of opinion on some issues, MBFR negotiations have been marked by like similarity of Allied views, though sometimes with one side of the Atlantic keen to move forward and the other to be cautious. The countries playing these two particular roles vary with changing governments. What remains constant is the Soviet wish to get U.S. troops out of Europe and to prevent West German forces from becoming any stronger--a set of objectives which fortunately tends to concentrate NATO minds.

A reasonably cohesive alliance position should also be possible on Confidence Building Measures (CBM) in the Madrid Conference on Security and Cooperation in Europe, if negotiators are cognizant of the danger that one ally or another may press for agreement to allay domestic political pressures rather than to reach a sound military position. Indeed it should not be forgotten that the primary reason for MBFR negotiations in the first place was to forestall U.S. Congressional pressure for American force withdrawals from Europe. Great prudence is required in balanced force reductions to prevent the weakening of defence. In this sense, arms control touches the very heart of security.

STRATEGY

For many years there have been underlying tensions within the Alliance over the formulation of an appropriate strategy. The doctrine of flexible response, introduced in 1967, was essentially designed to give an American president more options in Europe than just the early use of nuclear weapons, and it accordingly placed much more emphasis on conventional forces. Although Europeans accepted the idea of a flexible response, they were clearly opposed to any plans for fighting a protracted conventional war in Europe. On the contrary, it was their intention to develop primarily a strategy which was nuclear at heart, as the most effective way of deterring the Soviet Union and also of having the United States share the risks. While they accepted the idea from 1967 onwards that conventional forces should play an important defensive role and, therefore, had to be strengthened, they did not want those forces to be *too* strong. Preponderant conventional strength might lead the Soviet Union to the conclusion that nuclear weapons would not be used; thus rendering the deterrent less effective. Cynics dubbed this approach 'deterrence by conventional insufficiency'.

Today there are a number of problems with the strategy of flexible response, but two in particular should be firmly noted. The first is that if the conventional forces were insufficient when the strategy was introduced, they are probably more so now. To be sure, these forces have been strengthened over the years, but the Soviet Union has strengthened its own forces even more, so the relative balance is now worse than it was in 1967. The enduring imbalance has led to NATO being just as reliant on the early use of nuclear weapons as before, and with the prospect, furthermore, of less warning of impending attack. Only events in Poland with the problems they obviously pose for the Soviet Union, offer some bitter comfort.

The second problem arises from the fact that implicit in flexible response was the willingness to have recourse to nuclear weapons if the conventional defences could not hold, based on the idea that this could gain advantage for NATO. At the time, NATO had clear TNF superiority in battlefield nuclear weapons and could expect to be able to use them to restore a failing conventional position. Now it is the Soviet Union which has the superiority, and so is able to threaten to use these weapons on more than equal terms. It is thus extremely difficult to see how NATO could use TNF to gain advantage. The boot could be on the other foot.

From the viewpoint of Washington, the more vulnerable the United States is to strategic nuclear attack, the less attractive is a predominantly nuclear strategy in Europe, especially when the ability to exercise escalation dominance is doubtful. Greater emphasis on conventional forces therefore makes sense. Europeans, on the other hand, are likely to remain attached to an essentially nuclear strategy, since this threatens to carry the war to the Soviet homeland and to inflict immeasurably greater penalties for aggression, so providing stronger deterrence. It is pre-eminently a strategy for avoiding war, not fighting it, that Europe wants; although flexibility, the need to defend frontiers, and the ability to counter lesser threats provided by conventional forces must be retained as well. Such a strategy also happens to be cheaper than a purely conventional one, which could require far more men, equipment, and munitions stocks.

It is possible that new strategic ideas will come bubbling out of Washington--nuclear or conventional--as they tend to do with each new president. European governments will no doubt grin and bear it and try to go on doing what they have been doing. Something is, of course, being done to restore theatre nuclear deterrence, e.g. the current efforts to modernize LRTNF. The possibility of diversion of U.S. resources to the Gulf has also received some attention, although probably not enough. In this regard, it must be emphasized that opposition to the LRTNF deployment from anti-nuclear movements in a number of European countries rarely indicates support for putting conventional strength in place of nuclear capability; too often the anti-nuclear groups are also anti-defence and some are anti-NATO.

It has long been evident, however, that the conventional defences in Europe are not strong enough and so the United States may well press for improvements, not only in European forces, but also in U.S. conventional forces. Given sensible handling and an avoidance of theology, improvement of conventional strength should create no real reason for disunity. But there will be some difference of view over the development of the tactical concept: the prospect of a drawn-out conventional war in Europe has always looked more attractive from Arkansas than from Aachen.

CONCLUSION

The Alliance clearly has difficulties, but it always has had and no doubt always will. Indeed, not all of the problems have been discussed. There is friction over economic matters with resulting threats of linkage; arms sales to third countries have given rise to irritation, as did the way in which the Carter administration implemented its human rights and nuclear nonproliferation policies, despite the sympathy there was for the aims behind them. Differing attitudes towards volatile areas in the Third World, no longer simply a passive object of foreign policy, have also created tension. Certainly the allies did not emerge with any great cohesion from the events in Afghanistan and Iran, and it is by no means certain that future threats outside the Treaty area would find them in agreement on appropriate responses.

Some of this disarray--almost a standard word in the NATO vocabulary--is in response to attempts by members of the Alliance to respond to a changing world and, in turn, being changed themselves. The United States no longer enjoys unchallenged military superiority and its resources are now stretched to compete with Soviet power. European states are economically stronger than they were and more cohesive politically, and yet remain a group of sovereign nations dependent for their security on the United States. There is no sign that this security structure will change, or that Europeans wish it to. The Atlantic Alliance continues to be a symbiotic one in which each side depends upon the other.

Mutual dependence, however, is unequal: the United States remains dominant, particularly in the world outside Europe. The European allies therefore look to Washington for leadership and although they do not always like it when it is exercised, where security matters are concerned there is often no substitute. If Europeans are often quick to make plain what they don't like, they are much less able to agree among themselves on what they do.

The Alliance has been through a disturbing period and a few lessons ought to have been learned. The first is that while allies share a common security interest, the ways in which they prefer to realize it are more complex than they previously were. The second is that detente brought benefits which many in Europe will be reluctant to abandon--benefits which will continue to condition relations with the East. Perhaps only catastrophe in Poland could change this attitude materially. Thirdly, current attitudes towards arms control are symptomatic of differing political and security perspectives on either side of the Atlantic which will probably not change.

European security does, however, rest fundamentally on Atlantic unity. As the identity of interest remains strong, there is no reason why the Alliance should not endure. But there are difficulties which will have to be overcome and differences which will have to be accepted: after thirty years, it is, perhaps, surprising that there are not more. Recognition of this reality should not breed complacency as NATO faces difficult challenges. Preservation of unity within the Alliance depends on the willingness of its members to work hard at understanding each other.

FOOTNOTES

1. Henry A. Kissinger, The Troubled Partnership (New York: McGraw-Hill Book Company, 1965).

2. Karl Kaiser, Winston Lord, Thierry de Montbrial and David Watt, Western Security: What Has Changed? What Should Be Done? Report prepared jointly by the Forschungsinstitut der Deutschen Gesellschaft fur Auswartige Politik, the Council on Foreign Relations, Institut Français des Relations Internationales, and the Royal Institute of International Affairs, 1981.

3. NATO Review, (February 1981) p. 1.

4. A discussion of the problems posed by threats outside the NATO area is contained in a report by the Defence and Overseas Policy Working Group of the British Atlantic Committee entitled, A Global Strategy to Meet the Global Threat (London: British Atlantic Committee, February 1981).

5. Western Security, p. 28.

5
The Transformation of NATO: Parallel European Cooperation

Pierre Lellouche

Europeans enter the 1980s experiencing, for the first time since the cold war, a deep sense of concern--and even fear in some quarters--for the preservation of peace of their Continent. The decade began with speeches by European leaders, former President Giscard d'Estaing and Pope John Paul II, stressing the risks of a new world war, and polls conducted in several European countries throughout 1981 echoed similar qualms.

This concern is, of course, fueled by the rapid accumulation of crises over the past few years, ranging from Afghanistan, Poland, the Iran-Iraq war, and the breakdown of East-West détente--all of which have had a direct impact on the security of Europe. The sad irony is that although Europe has had to endure this avalanche of events without having any control over it, the basic setting of European security has been drastically changed.

Paradoxically, while new realities call for urgent and drastic actions on the part of all responsible European governments, these same realities seem to enhance the inertia of these governments, so that they appear both unwilling and unable to take such actions. Up to now, most European governments have endured passively what is in effect the restructuring of their entire security framework. They have only been capable of pushing through policies which amount in practice to

---

This chapter is a revised version of an article which appeared in Foreign Affairs (Spring 1981) under the title of "Europe and Her Defense". Reprinted by permission of Foreign Affairs 1981.

delaying tactics: the Warsaw and Moscow summits of last spring between former French President, Giscard d'Estaing, German Chancellor Helmut Schmidt and Soviet leader Leonid Brezhnev have not succeeded in restoring East-West détente in the absence of détente between the superpowers; and the European Community's "Venice initiative" of June 1980, calling for participation by the Palestine Liberation Organization in the settlement of the Arab-Israeli dispute, has yet to resolve Europe's strategic problems in the Middle East. Moreover, the stagnation of defense programs and expenditures in most European countries (with the exception of France) and the likely regression of their defense budgets in the coming year, illustrate a general reluctance to face up to new threats of the 1980s as well as the growing strains imposed by a continuing economic crisis throughout Western Europe.

The key questions for the Europeans--as well as for the West as a whole--remain to be faced and answered: how can the existing European security system adapt to the new political and strategic realities of the 1980s? What, specifically, can the Europeans themselves do for their own defense? And what would a modified European security arrangement imply for European defense cooperation as well as for the NATO alliance as a whole?

II

Today, amid great confusion, a new and more somber setting for European security is gradually emerging. The 1970s began with great hopes for a new era of détente between East and West and the promise of permanent stability in Europe. With the signing of the SALT I agreements in November 1972, nuclear war came to be seen as a mere theoretical possibility; the continuation of peace in Europe under a nuclear balance stabilized by arms control was now taken for granted. Few worried about European security, and, indeed, few in America worried about Europe as a whole. The Americans tended to concentrate on extricating themselves from their Vietnam quagmire and on building a new "structure of peace" with the Soviets. Meanwhile, the Europeans--and the West Germans in particular--felt freed from their obsession with security prevalent during the cold war years, and aimed at establishing their own détente relationship with the Soviets. It is typical of that period that Washington thought it necessary to launch a "Year of Europe" in 1973 to demonstrate to its allies America's continued interest in the commitment to the Old Continent. Equally telling of the prevailing mood was that of a 'superpower condominium' (détente being perceived as leading to entente), as well as about dangers of a renascent German nationalism in a Europe stabilized by détente.

Although many Europeans--including most governments on the Continent--would prefer to ignore them, it is now becoming clear that their defense in the 1980s will be shaped by the conjunction of three new realities.[1] First, the Soviet invasion of Afghanistan in December 1979 precipitated a major crisis between the superpowers that affected the overall climate of East-West relations. Although Europeans tried their best to reverse this trend, the very existence of détente--a key political condition of European security since the late 1960s--was called into question. Moreover, the prospects of détente were further undermined in the summer of 1980 by the eruption of the Polish crisis, the latter bringing the risk of another Soviet military intervention in Central Europe.

Politically, then, European security will have to be maintained during the 1980s within a new and potentially lasting phase of confrontation between the superpowers. Armed with renewed moral convictions and a resurgent nationalism, the United States under the Reagan Administration is aiming at restoring its overall power in world affairs and containing Soviet expansion in the Third World. For its part, the Soviet Union, conscious of its newly acquired global military might but wary of its internal weaknesses, remains preoccupied with the constant consolidation and expansion of its empire rather than the requirements of a genuine détente relationship with the United States. Whether the Europeans like it or not, this state of affairs will directly affect East-West relations as a whole, and European-Soviet relations in particular.

Second, militarily and strategically, the basic conditions of European security have also been subjected to fundamental alterations. Ever since 1977-78 the Europeans have been increasingly preoccupied with the gradual shift of the overall military balance in Europe in favor of the U.S.S.R. and about the impact of this evolution on the credibility of the U.S. nuclear guarantee. In the aftermath of Afghanistan, they face the prospect of a new arms race between the superpowers. In the meantime, however, arms control has become in European eyes a key condition for stability on the Continent as well as a somewhat bizarre justification, in the domestic politics of most European countries, for continued defense efforts. This new phase of military competition between the superpowers also means a great deal of American pressure for increased European defense efforts, at the very time when the continued deterioration of the economic situation in Europe, coupled with the emergence of a new wave of pacifist and neutralist sentiment in several European countries, make such commitments even more difficult to fulfill.

The balance of forces in Europe will continue to favor the Soviet Union throughout most of the 1980s. Given overall parity on the central strategic level, the growing Soviet superiority in Europe--both in conventional and theater nuclear forces (TNF)--will further weaken the credibility of NATO's strategy of "flexible response". In effect, the European members of NATO will increasingly find themselves caught in a strategic bind wherein:

1. their continued inferiority in conventional means will make them more and more vulnerable to a Soviet surprise attack with conventional forces; as a result, the Europeans will become increasingly dependent on first and early use of nuclear weapons by NATO;

2. yet, at the same time, the newly acquired Soviet superiority in theater nuclear systems, as well as parity at the strategic level, will in effect neutralize any attempt by NATO to escalate the conflict to nuclear weapons.

It is only toward the end of the decade that the new defense programs now being launched or accelerated in the United States will begin to affect some of the components of the military balance--in particular, at the central strategic level. As to the conventional and theater nuclear imbalances in Europe, these will only be partially offset in the mid-1980s by NATO's Long-Term Defense Program and TNF modernization program--assuming, of course, that both programs are fully implemented.[2]

Finally, on a wider geostrategic scale, the invasion of Afghanistan, coming after the extension of Soviet influence into Ethiopia and Yemen, has changed the strategic map of the Persian Gulf region, from which Europe now receives about 60 percent of her oil imports. The resulting reinforcement of Western naval forces (essentially American and French) in the area has expanded East-West confrontation beyond the traditional European theater into a region which is itself extremely volatile and unstable. Local regimes, meanwhile, are either reluctant or fearful to see the Persian Gulf area transformed into a new theater for East-West competition. To use Raymond Aron's words, "the Middle East is a void, but a void which refuses to be filled".

The promulgation of the Carter Doctrine, proclaiming the Gulf a vital U.S. interest and threatening the use of force to preserve the oil flow, and the eruption of the Iraq-Iran war in 1980, coming after the second dramatic oil price rise in the wake of the Islamic revolution in Iran the previous year, finally brought home to Europe the lesson which had been quickly forgotten after 1973; namely, that European security can no longer be geographically limited to the European theater alone. Although most European governments are reluctant to face this new reality, the fact remains that defending Europe in the 1980s will also mean protecting the raw materials and energy sources located in faraway regions--particularly in the Middle East and Africa--without which European democracies cannot survive.

Yet without adequate conventional means to back it up--the Rapid Deployment Force has yet to be turned into a credible instrument--the Carter Doctrine (which has apparently been maintained under Reagan) carries the risk of a very unpleasant alternative: either an early recourse to nuclear weapons which could then escalate into a major war in Europe and possibly between the superpowers, or a situation of 'Cuba in reverse' whereby the United States, having decided not to escalate to nuclear weapons, would suffer a military defeat on the ground, leaving the area under Soviet control.

Americans and Europeans have reacted in profoundly different ways to the transformation of the security environment in Europe as well as in the Third World. While events in the Gulf region brought about a new 'awakening' in America and a major shift toward a more assertive U.S. foreign policy, Europeans have tended to react with great caution, thereby triggering a growing irritation in the United States at what is perceived, at best, as selfishness on the part of its European allies, and at worst as proof that Europe is already sliding toward 'self-neutralization' or 'Finlandization'. So far neither side has come up with a coherent strategy to deal with the security equation of the 1980s. Instead, Americans and Europeans have tended to look for solutions belonging to the past.

Increasingly exasperated by the attitude of their European allies, more and more Americans are inclined to revive the old Atlantic system--in effect, to turn the clock back to the days of American nuclear superiority and absolute leadership in the Alliance. Hence, the temptation in many American quarters to try to strong-arm Europe and to threaten--in a new kind of 'Mansfieldism'--to abandon her to her own fate.

For their part, most Europeans still yearn for a miraculous return to the 'divine détente' of the 1970s, one which allowed them to enjoy at the same time the continued protection of the United States within the Alliance, and the dividends of European détente with their Eastern neighbors. Other Europeans--though a minority--still dream of a European Defense Community which would give a united Europe the means of its own defense and a new role in world affairs. In fact, neither the old Atlantic concept nor the notion of a European Defense Community corresponds to the political realities of both the Alliance and Western Europe today. Neither can provide the basis for realistic options for the future.

III

The magnitude of the transatlantic crisis triggered by the Afghan affair makes clear the structural transformations which have taken place in the Alliance over the past decade and a half.[3] Yet the current transatlantic crisis was already evident well before Afghanistan; it is enough to recall the various quarrels of the 1970s involving the October 1973 War, economic policy and energy, nuclear nonproliferation issues, the Middle East and the Camp David process, the 'neutron bomb' episode, and so forth. The longer historical record had shown that the Alliance did tend to unite in cases where the threat was really serious, e.g., the crises of Cuba and Berlin in the 1960s. But it was precisely this element of cohesion--imposed from the outside--which was missing in 1979-80, despite the gravity of Soviet behavior.

To be sure, several short-term factors did play a role in fueling quarrels within the Alliance. The lack of an adequate mechanism for Alliance consultation on crises arising outside NATO's boundaries was one of them. Similarly, the record of the Carter Administration--widely perceived in Europe as one of 'zigzagging', as well as the lack of more than rhetorical American reaction to earlier Soviet and Cuban interventions in Third World areas--led many Europeans to believe that the U.S. reaction to Afghanistan would only be a short-lived sign of displeasure (due in part to the presidential campaign), soon to be followed by the 'normal' pursuit of superpower dialogue.

More importantly, perhaps, the differences in attitudes throughout most of 1980 reflected a basic failure on the part of most Europeans to comprehend the magnitude of the shift which has been taking place in America over the past three to four years and which found its final resolution in the conjunction of the Iranian hostage crisis with the Afghan affair. For several months after Afghanistan, most European observers, including officials at the highest levels of government, were still convinced that the United States would go back to "business as usual" with the Soviets. Indeed, some went so far as to predict a "new Yalta" between the superpowers over the Persian Gulf. It was only with the November 1980 landslide which brought Ronald Reagan to the White House and a Republican majority to the Senate that Europe as a whole began to realize that she is now faced with a tougher, more nationalistic, and assertive America.

Yet these problems of communication and the resulting misunderstandings fail to explain the magnitude of the transatlantic split. It would be wrong to assume that once the international situation quiets down a little, and the new American administration shows more coherence and leadership, the Europeans will simply 'fall into line' and the Alliance will go on 'as usual'. In fact, the roots of the transatlantic crisis are to be found in two complementary historical trends going all the way back to the 1960s: the relative decline of U.S. power vis-à-vis both the Soviet Union and the European allies; and the gradual emergence of West Germany as a new pole of power in East-West relations in a Europe that has become--to use Fritz Stern's words--"semi-Gaullist".[4]

One area where this transformation has been visible for some time is economics: here the quarrels of the 1970s on economic policy (the "locomotive" theory urging Germany and Japan to stimulate their economies in a recession), the creation of the European Monetary System, and the controversy about nuclear energy and nonproliferation, all point to a new situation in which Europe has become as rich and as competitive as the United States and is now able to defend her own interests (as in the case of monetary or nuclear energy policies) against the wishes of the United States.

A much more complex and perhaps less visible evolution has been taking place in the political and security area. The main transformation here involves the area of East-West relations, or rather the way Soviet-American and Soviet-European relations have gradually diverged during the 1970s. What is at stake is a fundamental divergence between the respective commitments of Americans and Europeans to the process of détente.

For the United States, détente was a parenthesis in

its history. As Robert Tucker has rightly pointed out,[5] détente was for the United States a much less costly way to deal with the Soviet Union than the earlier policy of containment: it justified a drastic decrease in U.S. military spending throughout most of the 1970s and allowed the United States, in effect, to renounce unilaterally the use of force in its foreign policy. In substance, therefore, détente was heavily based on military components (especially arms control), with little else in terms of trade or human relations. Once the Americans gradually realized the magnitude of the shift in the military balance and as they became increasingly disappointed by the actual security benefits produced by the arms control process, the American pendulum gradually moved away from détente and back toward a more traditional form of power politics.

For the Europeans, however, and in particular for the Germans, the experience of détente did not--and indeed could not--parallel that of the United States. From the very beginning, détente in Europe has meant a very concrete, day-to-day set of human and economic relationships. It means the stabilization of the territorial status quo on the Continent and the continued safety of Berlin. Economically, it translates into an important market for European industrial goods and much-needed access to a new source of raw materials and energy. Détente should also permit the stabilization of defense efforts at modest levels (between two and three percent of the gross national product of most European nations). On a wider political level, détente has allowed the Europeans to enjoy more freedom of maneuver and has provided a convenient setting in which Europe can safely assert her own identity against the leader of the Alliance.

There are, however, three inherent problems in such a situation: the first is that, in politics, when commitments become too great, they also tend to turn into vulnerabilities; there comes a stage where it becomes politically (or economically) too costly to abandon one's commitment, even if the other side has blatantly broken the rules of the game. Clearly, in the case of Afghanistan, Europeans were reluctant to give up the dividends of détente, even if that meant accepting the Soviet notion of the divisibility of détente. The question thus becomes: Where does one draw the line? Would Poland be worth the price of détente? After all, if détente was divisible in the case of a nonaligned country subjected to direct aggression by the Soviet Union, why would it be less so in the case of a country which is recognized as an integral part of the Soviet empire?

The second problem is that the Western democracies have tended to be blinded by the short-term benefits of détente, and thus ended up forgetting that détente can only be based on a stable balance of forces. An unequal military balance can only produce an unequal political relationship. European countries have viewed détente and its corollary in the security area--i.e., arms control--as a convenient substitute for a continued defense effort. Indeed, as the Europeans' dependence on détente steadily increased over the past decade, their awareness of the central importance of the military balance declined proportionately, as did their willingness to incur the political and economic costs necessary to their defense policies. The danger here is that while the importance of détente in European politics has grown, détente has come to be based on an increasingly unfavorable military balance.

This danger is compounded by the fact that European security remains dependent on U.S. protection. This is where the gap between the respective commitments of the United States and Europe to détente produces the greatest problems. For there will come a time when Europe's commitment to détente may come into conflict with her commitment to the Alliance. Indeed, this is a point which the Soviet Union continuously presses upon the Europeans in its effort to decouple Europe from the United States politically as well as militarily.

Among all European countries, West Germany is certainly the one which is--given its partition and its location on the borders of the Soviet empire--the most committed to detente. It is also the one which has benefited most from what have been called the dividends of détente. Ostpolitik gave Germany the political dimension that the Federal Republic was lacking up until the 1970s: it permitted Germany's international recognition and, above all it turned the Federal Republic into the center of gravity of East-West relations in Europe. In the process, the United States (and, to a lesser degree, France) in many respects lost the initiative in dealings with the East. The Soviets in turn won a precious 'advocate' within NATO as well as the means to push forward their policy of decoupling European détente from U.S.-Soviet relations. For the Germans, the dividends of détente were clearly translated into human terms (with the return of 200,000 ethnic Germans) and in economic benefits (the Federal Republic alone represents about 45 to 50 percent of Western trade with the East). Détente has also allowed Germany to enjoy more freedom of maneuver diplomatically and to assert its own independence and interests against the United States.

But, as noted earlier, such a great commitment also means great vulnerabilities. These have been plainly demonstrated in Bonn's reluctance to join the United States in imposing economic sanctions on the U.S.S.R. after Afghanistan. In fact, it remains to be seen whether a durable German commitment to such sanctions could be obtained even in the case of a Soviet invasion of Poland. There are also political vulnerabilities. In the aftermath of Afghanistan, Germany did demonstrate its solidarity with Washington by boycotting the Moscow Olympics. Yet this gesture was largely offset by Chancellor Schmidt's trip to Moscow in June 1980 as well as by repeated German pressures on the United States to renew its dialogue with the USSR.

The main vulnerabilities lie, of course, in the security area. This is where Germany is most dependent both on the Soviet Union, as the potential aggressor, and on the United States, as its ultimate protector. Here, the first neutron bomb episode of 1977-78 and the laborious intra-Alliance negotiating process which led to the TNF decision in December 1979 to deploy intermediate-range nuclear missiles on German soil, illustrate Germany's fundamental dilemmas in an era of détente. The TNF decision also deserves a particular reference here because it accurately reflects the structural transformation that has taken place in the Alliance as a whole.

Ironically, Germany was the first European NATO country to raise the TNF issue in 1977, because of the wider implications of strategic nuclear parity for the continued validity of NATO's strategy of flexible response. Yet after having pressed for a remedy to the growing imbalance of forces at the theater nuclear level, the Germans soon found themselves caught between conflicting pressures from the United States and the U.S.S.R. The former demanded that the Europeans favoring a TNF program say so publicly; the latter threatened that any deployment of new, longer range nuclear missiles on European territory would be tantamount to ending détente and starting a new arms race. As a result, Germany found itself entrusted with a major decision-making power on nculear issues which it could not possibly use without risking a breakdown of its relationships with the East.

In essence, the 'solution' consisted for Germany in not deciding: Bonn announced a series of conditions for the deployment of the new TNF systems, including the so-called no-singularity provision, whereby Germany would deploy such weapons only if at least one other continental European nation also accepted the weapons on its territory. Another important condition was that deployment be linked to parallel arms control negotiations between the United States and the Soviet Union on the same systems. The end result of the TNF diplomatic ballet was twofold: the whole program became suspended in the domestic politics of Belgium, Holland and Italy, none of which is exactly enthusiastic about TNF; and in the absence of a ratified SALT II treaty, and therefore in the absence of any SALT III talks, a special negotiating forum had to be convened in order to satisfy the domestic political requirements of the European countries involved. After much hesitation in view of the post-Afghanistan situation, the Carter Administration did open the TNF talks in October 1980 in Geneva simply to save the program. Despite its obvious reluctance to do so, the Reagan Administration, under intense pressure from its European allies, had to agree to reconvene the talks a year later (November 1981) for the same reason. The final irony of this peculiar exercise in Kafkaesque diplomacy is that the negotiations are being opened without any allied consensus as to what the negotiating objectives should be, what weapons are to be considered in the talks, and what the impact of a failure would be on the 1979 decision on the deployment of the so-called 'Euro-missiles'.

Two things are clear however: first, even before they actually began, the TNF talks are loaded with an enormous political weight in Europe. Formidable expectations have been allowed to grow in Germany, in Holland and in Europe as a whole, to the point where any delay in the talks, any failure in reaching an agreement will most likely jeopardize the deployment decision, and will certainly be blamed by most Europeans on the United States. Sadly, all those who are familiar with the TNF problem agree that the subject is of such complexity (given the specific characteristics of the weapons involved and the basic geostrategic assymetry of both sides), that a successful outcome is by no means certain, and that, in any case, the talks are likely to last over many years.

This means--and this is the second observation that should be made here--that the very fact that the negotiations did open was a major victory for the Soviets. Not only will their vast superiority in intermediate range systems allow them to negotiate from a position of strength[6] but the TNF talks will also give them a permanent and highly effective leverage to influence European public opinion and to delay the deployment of NATO's systems when the weapons are produced (1983-84); moreover if Soviet insistence on including in the negotiations the US forward-based systems in Europe is accepted--as seems to be the case--the Soviets will have achieved a major breakthrough which they have been seeking from the very beginning of the SALT process in the late 1960s. Given Soviet superiority in theater nuclear weapons, and Moscow's growing influence on European public opinion, the talks therefore carry heavy risks for the Alliance as a whole.

With this background, the opening of the TNF talks has less to do with genuine arms control than with short term political expedient to try to resolve NATO's own internal political dilemmas. The trouble, however, is that the cure is only bound to aggravate the disease further. Indeed, it is becoming increasingly clear that the TNF decision, while militarily useful for European security, may well turn out to be a political disaster for the Alliance, with long lasting effects on the political fate of Western Europe.

IV

The gradual weakening of the Atlantic system does not imply that Europe has reached a stage where she is politically ready to take charge of her security. Indeed, one can even speak of a regression here, to the extent that in the late 1950s and early 1960s when Europe had her first doubts about the credibility of the U.S. guarantee, the natural reaction was to look for a European substitute, either by developing an independent nuclear capability (e.g., France) or broader European defense cooperation (e.g., the French-German talks between 1958 and 1963 and the 1962 Fouchet Plan proposing political and defense cooperation in Europe).[7] Today, while each of the countries in question has gone through a major defense debate at one stage or another since 1978-79, this has not led to any serious attempt at developing intra-European defense cooperation as a means to fill the gaps left by the declining validity of the American security guarantee.[8]

Instead--and this is what is really worrisome about the current mood in Europe--each of these governments reacted separately in trying to preserve the _status quo ante_ in the face of growing Soviet pressures and a new wave of pacifist sentiment throughout the Continent. While some governments, particularly in the small NATO countries, simply decided to cut down on their defense efforts, most Europeans tended to push forward with arms control initiatives (as in the case of TNF and confidence-building measures in Europe) in the hope that such negotiations would somehow reverse the adverse trends in the military balance, keep the dialogue alive with the Soviet Union, and facilitate domestic political support for the minimum defense policies compatible with their continued commitment to the Alliance.

In this context, virtually no political capital was invested in developing European defense cooperation. To be sure, a minority of Europeans continue to dream of a hypothetical 'third way' whereby a United Europe would take charge of her own defense. Similarly, the idea of possible Franco-German or Franco-British nuclear cooperation did surface at various times throughout the 1970s in several European countries. In practice, however, very little has been accomplished in that direction. To take the most recent episode, Great Britain, which had to decide upon the modernization of its deterrent force, never seriously considered 'the French option': for a variety of political and financial reasons, the new French M-4 submarine-launched ballistic missile was never a serious contender with the American Trident system which the British finally selected.

As for Germany, while officially strongly committed to the French-German entente, it remains totally opposed to any kind of military nuclear cooperation with France. The issue arose in the summer of 1979 when two French Gaullists, General Georges Buis and Alexandre Sanguinetti, launched a trial balloon proposing such cooperation. Although the proposal itself carried little political weight on the French side, the German government took great pains to reject it officially. More than ever, the Federal Republic holds to its non-nuclear status, which has become one of the cornerstones of its relationship with the East. Moreover, ever since the late 1950s and the early 1960s, when similar approaches were made by the French, Germany has done its best to avoid being put into a position where it has to choose between America and France for its protection.

Interestingly enough, the most positive evolution toward the idea of European defense cooperation is to be found in France. Until recently, the French enjoyed a very comfortable position indeed. The U.S. nuclear guarantee and NATO protected France's neighbors without infringing on France's independence. And France could capitalize on its national deterrent to establish itself as a major world actor, and indeed as a kind of arbitrator between the blocs. The German problem--France's traditional obsession--was solved, though not quite as the Gaullists would have liked it to be: for in the early 1960s the Germans had rejected General de Gaulle's proposal for forming France and Germany into the nucleus of an independent Europe outside NATO. Yet the Federal Republic's presence within the Alliance was still a convenient way to ensure the continued security, and therefore the stability, of a divided Germany.

The situation began to change in the late 1970s: the United States was no longer the dominant power, and the credibility of the U.S. nuclear guarantee was now in doubt throughout Europe. The neutron bomb episode and the TNF debate provoked in France the sudden realization that Germany, too, was having its own 'Gaullist' doubts about the United States. And, in French logic, a Germany that feels insecure means an unstable Germany and hence an unstable Europe. It also means that such a Germany would be tempted to solve its own security problem by purely German solutions: either by going nuclear, or more likely, given the situation in Europe, by looking for a separate accommodation with the Soviet Union. Obviously, neither outcome would be favorable to France.

It is therefore no accident that France's nuclear strategy, while still formally committed to the doctrine of independence defined under de Gaulle, has evolved considerably during former President Giscard d'Estaing's term in office. The evolution began in 1976 with the announcement of a new concept of an 'enlarged sanctuary' and 'forward battle'. It was later confirmed by repeated official statements, including those from Giscard himself, to the effect that France's security was now inseparable from the security of her European neighbors, and of Germany in particular. The purely 'national' deterrent concept in force a decade ago thus gradually gave way to a wider posture which took into account the European theater as a whole.

In practice however, the evolution of French thinking about European security failed to be translated into meaningful actions during Giscard's term in office, let alone into a full-fledged diplomatic initiative. Given strong domestic resistance from both the Gaullists and the communists, who are prompt to denounce any evolution of France's defense policy as "Atlanticism", Giscard's treatment of the European defense issue remained extremely cautious. France chose, for example, not to take sides in the TNF debate, although Giscard's support could surely have helped Helmut Schmidt in coping with the left wing of his socialist party earlier in the TNF battle. Instead, theater nuclear weapons were treated officially as NATO business. At the same time, however, France did announce an ambitious program of modernization of her own nuclear forces and let it be known--unofficially--that she was supporting a similar modernization of the part of her NATO allies. Similarly, while Giscard's officials often stressed the inherent link between France's security and European security, they also took great pains to remain as vague as possible when it came to defining the actual contribution of French forces, including nuclear forces, to the security of the Continent.

Unfortunately, the ambiguity of French policy in the European security area, has been only partly removed under the new administration of President François Mitterrand. To be sure, the new socialist Government, immediately upon coming into office, adopted a much more dynamic attitude on the TNF issue. Openly criticizing the USSR's "overwhelming military superiority in Europe", France now supports NATO's decision in both its components.

The deployment of the new Pershing and Cruise missiles is seen as an essential condition to restoring a stable military balance in Europe; and the negotiations are seen as a means to improve European security (although France is still intent on rejecting any participation in the TNF talks). As result, France is now playing an important role in helping indirectly the United States to secure Germany's as well as other Europeans' continued commitment to the NATO decision. However, aside from the TNF dossier, French strategic posture as a whole remains as ambiguous as ever in terms of France's commitment to the security of its neighbors. Indeed, the first statements made by President Mitterrand in this respect[9], which reflect a general tendency among socialist defense experts and officials, point to a more 'Gaullist' view of French deterrence doctrine. Contrary to Giscard, who envisioned France's participation in a "forward battle", as well as a concept of "enlarged sanctuarization" for the Force de Frappe, Mitterrand is inclined to revert back to a narrower 'Gaullist' and 'nationalistic' deterrence doctrine, in which France would take little responsibility for the fate of its European neighbors[10].

General inertia and inability on the part of key European nations to move toward greater cooperation in the security area reflects the continued divisions and basic differences of interest among the various Europeans on the global political plane. In fact, despite some progress in European political cooperation, and despite the French-German entente under Giscard and Schmidt, intra-European divisions have increased in recent years. The enlargement of the European Community has produced dilution which threatens to convert the Community into little more than a free-trade area. Furthermore, the gap is widening between the large and small members of the Community as, increasingly, serious political business is negotiated on a bilateral basis among France, Germany and the United Kingdom with little involvement of the smaller members of the Community. And when the Community as a whole takes a political stand, as in the case of the June 1980 Venice initiative on the Middle-East, it tends to be limited to words in the absence of appropriate means (i.e. political and military leverage) necessary for implementation.

The future of the French-German entente, which is often cited as the one example of progress toward European unity, is now an open question in the aftermath of the recent change of government in France. As a matter of fact, even under Giscard d'Estaing and Helmut Schmidt, Franco-German cooperation was flawed with basic ambiguities and conflicting interests. To Giscard, who in fact never gave up on the Gaullist idea of German withdrawal from NATO, the alliance with the Federal Republic was the first step toward building a new Europe, one that could, in Giscard's words, "assert its own voice in world affairs". But, in the French view, this new Europe was not aimed at reunifying Germany: in that sense, most French leaders continued to share the basic Gaullist concept that France and the USSR were somehow 'natural' allies when it comes to keeping Germany divided.

To the Germans, the objective was--and remains--to preserve the status quo both with the NATO Alliance and with the East. The alliance with France therefore serves two useful purposes: first, it helps to bring France closer to the Atlantic Alliance and second, it allows Germany more diplomatic leeway in dealings with Washington, particularly with regard to protecting Ostpolitik and the Federal Republic commitments to European détente. This 'French card' was particularly useful in the aftermath of Afghanistan, e.g. the Paris communiqué of February 1980 helped shelter Germany from American pressures and former President Giscard d'Estaing's trip to Warsaw in May paved the way for Chancellor Schmidt's own visit to Moscow the following month.

Ambiguities of this magnitude were bound to lead to strains. Indeed, as events unfolded since the spring of 1980, basic divergencies between Paris and Bonn gradually developed. While France stiffened its attitude toward Moscow following the failure of the Warsaw meeting and the threat of another Soviet action in Poland, Germany persisted in its objective to preserve European détente and was hesitant to envisage serious sanctions in the case of an invasion of Poland. Moreover, whereas France considerably increased her naval presence in the

Indian Ocean and announced an ambitious program of defense modernization with a corresponding increase in military expenditures, Germany categorically refused to envisage a military role for itself beyond NATO's boundaries, was still hesitant about the TNF program, and failed to reach the three-percent target set by NATO for annual increases of defense expenditures. By the end of 1980, the French-German entente began to show visible cracks for the first time.

What direction French-German relations will take in the aftermath of the French elections of May-June 1981 remains unclear. As noted earlier, Socialist France has given strong support to Chancellor Schmidt in the TNF battle; this may be the occasion to rebuild a healthier French-German link devoid of the ambiguities of the past. However, this improvement is by no means certain. The French--particularly the Socialists--are increasingly distrubed by the neutralist trends evident in West Germany; hence the traditional fear of 'reunification' is once again apparent. Similarly, many Germans--ironically, socialists as well--find Mitterrand's position on East-West issues too 'Reaganian' for their taste and too harmful to détente. The odds are, therefore, that differences on security issues, in addition to radically opposed views on economic policy will seriously hamper the development of a new French-German entente which could in turn provide the basis for wider European cooperation in the political and strategic area.

The irony of this situation is that France, which used to be considered the 'black sheep' of the Alliance, is now the one European nation that shows the greatest readiness to safeguard its security in the face of new threats arising in Europe. The situation is now exactly the reverse of what it was during the 1960s. As President Reagan discovered--to his surprise and delight--during the July 1981 Ottawa summit, the defense policies of socialist France are now objectiveley, if not officially, more similar to those of the United States than to any other European nation in facing the new realities of the East-West security environment.

V

Although the need for an urgent and fundamental restructuring of the European security system is clear, it is equally obvious that the choices before us are few and rather poor. Given the realities of both the NATO Alliance and of Europe today, neither the return to the old Atlantic system nor the establishment of a hypothetical European Defense Community are realistic options for maintaining European security in the 1980s. However tempting the nostalgia for the 1960s, the United States can neither restore the absolute nuclear superiority it once enjoyed nor reestablish its dominant leadership over Europe. Given its present internal contradictions, however, the Alliance can hardly be expected to last for another 30 years without either a major breakdown or a major transformation. On the other hand, in the absence of political will among key European nations to take their security into their own hands, it is hard to see how an autonomous European security entity could be established, even in the very long term.

In essence, the only realistic option for preserving European defense in the 1980s will have to be of a hybrid nature, one that accurately reflects the historical stage at which Europe now finds itself, namely halfway between a much weakened Atlantic system and a still embryonic European framework.

The recognition of this fact points to a necessarily pragmatic, if not modest, approach aimed at achieving realistic objectives. Such an approach assumes that Americans and Europeans alike abandon their traditional tendency to think of the Alliance and of European defense cooperation in mutually exclusive terms. For far too long now, the Americans as well as most Europeans have refused to envisage any European alternative to NATO. This worked as a convenient justification for the continuation of both the U.S. dominance over the allies and the passivity of most European nations in ensuring their own security. The opposite tendency was, for some Europeans (the French, in particular), to consider that Europe could only exist if she gave herself the means to protect her own security outside NATO. In effect, this logically sound but unrealistic approach served as an equally convenient justification for the general inertia that has characterized European defense cooperation since 1954.

Today, our objective should be to reconcile the Alliance with a genuine effort toward European defense cooperation. Gradually improving defense cooperation among the key European nations, in parallel to NATO, would:

1. encourage a greater European contribution and responsibility in the defense of the Continent;

2. compensate for the decline of the credibility of the U.S. guarantee afforded within NATO; and

3. allow American resources and personnel necessary for the protection of vital Western interests to be used beyond NATO's territorial boundaries, as well as gradually open the way for a wider European military role in these regions.

To do these things would not require any new institution or an impracticable and risky renegotiation of the 1949 NATO treaty. Nor would it imply for the European nations involved the establishment of a specific regional body, let alone a supranational one. Instead, the objective should be to work upon--and, in effect, to enhance--the basic complementarity which already exists both at the Alliance level and in Europe between the various components of the overall Western deterrent force. Here, the precedent of the 1962 Fouchet Plan, which called for gradual political as well as defense cooperation among European states, serves as a useful model. Although the plan was rejected at the time as insufficiently 'European', the basic approach of the proposal, namely, that of an evolving cooperation among states, was later proven right and even embedded in the evolution of European institutions and policies.

Militarily, the objective of a cooperative defense effort among the major European powers would be to remedy the most urgent weaknesses in the Alliance deterrent posture resulting from the growing inferiority of Western conventional forces on the Continent and the declining credibility of NATO's first use of nuclear weapons.

Such weaknesses could have the gravest military implications, should the Soviets decide, especially during a crisis, to resort to the 'conventional option'. This situation also carries heavy political risks, as the Soviets will certainly try to translate their local military superiority in Europe into political gains, thereby achieving in the long run the 'victory' for which they are really aiming, namely the political control of Western Europe <u>without</u> resort to war.

Such a situation demands that Europeans urgently undertake a dual effort--going well beyond NATO's current plans--aimed at raising the nuclear threshold through reinforcing conventional capabilities, and achieving the means and defining the doctrine necessary to restore the credibility of the first use of nuclear weapons.

This dual effort would be based on the idea of reinforcing the operational and structural complementarity among the forces of the three major European countries, namely France, the United Kingdom and the Federal Republic of Germany. Although lack of space prevents going into many details, the basic guidelines for such an effort can be proposed.

With respect to conventional forces, the Europeans will have to face an increasingly unfavorable situation given (1) the growing Soviet capacity to launch a surprise attack, and (2) the tendency on the part of the United States to move forces and equipment out of Europe for contingencies arising in Third World regions (in particular, the Persian Gulf area). Improving the conventional military balance between East and West will imply, at the outset, that a number of financial, and therefore political, choices have to be made. Such an effort will require either a major increase of defense expenditures well beyond the two to three percent of the gross national product now devoted by the Europeans to their defense, or the rationalization of the various national programs now undertaken separately.

Given the economic, social and domestic political constraints at work in most European countries, a drastic increase of European defense budgets seem unrealistic. This means that one has to do better with what one already has. And here much could be done in terms of rationalizing arms procurement policies among the key European countries. In fact, intra-European cooperation in this area is already well on its way, particularly between France and Germany, and in some instances between France and the United Kingdom. A rationalization of weapons-production programs among these three nations could be further developed in spite of the complex technological and economic obstacles involved. Such a rationalization would avoid the dispersion of scarce resources and lead to better weapons at a lower unit price.

Going beyond the issue of arms-procurement policies, the main effort of rationalization should involve the overall conception of the defense forces of the three countries. The objective here should be to establish a "division of labor" among the three national defense forces. To a large extent, this specialization already exists: the Bundeswehr is the strongest conventional European army today, whereas France and Britain are, preeminently, nuclear powers. In the future, this specialization should be reinforced by turning it into an effective complementarity both at the operational and financial level. Indeed, Britain and France already face increasing financial difficulties in financing simultaneously the modernization of their nuclear arsenals and that of their conventional forces (in the case of France, one should add the financing of special intervention forces earmarked for Third World areas). Rather than 'sprinkling' scarce resources in too many directions, both countries should opt for more limited but better equipped conventional forces than is presently the case with the British Army of the Rhine and the First French Army. In so doing, additional resources would be available for both the essential modernization of two European nuclear forces and the creation or reinforcement of mobile intervention forces.

With respect to nuclear weapons, it is clear that both the French and British forces will be called upon to play an increasingly important role in the necessary restructuring of the Alliance nuclear posture. Indeed, this process has to some extent already started.

As long as the U.S. nuclear guarantee was seen as clearly protecting the non-nuclear members of the Alliance, the two European nuclear forces had only a marginal--if not insignificant--role in the overall deterrent posture of the Alliance. France--and to a lesser extent Britain--could therefore enjoy the political benefits stemming from their nuclear status without undertaking any direct responsibility in the defense of the Continent as a whole. Today the situation has changed. The gradual decline in the credibility of the U.S. nuclear guarantee during the past decase had propelled both the French and British forces into an increasingly important European role although, ironically, neither the French nor the British really desired such a role.

In practice, the contribution of both European nuclear forces to the defense of the Continent--which is already recognized in NATO's Ottawa Declaration of 1974--will continue to grow as the French and British arsenals are modernized. The development on the French side of MIRVed M-4 submarine-launched ballistic missiles (SLBMs) beginning in 1985, as well as Trident SLBMs equipped with Chevaline warheads on the British side, will give both countries a deterrent power capable of protecting much more than their respective territories.

In the future, one of the key objectives of European defense cooperation should be to accelerate this evolution by broadening the deterrent effect of both forces to include explicitly the European theater as a whole. In practice, this would be achieved by entrusting both European nuclear forces with the essential task of triggering nuclear escalation in the event of Soviet aggression on the Continent. To the extent that the

Soviets may have doubts as to the readiness of the United States to resort to the first use of nuclear weapons for the defense of Europe, such doubts will not be possible if the Europeans commit themselves and have the capability of triggering this first use for the defense of their Continent.

When added to the existing American guarantee, this broadening of the deterrent role of the French and British nuclear forces to Germany and to the whole of Western Europe would bring two major advantages: first, the present decline of the credibility of the American guarantee would be compensated for, and, second, the coupling of European defense with the U.S. central systems, far from being diminished, would in fact be reinforced.

To be sure, implementing such a scheme presupposes the solution of many intra-European problems mentioned earlier. It also implies that the threat of French and British nuclear first use must be credible to the Soviets politically as well as militarily. In turn, this calls for an increase in the nuclear capabilities of both France[11] and Britain, as well as for a certain visibility of the new deterrent posture. Such visibility could be achieved by the deployment in West Germany of French and British intermediate-range systems.[12] This European arrangement, which would function in parallel with NATO, would in the longer run be reinforced by a series of bilateral "double-key" agreements between Paris and Bonn as well as between London and Bonn, and possibly by the definition of joint targeting plans.

VI

The guidelines set forth in the preceding section are no doubt imperfect. Many will view them as too ambitious and unrealistic; others will find them too modest and insufficient to resolve European security issues in the 1980s. As such, however, they illustrate the immense complexity of the problems now facing us. In the absence of a purely 'Atlantic' solution or of an alternate European one, Europeans are condemned to a pragmatic and difficult route. But it is one that can preserve both the Alliance, despite its internal contradictions, and the long-term chances of meaningful European defense cooperation.

There is, however, one other route open to the Europeans, one that is surely more convenient, at least in the short run, and requires considerably less effort.

This is the route of inertia, which has been followed by most European governments over the past ten years, notwithstanding the drastic transformation which has taken place in the international security environment. Such a path carries three sets of potential dangers: those involving European relations with the United States, with the Soviet Union, and among the Europeans themselves.

In the first instance, it is clear that the Europeans cannot hope to maintain the attitude they have adopted since Afghanistan without risking a major crisis in--and a possible breakdown of--the transatlantic relationship. The Europeans cannot simultaneously try to pursue détente with the Soviets as if nothing had happened--and therefore decouple themselves politically from the Americans--and demand that the military coupling be maintained as usual. The ultimate price to be paid by the Europeans for keeping the dividends of détente may therefore have to be the dissolution of the Atlantic Alliance itself.

Toward the Soviet Union, the present European attitude, which consists of accepting in practice the Soviet notion of the divisibility of détente, is equally dangerous. As the dividends of détente turn into paralyzing vulnerabilities, the European obsession with preserving their peace may well lead in the long run to the end of 'Western' Europe as an independent entity.

Finally, a third set of dangers threatens the Europeans themselves. These are perhaps the most likely and the most damaging for Europe as a whole. In view of Europe's deep internal divisions and given the absence of an all-powerful American leader, or of a substitute European directorate, there is a real danger that each European country will gradually be led to look for its own solutions to its security problems. Some would doubtless choose to return to the American strategic shelter; others would look for an accommodation with Moscow; and still others would entrench themselves behind an exclusively national nuclear deterrent. In the end, Europe as a whole would fall victim to such a 'Balkanization' process, which is already visible in certain countries.

VII

Above and beyond all the political and strategic problems which are threatening the security of the Continent, the fundamental question is whether the Europeans still want to exist with their own culture and civilization in a rapidly changing and dangerous world. Or, conversely, whether they simply want to watch history pass by with the sole ambition of preserving their peace and their material well-being at any cost.

However strong the temptation to do so, it would be illusory for some Europeans--or all Europeans--to believe that they can become a 'large Switzerland', rich, neutral and protected from the dangers of the outside world. For if Switzerland, or indeed Finland, or Austria, exists as such today, it is because other Europeans have shown the will to exist as independent nations ready to defend themselves. And although it has become fashionable to use such terms, there will not be in Europe any general 'Finlandization' or 'Euroneutralization': for there is, in the final analysis, no middle way between defense and enslavement.

FOOTNOTES

1. The following discussion summarizes a much more detailed analysis published in Pierre Lellouche, ed, La Sécurité de l'Europe dans les Années 80, IFRI/ ECONOMICA, 1980.

2. An analysis of NATO's Long-Term Defense Program (LTDP) and of the Theater Nuclear Force (TNF) modernization program are to be found in the contributions of Richard Burt, Coit Blacker and Farook Hussain to the aforementioned volume.

3. The transatlantic crisis is analyzed in depth in Karl Kaiser, Winston Lord, Thierry de Montbrial and David Watt, Western Security: What has changed? What should be done? (New York: Council on Foreign Relations, Inc., February 1981). See also Dominique Moisi, "Les Nouveaux Malentendus Transatlantiques," in Lellouche, La Securité de l'Europe, 1980.

4. See Fritz Stern, "Germany in a Semi-Gaullist Europe," Foreign Affairs, Spring 1980, pp 867-86.

5. See Robert W. Tucker, "America in Decline. The Foreign Policy of 'Maturity'", Foreign Affairs, "America and the World 1979", pp. 449 84.

6. See the Military Balance, 1980-81 (London: International Institute for Strategic Studies 1980), pp. 116-117. The imbalance is particularly evident at the level of long-range theater missiles based in Europe, such as the Soviet SS-20s and NATO's cruise missiles and Pershing IIs, a category of weapons which will presumably be a key component of the TNF talks. At the present rate of deployment of the SS-20 (between 60 and 100 per year) and given existing deployments, the Soviet Union will possess by the end of 1983 (at which date NATO's TNF will begin to be deployed) between 340 and 460 such missiles, each armed with three warheads. (This would mean between 1,020 and 1,380 warheads, in addition to some 440 older SS-4 and 5, as against NATO's 108 Pershings and 464 cruise missiles.)

7. See Wilfrid L. Kohl, French Nuclear Diplomacy (Princeton: Princeton University Press, 1971), Chps. 2 and 7.

8. See Pierre Hassner, "Europe and the Contradictions in American Policy," in Richard Rosecrance, ed., America as an Ordinary Country (Ithaca Cornell

University Press, 1976).

9. See in particular his press conference of 25 September 1981, Le Monde (26 September 1981).

10. At the time of this writing (October 1981) it is however too early to tell whether this trend will actually be confirmed in the future. Some segments of the Socialist Party remain committed to a more "European" concept of French defense policy, as evidenced in particular in Prime Minister Pierre Mauroy's speech to the Institut des Hautes Etudes de Defense Nationales on 14 September 1981. The test for future French strategic posture will come in 1982-83 with the final decision to deploy--or not deploy--the neutron bomb, a weapon which has no relevance in a purely "national" and "Gaullist" defense concept.

11. In this respect, it is encouraging to note that the Mitterand government recently announced its decision to build a seventh nuclear submarine armed with M-4 missiles.

12. This could involve, for example, Mirage IV, Mirage 200 and Vulcan bombers as well as British ground-launched cruise missiles and the new French generation of mobile MRBMs.

6
U.S. Policy, the Press, and the Atlantic Alliance

Marten van Heuven

INTRODUCTION

United States' policy in Europe since the election of President Reagan suggests that the NATO countries need to build a new political consensus to restore Western cohesion, to reaffirm alliance vitality, and to complement the new dynamism in Washington which is focussed on stabilizing Soviet behavior. It is a policy perspective which is important as a new foundation for sustained and even improved allied defense effort; it is also important as a demonstration to Western and Soviet audiences that America and Europe are coming together on the question of dealing with the Soviet Union.

Such a framework should be built on three elements:

1. A consensus that sustained and substantial force improvements are necessary to restrain the Soviet Union;

2. A coordinated Western effort to promote stability in key regions by restraining Soviet behavior; and

3. Effective use of arms control, where possible, as a tool for restraint of Soviet capabilities and behavior rather than as an end in itself.

To complement this framework, NATO should aim to convey a sense of vitality of the Alliance as an association of free nations with common values. The possible entry of Spain into the Alliance would be an example of the vigor, attractiveness, growth, and democratic values of NATO--in marked contrast to the Warsaw Pact.

In recent years, European confidence in the United States and European understanding of American thinking have been eroded by unpredictability and by reduced confidence in the American strategic deterrent. Moreover, there are abiding differences in perspective: some allies perceive a greater political and economic stake in good relations with the Soviet Union than the United States does. On the other hand, America's allies have an interest in working out an agreed and effective alliance strategy with Washington. The key task at present is to strengthen the common political base among the allies and to close the confidence gap. For the United States, this task means building confidence for the objectives of the Reagan administration. There will be a premium on steadiness, predictability, consultation and consistent policy signals; however, it will not be characterized by hyper-sensitivity in Washington to allied concerns which could paralyze needed initiatives. What it does imply is a serious effort at mature confidence building, in which the United States sets high standards for itself (as in defense efforts) and gains allied support through steady leadership, urging allies to accept not only Washington's view of the nature of the Soviet threat, but also the increased defense effort this entails for all alliance members.

Thus it is possible to build a political base for concrete actions to strengthen Western defense and, at the same time, to show Western opinion makers and Soviet leaders that the Alliance is moving cohesively in its approach to central questions of East-West relations. Such an approach will strengthen NATO as the United States engages further in contacts with Moscow and prepares for high level discussions with the Soviet Union.

ALLIANCE CONSULTATIONS

As Harlan Cleveland once remarked, "The nature of allies is that they expect to be consulted"--an expectation which keeps the principle of consultation alive and the practice so lively. The advantages seem obvious since the country which begins the consultation process usually gains an advantage by involving its partners not only in policy issues, but in shared responsibility as well. Consultation, moreover, builds support; decisions in which countries have a voice acquire strength and durability. But there are also disadvantages: when a country consults, it loses some of its freedom of action and options can narrow. There may even be a sense that consultation subordinates national policy to collective decision. France's behavior within the Atlantic Alliance has, at times, reflected such considerations.

On balance, however, the argument favoring consultation within the Alliance is overwhelming. In defense,

NATO manages common programs involving large sums of money. Even in those areas where members retain their national freedom of action, consultation is the essential element without which the Alliance defense effort would make little sense. To quote Harlan Cleveland once more, "The best antidote for uncoordinated stupidity among friends is long, candid and often tedious talk about real problems".

How, then, should consultation proceed? Students of NATO affairs are familiar with the whole range of permutations which have characterized the organizational development of the Alliance and which have provided a wide variety of fora for consultation: to wit, the NATO Council of Fifteen, the Defense Planning Committee with fourteen members, the Summit Seven, the Five (when Italy was chairing the European Community), and now the Berlin Working Group with four members. To complement these multilateral efforts, there has been a recent and decided increase in bilateral activity. While these procedures are testimony to the ingenuity of their architects to devise formats which serve substance, occasionally they have gone awry. The Nuclear Planning Group is a case in point. Created originally to promote the personal involvement of NATO defense ministers in the study and handling of complex and difficult issues of nuclear deterrence, pressures for enlargement have caused the original intimate and informal format to give way to a stylized and formal process involving thirteen defense ministers. The last meeting of the Nuclear Planning Group in Bonn was marked more by the protocol which surrounded it and by marginal discussion on Poland than with nuclear planning. It would not be surprising if eventually someone were to reinvent the original format under a different name.

The report of the four foreign affairs institutes which appeared in January 1981 has set forth some interesting suggestions regarding alliance consultation, particularly with a view to addressing new Alliance-related issues which emerged in the Middle East and Persian Gulf areas.[1] Although these suggestions have been imaginative and useful, some of the procedures suggested are, perhaps, too formalistic. There is no perfect formula for intra-alliance consultations; in practice, NATO is likely to continue much as it has before. With respect to security issues, the range of subjects for consultation now extends well beyond NATO, and is already global with respect to economic and other problems. A broad range of fora and methods is required to serve allied consultation purposes--some of these will be outside the formal structure of NATO, but most will be within. As the preservation of flexibility is essential, many points of contact and consultation will have to be ad hoc; they will be neither neat nor orderly, and some will work better than others. Potential participants may be excluded; nevertheless, the members of NATO have no alternative but to proceed more or less as they have in the past.

THE PRESS AND PUBLIC OPINION

The press today has assumed a political importance influencing international relations--and Alliance relationships in particular--to a degree greater than before. It is a dominance which is often overlooked in attempts to assess foreign policy and alliance relations. A local paper in Bonn provides a case in point. It never ceases to emphasize the need for a '<u>General-Konzept</u>' and it has not spared Washington. In February 1981, the paper gave evidence of more than the usual anxiety as it engaged in a game of "He loves me, he loves me not", and drew the conclusion that because Mrs. Thatcher and Mr. Francois-Poncet managed to visit the newly-elected President of the United States before the West German Foreign Minister, Mr. Genscher, the Federal Republic had now dropped somehow to third place in Washington's affections. Even more recently, the paper wagged an admonishing finger in the direction of the United States, declaring that its patience was running out with American procrastination with respect to arms control. Some of this hyperbole, of course, has to be taken with a grain of salt--occasionally such interludes are even amusing--but they mask a fundamental fact that, at times, the press conveys only a partial and, therefore, misleading impression.

During 1980, press stories focussed in particular on the relationship between Chancellor Schmidt and President Carter. A number of respected commentators sketched a dark picture which had an air of unreality for those engaged in the daily bilateral affairs of the United States and the Federal Republic of Germany. At other times, the press has a capacity for what might be called the 'foul-up factor'. In February 1981, Secretary of Defense Weinberger commented about the enhanced radiation warhead. Subsequently, the press reported that Secretary Haig had advised the European allies to disregard Secretary Weinberger's comments. Someone took a speculative newspaper piece, matched it with background information, and then interpreted what the U.S. spokesman had said in Washington. Journalistic speculation and lack of concern for accuracy not only makes the coordination of alliance relations difficult; it also forces diplomats on both sides of the Atlantic to expand inordinate energy and time clarifying subsequent misunderstanding.

Clearly the perspective of the press is different from that of officials operating at the working level of foreign relations; namely, the press, by disposition, is apt to focus on differences--diplomats are more likely to seek common elements upon which cordial and mutually advantageous policies can be built. The problem of those engaged in the conduct of foreign affairs is, fundamentally, that the press is now capable of setting a mood which can inordinately influence the conduct of international affairs. Added to the capacity of the press to direct attention toward or away from certain issues, this influence makes the press a formidable partner in the business of international relations.

Indeed, gains in the influence of the press are not limited solely to international affairs. In a recent book on U.S. domestic politics, Professor Barber concludes that the domestic press is now the single most important factor in determining success or failure of presidential candidates in the United States.[2] The lesson, it seems, is simple--the press is an important, even vital element of our society. It helps guarantee freedom and it is a powerful ally in the constant struggle against closed societies; therefore, public officials must maintain close relations with the press. Surely it is better to seek out the press in an effort to ensure accuracy of its reporting rather than to avoid contact and risk a distorted version. At the same time, a dose of healthy reserve about what the press reports is not out of place and will modify the danger of permitting the press to set the mood and the pace of international and domestic affairs.

THE LRTNF AND PUBLIC OPINION

Throughout much of 1981, NATO has been embroiled in a public controversy over the placement of long range theater nuclear weapons in Western Europe. Three years ago a senior colleague in Washington commented that the issue of deploying LRTNF would likely occupy the central position in the bilateral relationship between Bonn and Washington. This prediction has proved accurate and the observation continues to hold true. The Alliance approach to LRTNF at present is uneasy: two prospective basing countries--Belgium and the Netherlands--have given indications of reserve. There is also demonstrated unease in West Germany which seems to be increasing; but the trends there are also visible elsewhere. Germans do not have a monopoly on pacifism: the trend is even stronger in the Netherlands and in Scandinavia. Inclination to measure the decision to deploy nuclear weapons with a moral yardstick can be found in many countries.

The role of German church groups, however, deserves special attention. Increasingly, anti-nuclear weapons sentiment can be seen within the evangelical church and among catholic youth. This trend, no doubt, reflects latent feelings long present within Germany, but, at the same time, it derives sustenance from similar groups abroad. Both the Anglican Bishops and the Mormon Church in the United States have taken positions which, in effect, oppose further deployment of nuclear weapons on moral grounds.

It is obvious that since NATO took the so-called 'double decision' to deploy 572 cruise missiles and Pershing Two missiles, and also to engage in arms control, the trend against deployment has accelerated: an acceleration which has been given impetus by a gap in public understanding. Not long ago, a German politician expressed doubt that most of his constituents understand what _Nachruestung_ (disarmament) means. Many people today have come to regard nuclear weapons as an implement for fighting war and tend to ignore that their principal function is deterrence; a concept which remains at the heart of Alliance strategy to safeguard Western interests and to maintain peace. The noisy Soviet campaign to keep NATO from proceeding with its deployment decision makes this task a challenging one, but it is both right and necessary to meet it. And indeed Soviet attempt to influence Western public opinion has one positive aspect: it is an indication that, at long last, NATO's decision to modernize and to negotiate has caught Moscow's attention. Perhaps now a useful discussion designed to arrive at the lowest possible balance of these forces can begin.

The lesson seems inevitable: the NATO countries should adhere to the deployment decision. A British official recently observed, quite correctly, that abhorrence of war is no substitute for realistic plans to prevent it. What will be required, however, is sustained leadership by allied governments to explain to their publics what Alliance policy is and, in this specific case, that the acquisition and deployment of weapons is designed to enhance the maintenance of an East-West balance and to preserve the peace. European defense ministers have emphasized recently the need to keep public opinion informed. Wide dissemination of information is certainly a step in the right direction.

George Washington once said, "To be prepared for war is one of the most effective means of preserving peace." The Atlantic Alliance today needs the cooperation of both its members and the press to ensure its continued capacity to preserve the peace. One must optimistically conclude that out of the seeming cacophony of Western voices and the glare of publicity, NATO will stand by its 'double decision'.

FOOTNOTES

1. Karl Kaiser, Winston Lord, Thierry de Montbrial and David Watt, Western Security: What Has Changed? What Should Be Done? Report prepared jointly by the Forschungsinstitut der Deutschen Gesellschaft fur Auswartige Politik, Council on Foreign Relations, Institut Français des Relations Internationales, and the Royal Institute of International Affairs, 1981.

2. James D. Barber, Presidential Character: Predicting Performance in the White House (Englewood Cliffs, N.J.: Prentice-Hall, Inc., 1977).

7
The Institutional Implications of NATO in a Global Milieu

Derek C. Arnould

INTRODUCTION

The 1980s have ushered in a new time of introspection within NATO and a rethinking of the whole East-West relationship in the wake of many shattered illusions. This rethinking takes place not only against the background of dramatic events in Eastern Europe, Afghanistan and Africa, but also against a new wave of public questioning of the concept of collective defence as it is embodied in the North Atlantic Treaty Organization. Public opinion has been roused in many member countries to cast doubt upon the long-held basis of NATO policy, i.e. a credible deterrence and defence coupled with the pursuit of dialogue and negotiations with the East.

The fact that these shattered illusions have not been confined to the West should not be a source of comfort for those who prefer to ignore the obvious implications for future NATO policy and modes of operation. Although the system of Soviet military control of its partners is too fundamental to dismember and will, therefore, be preserved under some guise or other, there is equally no doubt that the train of events in Poland set in motion in July 1981 will sooner or later alter the relationships between the Soviet Union and the countries of its buffer zone with the West. Likewise, the invasion of Afghanistan has sown the seed of doubt in the minds of Eastern European leaders. Despite appropriate expressions and appropriate messages sent more or less promptly, the East Europeans have made it clear to Western interlocutors, privately but at high levels, that they consider the Afghanistan adventure a serious mistake.

In classic dichotomy, Eastern Europe remains both the essential defensive buffer with the West and the Achilles heel of the Soviet system. Much has been written about the relative value of the Eastern partners of the Soviet Union within the Warsaw Pact, i.e. reliability of the military in some countries of the Pact is not considered very high by many observers, at least in the framework of the scenarios envisaging a Soviet move against the West. It is only in the unimaginable situation of an aggressive Western move into the East that a certain reliability might be assured. Nevertheless, the Eastern European partners of the Soviet Union continue to serve their purpose as a passive buffer zone, and a major upheaval would be required to change this situation. Whether or not recent events in Poland represent a 'major upheaval' remains to be seen.

Perhaps another set of shattered illusions can be discerned in the economic situation prevailing in Eastern Europe. Economists predict, and indeed it is already evident, that these economies have entered into a very difficult period of stagnation and poor economic performance, with little hope of an early transition to something better. Economic problems facing that part of the world have raised, more or less audibly in different countries, fundamental questions about the appropriateness of the Soviet economic pattern which has been imposed upon them for more than three decades. Clearly, these changes and trends in Eastern Europe must be the subject of intense examination so that conclusions can be drawn for wise and understanding Western policies to be pursued over the next difficult, if not to say, dangerous years. Development of those policies is precisely the current challenge to NATO.

THE MECHANISMS OF CONSULTATION BEYOND NATO

NATO was born in 1949 into a simpler world of East and West and in response to a challenge in Europe. It has had to adapt itself over the years to new and different circumstances, but it is only in the last year or two that full realisation of the implications of multipolarity for Western decision-making and action has become apparent. Some years ago NATO began the examination of a phenomenon which has been called the 'diffusion of power'. The Atlantic Policy Advisory Group met in Canada in 1978 to take a first look at the question of new centres of power which affect world decision-making. The report of this group noted the shift from the bipolar world of earlier years to a tripolar world with Peking as the third pole. It also identified a great many other centres which had assumed, for a variety of reasons, a certain amount of power and certain ability to influence events. The obvious example is OPEC, and perhaps more particularly, the oil producers of the Arabian Peninsula and other Near Eastern countries which have had such a sharp impact on the world since 1973.

Recognition that the world was becoming a more complex place was heightened by actions of the Soviet Union in the former Portuguese African colonies and on the two sides of the entrance to the Red Sea, but it took the unexpected invasion of Afghanistan, with its strategic implications, to demonstrate the need for members of NATO to look beyond the traditional NATO area in their quest for continued security. There is no lack of awareness, therefore, of the new dimensions of the problem that faces the sovereign nations of NATO, but what is less apparent is the question of its impact on NATO as an organization. Although early in its existence, NATO asserted its right--indeed its duty--to consult, review and analyse events beyond the geographical limits set forth in the North Atlantic Treaty, the problem of its limited scope has never been seen so acutely as now.

In the Communiqué of the Rome ministerial meeting in April 1981, the Foreign Ministers of the NATO members discussed at length what has come to be known as the 'out-of-area problem'. Paragraph seven of the Communiqué is a departure, in many ways, from the traditional outlook of the allies, and its implications for the future are well worth examining. The main theme of this new language is the assertion that the individual NATO members are neither prepared to allow membership in NATO to hamper their efforts to ensure their security interests in areas not covered by the Treaty, nor to hamper their adherence to defence arrangements not envisaged in the Treaty.

In addition to consultation within the Atlantic Policy Advisory Group discussed above, experts have met twice a year since the early 1960s to examine all the regions of the world. The North Atlantic Council has discussed and analysed events in China, the Middle East, the Far East and elsewhere over many years. But consultation--that fundamental mechanism through which the North Atlantic Alliance has remained relevent and contemporary--is seen currently as inadequate. According to its basic Treaty, NATO exists as a defensive organization to react to aggression against its members. Its basic document contains no brief to take action elsewhere in the world. The full meaning of the Soviet Union's projection of power without any geographical limits has only recently been clearly perceived. There has been much discussion in Western circles about the vulnerability of the Western industrialised countries to interdiction of the trade routes that carry raw materials so essential to their economies. Oil is perhaps uppermost in the minds of Europeans because of their heavy dependence on supplies from the Persian Gulf. Additionally, NATO is confronted with the terrible dilemma of South Africa which occupies such a vital strategic location astride Western trade routes, but whose unacceptable internal policies pose moral dilemmas for Western strategic cooperation.

Equally problematical for Western security interests has been Soviet involvement in the Third World. While there is no doubt about Soviet motives in taking advantage of internal situations in the People's Democratic Republic of Yemen, Ethiopia and elsewhere to establish a strategic position, Soviet policy is sometimes viewed too simply as the subversion of existing governments on the basis of some long-term strategic plan. What must be recognized is that the Soviet Union is ideologically conditioned to champion the more radical factions in the internal struggles of countries seeking a more equitably balanced society. In the West there is much sympathy for Third World attempts to modernise their societies and to alter them according to the requirements of modern democratic communities in a post-colonial age. This sympathy is, however, tempered by rejection of the idea that victory of one form of totalitarianism or oligarchy over another is the solution. Thus the demand for change, coupled with the tendency to replace one dictatorship with another, creates a dilemma in much of the contemporary world, particularly in Central and South America. It is a dilemma also in Africa. Recent attempts by five Western countries (France, Britain, West Germany, Canada and the United States), all members of NATO, to prevent transfer from colonial master to totalitarian regime in Namibia is a case in point.

The Contact Group on Namibia provides insight into how NATO responds to problems outside its traditional area. The countries in this group met originally because their presence as the five Western members of the United Nations Security Council coincided with a new effort to find a broadly acceptable solution to the Namibia question. The group remains intact even though the two non-permanent Western members of the Council--Canada and the Federal Republic of Germany--are no longer members. As NATO members, the five report their progress, or lack thereof, to other members of the organization--a consultative process which stimulates discussion, suggestions, and points of view on how to resolve the conflict. The Namibian case is primarily political in nature; however, the Zaire situation provides a good example of certain NATO nations acting in concert in a military or quasi-military way. Belgium,

France, Britain and the United States, four NATO nations, have given assistance to the government of Zaire. In the case of two nations, the aid was military; in the others it was directed toward logistics and humanitarian assistance. As in the Namibian example, consultation took place which brought about general understanding among the allies of the motives and purposes of the actions of the four. It was a relatively short and successful operation; thus there was little controversy.

In the case of larger out-of-area questions--especially questions of confrontation between the Soviet Union and Western interests--the terms of reference are no longer Alliance interests, but rather of the interests of its individual sovereign members which, of course, go well beyond the interests of collective security. What sort of organization can coordinate the activities of the naval forces in the Indian Ocean and the Gulf area? As many as four members of NATO have, or have had, naval units in that area. The United States has the largest force, but France, Britain and West Germany have been represented as well. By the nature of the North Atlantic Treaty, there is no mechanism through which the admirals and other representatives of the military can meet together at NATO Headquarters or Supreme Headquarters Allied Power Europe (SHAPE) to plan activities outside the Treaty area. The consultative mechanism continues to work, and the fifteen are kept fully informed of the activities of those members who have forces in the Indian Ocean and the Gulf. But all this is not quite enough. NATO must consider the possibility that other countries will want to be involved in the Pacific or Indian Ocean. Japan, Australia and New Zealand are possibilities; there may be others at different times or in different circumstances. Thus the central question becomes: how to extend the consultative mechanism to non-NATO countries, especially as some of them may be reluctant to be associated too closely or visibly with NATO as such, but who nonetheless believe that they have interests to defend in concert with some other Western countries?

ALTERNATIVE ORGANIZATIONAL SCHEMES

Proposals for new mechanisms to extend NATO to other areas have been suggested from numerous sources, but the fifteen NATO members have responded cautiously. Certainly, consultations could take place in Brussels, or in any of the allied capitals, with other countries concerned about any given situation in various areas of the world. Consultation, as such, presents no difficulty, either practically or philosophically. Developing specific plans and meeting with military staffs to consider all the practical aspects of a common operation somewhere abroad, however, is a more complex task with a different set of expectations and requirements. There is no ready solution, but the sentiment that such a solution must be found has clearly increased.

Two recent studies have proposed suggestions for new mechanisms, but a great deal more thinking will have to go into the matter before the final solutions are found.[1] There is a deep suspicion among many of the nations of NATO--including Canada and Italy, which in European terms is by no means small--of limited inner councils, of directoires, of special groupings within the larger group. It is useful to recall the outcry at the ill-conceived meeting in Guadaloupe a few years ago and the rejection of earlier Gaullist ideas of a directoire to understand this point. At the same time, there is no doubt that some allies are able and willing to act far afield and others are not. The essential task is, however, to ensure that the creation of new mechanisms does not destroy the valuable existing ones of NATO that bring together small and large on the basis of equality, at least in terms of their voice at the Council table.

A third approach has been suggested, i.e. that the Economic Summit of the Seven might enlarge its horizons to embrace political questions. In fact, this enlargement was evident in Venice in 1980. But a meeting of heads of state, by its very nature, cannot engage in the long-term detailed work which is required to render policy concepts operable. The summit group can only point in generally agreed directions, with the detailed work being done elsewhere. Of course, a secretariat could be created, but does the world need yet another such body?

Over the years, through its various exercises in introspection such as the 'Three Wise Men's' report of 1956, the Harmel Report on Future Tasks of 1967, the Ottawa Declaration on Atlantic Relations of 1974, and the 1978 Report on East-West Relations, plus a great many other less publicised common analyses, ample evidence has been given to the great adaptability of NATO's existing mechanism to new situations. There has been only limited experience in considering the views of non-members; however, even that has been accomplished on occasion. Creating an actual cooperative mechanism of planning staffs for dealing with problems outside the NATO area and possibly involving nations not signatories of the North Atlantic Treaty must be approached cautiously. It is, perhaps, pertinent to question whether such new organizations do not raise once again the ghost of the Dullesian containment policy, a policy based on overwhelming force on the Western side which clearly does not exist at the present time. Certainly one cannot dismiss the possibility of some mechanism being created for dealing with practical questions in a purely practical way. The Western nations have shown themselves infinitely inventive and adaptable; there is no reason to believe that they will not continue to be so. At the same time, great care must be taken that an effort to redress the balance between East and West--stressing the word balance--does not stimulate a new wave of paranoia in the Soviet Union. Increased Soviet paranoia would be dangerous, especially at a time when Moscow is on the threshold of sweeping changes in leadership brought about as the grim reaper hovers over that conclave of elderly and essentially cautious invalids.

NATO has been successful because it has not been a purely military organization, but has stressed, throughout its existence, the need to ease the underlying atmosphere of mistrust and lack of comprehension between East and West as well as to seek political and diplomatic methods of making essentially unnecessary, or at least less necessary, the confrontation of manpower and ever more efficient weapons of destruction that mark the relationship between East and West today. The political pillar of NATO must continue to be given the full attention that it has received thus far. Indeed, there is no danger that it will not, because the mood of the allies is to continue a dialogue, despite being disillusioned and disenchanted by the events of 1979 and 1980, and even earlier, when the Soviet Union took advantage of a long period of reduction in Western military expenditures to enhance its capabilities. But if the will to negotiate and discuss with the East is now without illusion, it is nonetheless strong.

Again and again one hears in NATO circles the complaint that every objective and rational analysis of the situation of the Soviet Union points to the desperate need of that country to devote greater resources to the well-being of its people, to enhance its inadequate infrastructure, and to utilize its raw materials for future development. It seems obvious that this should be achieved through a slackening, at least somewhat, of the pace of its huge military programme of modernization. Therefore, in the necessary work of reestablishing a mutually confident balance between East and West, attention must be paid to fostering in every way possible, a mood in the Soviet Union of sufficient trust to allow the various arms control negotiations in which

East and West are engaged to go forward toward positive results, despite the years of virtual stalemate. It should be equally obvious that trust must be reciprocal. While the new administration in Washington needs time to review the various arms negotiations, there is a feeling in NATO that this work should be pursued energetically and quickly.

ALLIANCE POLICY AND PUBLIC OPINION

NATO members are only too conscious of the impatience of a growing section of their populations. Certainly some of this earnest drive for disarmament at any cost has been insufficiently considered by its authors and supporters, and some have not fully appreciated the alternatives for governments. Popular support, however, can no longer be taken for granted, and Western publics must be given cogent reasons for not only the security concerns of governments, but also for the increased costs of providing a credible defence. At the same time, governments must pursue, as a necessary corollary, every possibility for putting an end to the arms confrontation that makes these expenditures an essential requirement. Furthermore, the relevance and the appropriateness of NATO's way of resolving these problems needs the constant attention of thinkers on both sides of the Atlantic. The dimensions of the problems themselves need to be given the fullest public airing, so that the citizens of NATO countries fully understand what is involved and are prepared to accept the consequences of their demands to pursue any particular policy in the name of the peace and stability that all desire.

The image of NATO as a mindless war machine is a favourite caricature of Moscow's propagandists. It is important for the public to understand what NATO actually is today: a useful, even indispensable, mechanism for channelling the collective thinking and negotiating skills of fifteen Western democracies toward arms control and disarmament, toward contacts and cooperation between East and West; a mechanism that through a credible military deterrent underlines its seriousness as a negotiating partner. It is something that we should not lightly throw away or discount in the pursuit of something new for the sake of newness.

FOOTNOTES

1. See "A Global Strategy to Meet the Global Threat: A British Initiative," The British Atlantic Committee, February 1981 and Karl Kaiser, Winston Lord, Thierry de Montbrial and David Watt, "Western Security: What Has Changed? What Should Be Done?". Report jointly prepared by the Forschungsinstitut der Deutschen Gesellschaft fur Auswartige Politik, the Council in Foreign Relations, the Institut Français des Relations Internationales, and the Royal Institute of International Affairs, 1981.

Part III

The Warsaw Treaty Organisation

8
Devolution in the Warsaw Treaty Organisation

Malcolm Mackintosh

WHITHER THE WARSAW PACT?

The Soviet Union's relationships with the countries of Eastern Europe, particularly during the coming decade, are critical not only to the task of assessing how Soviet military control over the area will be maintained, but also to understanding the attitudes of the Eastern European governments towards membership in the Warsaw Treaty Organisation. Firstly, any examination of Soviet control requires a look at Soviet attitudes to military power and the use of force in external relations, with particular reference to Eastern Europe: attitudes which are unlikely to change in the foreseeable future. Secondly, it requires a description of the Soviet Union's military buffer zone in Eastern Europe as well as the nature, organisation, and role of the Warsaw Pact which provides the machinery for Soviet military control of the area. Finally, it requires consideration of how the Warsaw Pact may develop, particularly with regard to Soviet planning for the alliance in the context of possible changes in the Eastern European regimes. In the context of change, issues of national identity and history which may affect the Soviet-East European relationship in the military and strategic field assume renewed importance.

Clearly, some attention must be focussed on the future of Poland: its internal crisis and its difficult relations with the Soviet Union and other Warsaw Pact allies. It is impossible to predict how the Soviet Union will react ultimately to events in Poland; therefore, any discussion of devolution of the Pact must remain speculative. It seems safe to assume, however, that Brezhnev and his colleagues--or their successors--will not relinquish either political or military control over Eastern Europe. In this sense, some form of Warsaw Pact alliance will continue to exist; but its nature and its operational aims and capabilities, in the various situations which may develop, would be very hard to assess with any of the confidence prevalent before events in Poland changed the situation in Eastern Europe so unexpectedly.

THE SOVIET ATTITUDE TO MILITARY POWER

Upon considering possible devolution of the Warsaw Treaty Organisation, some appreciation of the long-standing and traditional Russian, as well as Soviet, concept of the importance of military power may be helpful, particularly to understand Soviet aims and motives in maintaining permanent military control over the countries of Eastern Europe. Russia has felt vulnerable to external military pressure ever since it attempted to create a national state in the vast plains of the northern parts of the Eurasian land mass. Lacking natural defences, the Russians found their territory overrun by Tartars and Mongols from the East, by Turks from the South, and attacked by Poles, Swedes, French and Germans from the West. Historical experience fostered in the Russians a deep sense of the need to amass military power and to entrust their survival exclusively to their own military effort. It also led them to feel an overriding suspicion of the aims, ambitions, and superiorities of other nations--at first in military affairs, and later in economic and technological terms. The Russians feel, therefore, that the preservation of the state and its power necessitates not only self-reliance, but also avoiding too much trust in political or diplomatic arrangements with potentially hostile countries on defence issues.

These historical and traditional attitudes to military power and defence combine today with more recent political and ideological trends to form the current and the likely future Soviet attitude to military power. Preservation of the Soviet system, wherever it exists, as well as defence of its homeland and its client states are the first priorities of the Soviet armed forces. Defence issues have played an important part in Soviet attempts to protect their frontiers by establishing pro-Soviet regimes in neighbouring states close to the Soviet border; in other words, the long-standing tradition of the 'buffer zone'. The most important of these zones, most of which were set up after the Second World War, is Eastern Europe, but the pattern exists today in Mongolia and in Afghanistan as well.

Military power is also essential to the Russians in maintaining the status of the Soviet Union as a superpower. It must be available to support or carry out tasks overseas--on an opportunistic basis--to expand Soviet influence and to encourage, where appropriate, additional countries and regimes to become friendly and then obedient to the Soviet Union. This policy summarises, in effect, the role of Soviet communist ideology in Moscow's foreign policy towards the Third World--much of which relies on powerful backing provided by the large and sophisticated armed forces which the Soviet Union has built, particularly in the last two decades.

SOVIET MILITARY CONTROL OVER EASTERN EUROPE

The military and strategic factors involved in Soviet control of Eastern Europe can be seen, in realistic terms, against this general background of fear and vulnerability. In the last year of the Second World War, the victorious Soviet Army occupied both Allied and Axis countries of East and Central Europe up to the demarcation lines in Germany and Austria which had been agreed with the Western Allies at wartime conferences in Teheran and Yalta. At the same time, collaboration with communist-led resistance movements in Yugoslavia and Albania (to which Britain and the United States also gave aid and support) brought two additional countries into the Soviet camp at the end of the war. The final composition of what was to become the 'Eastern Bloc' was not decided until 1948, after the incorporation of Czechoslovakia, the defection of Yugoslavia, and the Soviet agreement to allow Finland a form of neutrality acceptable to the Soviet Union. By 1945 the countries of East and Central Europe which had been reached by the Soviet Army during the war had acquired the status--in military and political terms-- of a buffer zone which has, with a few exceptions and uncertainties, remained in place until the present day.

The role of a buffer zone in Soviet political and military thinking is, on the whole, a fairly straightforward one. Politically, the zone in Eastern Europe protects the Soviet Union from direct territorial contact with non-communist countries (excepting Berlin, Northern Norway and Eastern Turkey) and helps to fulfill the ideological requirements of the Soviet Communist Party in its relationship with neighbouring states. It also enables the Communist Party in Moscow to ensure that Soviet standards and Soviet practices in administration, accountability and authority (including the superior status automatically given to Soviet citizens and officials in most East European countries) are followed and obeyed in the countries concerned. Control of the buffer zone allows the Soviet security services to operate freely throughout the area; thus providing the KGB, among other benefits, with authority to overrule its East European opposite numbers in defining and handling security issues. Economically and technologically, access to the resources of the buffer zone countries in manpower, skills, and material is available to the Soviet Union; methods of access have ranged from outright seizure in the Stalinist era to the more sophisticated arrangements of recent years through bilateral contracts or through the Council for Mutual Economic Assistance (CMEA).

The buffer zone performs two important military functions for the Soviet Union: it provides the Soviet Armed Forces with space for deployment and maneouvre in depth, well forward of the Soviet frontier, and it provides adequate territorial space for locating and training the large ground and air forces on which Russian tradition insists for military purposes. Soviet control of the buffer zone enables the Russians to choose the strength and concentration areas of their forces; for example, the nineteen Soviet divisions now stationed in East Germany to cover the main axis of operations in the North German plain and the smaller forces deployed on the southern flank in Hungary and Czechoslovakia, four and five divisions, respectively. Reflecting their more independent or special positions, Romania and Bulgaria have no Soviet forces deployed on their territory.

In terms of planning offensive operations against Western Europe, possession of the zone enables the Soviet Union to concentrate--in conditions of the strictest secrecy--the forces considered necessary by the Soviet General Staff for an attack on NATO which could occur well to the west of Soviet territory. Soviet planning includes the advance preparation of lines of communication and reinforcement routes from the Soviet Union, the dispersal of air and naval forces, and the pre-positioning of arms, ammunition, and supplies necessary for such a campaign in the event of a general war in Europe.

Control of Eastern Europe also enables the Russians to utilize the military manpower and skills of the East European countries. The machinery set up to achieve this goal is, of course, the Warsaw Pact. The Russians recognise, especially in the light of their own suspiciousness and mistrust of other nations, that East European nationalism and pride in historical achievements can create problems for a Soviet High Command expecting absolute obedience and military efficiency from its East European allies in all possible situations. Whatever happens in Poland, these problems--which are likely to be even more serious in the future--

are in the forefront of Soviet thinking on the European balance today. Since so much of Soviet planning in Europe concerns the organisation of a buffer zone in Eastern Europe, the structure and role of the Warsaw Pact provides a useful focus for analysis.

THE WARSAW PACT: MILITARY STRUCTURE AND ORGANISATION

The Soviet Union and its East European allies--Poland, East Germany, Czechoslovakia, Hungary, Romania, and Bulgaria--have been organised for political and military purposes in the Warsaw Pact since 1955, the only defector being Albania in 1961. Politically, the Warsaw Pact was deliberately modelled on NATO. It has a Political Consultative Committee with a civilian secretary-general, a military commander-in-chief appointed from the strongest power, and a combined staff. The Consultative Committee is supposed to meet at regular intervals to discuss foreign and military policy and to formulate political initiatives in East-West relations in Europe. Here any similarity with NATO ends. The Consultative Committee is largely a transmission belt for Soviet instructions and recommendations; some debate certainly takes place, but no basic divergencies are permitted in foreign policy, at least as expressed in public communiques. There is good evidence that in recent years disagreements within the Pact have occurred: for example, over Romanian insistence on following an independent foreign policy, on refusing to commit troops to Warsaw Pact exercises on other members' territory, and on resisting Soviet demands for an increased defence budget. The Warsaw Pact still maintains an official position that it would dissolve itself in return for the dissolution of NATO; although, of course, the Soviet Union has bilateral political and military treaties with all its East European allies which would continue to exist after the demise of the Warsaw Pact.

In military terms, the Warsaw Pact headquarters has grown from a directorate in the Soviet General Staff in 1955 to a large, multinational staff attached to the Soviet Ministry of Defence in Moscow. Its High Command at present consists of the following: the Soviet Commander-in-Chief, Marshal Kulikov, who is advised by two consultative bodies--a Committee of National Defence Ministers of all member countries, and a Military Council. The Military Council, which includes a senior officer from each country plus the Soviet Chief of Staff and a Soviet political officer, appears to meet regularly and does give the East European forces a stronger voice in military matters than was the case before the

Czechoslovakian crisis in 1968. The Pact also has a Soviet Inspector-General and a Deputy Commander-in-Chief for Armaments who appear to be members of the Military Council.

Subordinate to the Commander-in-Chief is the combined staff of the Pact, headed by General Gribkov, and deputy chiefs of staff drawn from each member country, as well as a Soviet political officer. The headquarters also administers the Soviet military missions in each of the East European capitals. These missions are normally located within the Ministries of Defence of member countries, and have considerable powers over training programmes and weapons utilisation in the forces concerned.

The most important feature of the Warsaw Pact's military organisation is that the headquarters apparently has no operational capability in peacetime; for example, it has no logistic branch, transportation, or supply services organisations--all of which are provided by the Soviet Ministry of Defence. Moreover, the air defence of the buffer zone is the responsibility of the Soviet Strategic Air Defence Command. Each of the non-Soviet Warsaw Pact (NSWP) countries is the equivalent of a Soviet Air Defence District and the national air defence forces are linked directly to the headquarters of the Strategic Air Defence Command in Moscow.

The conclusion, therefore, is that the Warsaw Pact's military headquarters, as constituted at present, is a peacetime organisation only. In wartime, the Soviet High Command, supported by the Soviet General Staff, would take command of whatever East European forces were available, properly trained, and considered politically reliable for the task in hand. Despite the uncertainties of the Polish situation, the Soviet Union continues to believe that the current structure and military capabilities of the Warsaw Pact countries are satisfactory. The troops appear to be well armed and exercised, and most senior officers are trained in the Soviet Union. Military service is an accepted part of life for the overwhelming majority of the young people in Eastern Europe. Morale and the sense of motivation obviously vary from country to country; but, on the whole, the present Soviet leaders probably consider that the existing alliance is consistent with their buffer zone concept of defence and offence, even taking at least some of the East European national characteristics and loyalties into account.

SOVIET PLANNING AND THE FUTURE OF THE WARSAW TREATY ORGANISATION

If the Soviet Union under its present or succession leadership could guarantee the continatuion of existing control over Eastern Europe--politically, ideologically, militarily and economically--and that the East European regimes would remain loyal, it would certainly do so, with all branches of the forces duly modernised in weapons, organisation, and training. However, Poland's current crisis, Romania's independent position, and Hungary's divergent economic policies have shown Soviet leaders that some form of evolution in their relationships within the alliance may occur, and that the Soviet Union itself must do some planning for the future of the Warsaw Pact. If the Soviet Union were to request an internal planning paper, perhaps by political and military experts prepared in Moscow for the Politburo, what would it contain?

Certainly such a planning document would begin by stressing the unchanging need for Soviet political control over all the countries of Eastern Europe, perhaps expressed with the hope that in due course both Yugoslavia and Albania might return to the fold, either voluntarily or perhaps as a result of Soviet or Warsaw Pact action, directly or indirectly. The authors of the paper would also assume that Eastern Europe must remain a buffer zone, protecting the Soviet frontiers and allowing Soviet forces freedom to deploy for defensive or offensive purposes. In other words, Soviet military control over the area must be retained--and it must be effective.

Following these assumptions, an important section of the paper would probably raise some international issues, primarily the future Soviet-American political, military, and commercial relationship, the SALT process, the strength or weaknesses of the Western alliance in Europe, the possible addition of Spain to NATO (and the likely Soviet response), the situation on the north and south flanks in Europe, and the future of East-West arms control negotiations on the continent. No doubt the paper would seriously consider economic factors relevant to the Warsaw Pact in the 1980s: the financial and commercial status of Warsaw Pact countries and the energy situation in Western and Eastern Europe, especially the oil and gas requirements of East European countries. The role of energy in underpinning East European dependence on the Soviet Union may be of great importance in the devolution of the Warsaw Pact. Finally, the planning document would address a subject which would be central to any Soviet analysis of the future of the

Pact: the policies of the individual East European countries and their likely future relationship with the Soviet Union on political and military issues.

A Soviet planning paper on this subject would have to begin with Poland. Poland's central geographical position in Eastern Europe and along the Soviet frontier would give it this priority, even if the revolutionary events of 1980-1981 had not taken place. The Soviet authors would begin by recalling the history of Russian-Polish relations. The Poles are a Slavic people whose flat and open territory historically posed serious problems to its leaders which led, at the height of Polish national power, to expansionist policies in search of security and military strength. At one time, Poland included most of the Ukraine and the Baltic States and a Polish Army once occupied Moscow. Polish power collapsed, however, in the 18th century and the country was divided among its larger neighbours. Poland, nevertheless, had made a significant imprint on European civilisation, and her people remain devout Catholics, as the role of the Church in the current crisis has shown so vividly. Indeed, Polish soldiers won enviable reputations during the risings in 1831 and 1863 and the Second World War for courage and endurance in adversity.

Poland has to be recognised as a formidable nation with an unrivalled sense of pride in nationhood and history. It was most unfortunate, in Soviet eyes, that Poland was where a workers' movement (Solidarity) developed which suggested the possibility of a new political party. Solidarity rivaled the official Polish Communist Party which, according to Marxism-Leninism, should be the sole element of authority and exercise the 'leading role' in a communist country allied and subordinate to the Soviet Union. During this crisis, the present Polish Party leader, General Jaruzelski, was faced with the almost impossible task of demonstrating continuing obedience to the Soviet Union while simultaneously accepting Polish nationalism and its search for political freedom so closely identified with the Solidarity movement.

Apparently, the Russians refrained from using force to restore the pre-Solidarity situation in Poland because the Soviet government was reluctant to assume the responsibility of administering an occupied Poland, particularly given that country's traditions, history and economic difficulties. The Russians are aware that without a return to Party orthodoxy on Soviet terms, not only will the Soviet Union suffer a major setback ideologically and politically at home and in Eastern Europe, but the Warsaw Pact may cease to exist as a viable military organisation. It seems likely that the authors of any Soviet planning paper would assume that such a situation is, in fact, intolerable, and that some form of direct Soviet action internally, or in the form of an external invasion--hopefully upon the invitation of 'healthy forces' in Poland--might have to be taken to restore the position of the Polish Party and to prevent the possible disintegration of the Warsaw Pact.

If the Soviet Union is forced, in the end, to military action in Poland, it would expect to maintain a strong force of Soviet troops in Poland for an indefinite period--perhaps ten to twelve divisions. These troops would help in the maintenance of order in the country and secure the vital lines of communication and logistics through Poland to East Germany, as well as carrying out the full range of air defence tasks within Polish air space. In strictly military terms the occupation of Poland, difficult and costly though it may be in bloodshed, disturbance and financial and economic commitments, could do something to preserve the Warsaw Pact in approximately the same form as it is today. Certainly it is important for the Russians that firm action in Poland stamps out any danger of the Polish 'infection' spreading to the other East European countries. Whatever the outcome of events in Poland, this nationalistic and religious population will remain a thorny problem for Soviet planners.

Czechoslovakia, now firmly in the hands of obedient, pro-Soviet hardliners like Husak and Bilak, has never shared Poland's pride in military achievements. Czechoslovakian opposition to Soviet domination has been intellectual and political. Its military efficiency or reliability in war is uncertain, in Soviet minds, partly because of the armed forces' lack of combat experience. If Soviet action is necessary to restore and maintain the pre-1980 situation in Poland, Czechoslovakia will maintain its role and loyalty to a Warsaw Pact modelled on the present alliance.

Hungary has proved to be a more difficult country to keep within the Soviet orbit. The suddenness and ferocity of the Hungarian rising in 1956 took the Russians by surprise; when the rising was over, the Soviet Union's initially harsh discipline and methods eventually gave way to a more flexible attitude to Hungarian nationalism, particularly in the economic and commercial fields. Today, Hungary's economic and trade policies, under the direction of Janos Kadar, seem to be the most liberal in Eastern Europe. However, Hungarians and Russians are deeply suspicious of each other for national reasons: the language barrier is almost insurmountable, the Hungarians have strong affinity for Western Europe through their historical and national traditions. Politically and militarily, Hungary is a stable member of the Soviet bloc and will not press for change in the present Warsaw Pact arrangements, if Soviet control of the alliance remains effective and unimpaired.

Turning now to the Balkans, Romania creates serious difficulties for the Russians. The Russians know that the Romanians are of mixed race: part Latin (like their language), part Slav, and part Turkish, with elements of long-forgotten Asiatic tribes which settled in the Danube valley in early medieval times. Romanians have tended to regard themselves as West Europeans, close to France and Italy; in fact, their political character has been shaped by centuries of Balkan history. Romania's present leader, Nicolae Ceausescu, is ruthless and authoritarian, and his communist regime in Romania is marked by unwavering rigidity. Romania, under Ceausescu's leadership, is in many senses a rebel against Soviet rule, but Ceausescu is a skilful rebel, and has avoided giving the Soviet Union an excuse to expel or overthrow him even on issues of defence expenditure--in spite of the attraction this option may have had for Soviet leaders in the past. The Romanian leaders, however, were dismayed by some aspects of the Polish situation and may have preferred a return to single Party control under Soviet authority to prevent a spread of Solidarity tendencies into Romania. The Romanians may hope for a peaceful solution to the Polish crisis and a continuation of the predictable and even rigid Soviet domination of the Warsaw Pact organisation. They have, after all, learnt to outwit the Soviet Union on military matters in the last decade, using traditional Balkan tactics. They would probably rather continue these policies in circumstances which they understand than have to face up to new and unknown forces which might appear if the Warsaw Pact changed its character significantly in the wake of the Polish crisis.

Little needs to be said about Bulgaria which has never given the Soviet Union any real trouble. Since 1944 the Bulgarians have been docile and subservient to the Russians, to whom the ordinary Bulgarian feels a sense of respect and even friendship--unlike the Poles or the Romanians. The Bulgarians are hard workers and traditionally disciplined and responsive to authority. They can be expected to continue their allegiance to the Russians indefinitely under their present rulers, and would accept any form of Warsaw Treaty Organisation sponsored by the Soviet Union.

With reference to East Germany, it can be assumed that the Soviet planning report would reflect some of the traditional ambivalence shown by the Russians for their hard-working, disciplined, authoritarian, and exceptionally efficient former opponents, whose separate state they set up after the Second World War. The Russians know well that East Germany has moved into a phase of economic and industrial development which is not only efficient, but of considerable value to the Soviet economy. Their very efficiency is, surely, in some ways a matter of envy to the Russians. East German leaders show no visible tendencies to question Soviet domination; if anything, especially on local, German matters, they seem to support a hard line, sometimes more extreme than the Soviet Union itself. East German loyalty should not obscure, however, their potential to cause problems for the Russians who are very careful to keep the East German party and government under close observation and control.

The Soviet Union regards the presence of a large number of Soviet forces on East German soil as absolutely essential to the control of their buffer zone and their ability to exert military pressure in Europe. The East Germans also need these forces to maintain their existence as an independent state, as one of two Germanies. East Germany would certainly oppose any change in the status or organisation of the Warsaw Pact, and would act to prevent any such alterations resulting from the crisis in Poland.

The judgement of this hypothetical Soviet planning paper, then, would probably be that the Warsaw Pact countries, under their present or similar succession leaderships, would prefer the Pact's existing structures and Soviet control to remain broadly unchanged in the next decade. The uncertain factor, at the moment, is the situation in Poland: if the Polish Communist Party fails to regain total control of the country, Poland, geographically the central bastion of the Warsaw Pact in Eastern Europe, could threaten the disintegration of the alliance. This danger may indeed have brought some members of the Pact, who were previously emphasising differing priorities, to an awareness of the risks of change.

While hoping for a successful and orderly solution to the Polish problem, for an unchanged Warsaw Treaty Organisation, and for the general acceptance of Soviet economic and commercial requirements by the East Europeans within CMEA, the Russians characteristically would not ignore the possibility of other situations developing.

We cannot predict all possible outcomes of the Polish crisis, but the emergence of Solidarity in that country in 1980-1981 raises the question of how the Soviets would react to any situation in Eastern Europe which poses a political threat to allegiance to the Warsaw Pact. In other words, what could the Soviet Union do to preserve its buffer zone if, for whatever reason, the Soviet Government felt unable to re-establish Soviet control over a Pact ally?

It is likely that the Soviet Union would, in these hypothetical circumstances, adopt a strategy of relying on its own forces and resources to retain as many of its existing advantages as possible. First of all, Soviet military doctrine would decree that Eastern Europe and Western Russian should comprise a single theatre of war, with a peacetime Commander-in-Chief who may or may not be Commander-in-Chief of the Warsaw Pact. Secondly, the Soviet Union would marshal its main forces in the western military districts of the Soviet Union: the Baltic, the Belorussian, the Carpathian, the Kiev and the Odessa Military Districts, armed and trained to move very rapidly into and across Poland, East Germany, Czechoslovakia, Hungary, Romania and Bulgaria at short notice, in response to the defensive or offensive needs of the Soviet foreign and military policy, with or without national opposition.

At the same time, the Soviet Union would retain some allied forces, relying perhaps on the defence treaties it has with those countries which support the existing structure of the Pact, in order to maintain an active Soviet military presence along the frontiers of the buffer zone. In particular, East Germany would permit a strong Soviet Group of Forces, and so would Czechoslovakia and Hungary. The Russians could also deploy troops to Bulgaria: a proposal which any foreseeable Bulgarian government would readily accept. In the last instance, future Soviet policy options towards Yugoslavia would also benefit from such new deployments of Soviet troops and facilities.

Despite its hypothetical nature, this scenario is generally consistent with Soviet military doctrine when applied to complex situations in a border area close to the Soviet Union. It would be, of course, a 'last resort' policy, to be undertaken only if Poland's political revolution remained unchallenged and, for whatever reason, direct Soviet intervention had proved impractical.

Any interpretation of Soviet planning remains speculative, if only because of the secretive character of

Soviet policy making, and the uncertain future of the Polish situation. If the Soviet Union succeeds in reversing the present political trends in Poland by eliminating Solidarity from Polish political life, by whatever means, the pressures to retain the discipline and control of the existing Warsaw Pact structure will be very strong even in potentially critical regimes such as the Romanian one. If the Poles were to complete their revolution successfully, the Soviet Union would simply re-fashion its military doctrine and force deployments to enable it to pursue its policies in Europe with reduced dependence on Polish facilities and cooperation--in spite of the inevitable defects in military capabilities. One thing is certain: whatever option is pursued (and there are many possible variations to those described above), the Soviet Union will never give up its political and military control over Eastern Europe: the buffer zone is here to stay.

9
The Warsaw Pact: A Study of Vulnerabilities, Tension, and Reliability

Ivan Volgyes

More than six decades have passed since the successful October Revolution led by the Bolsheviks created the first Soviet state in Russia, more than thirty-five years since the first Communist states were created in the heart of Eastern Europe by the victorious Soviet armies, and more than a quarter of a century since the Warsaw Treaty Organization (WTO) was formally organized. By any test of time such historical periods are certainly adequate for detached historical analyses of the stresses and tension that have developed between the military and society in Eastern Europe on the one hand, and within the alliance, on the other.

PECULIARITIES OF COMMUNIST MILITARY POLITICS

The armed forces of the Communist states of Europe, at first glance, obviously fulfill the traditional role played by armed forces everywhere: to provide the backbone of domestic defense for the regime against enemies from the outside and the inside. There is obviously nothing peculiar about such a role; the army of every state and every nation fulfills these same functions.[1] The army in the states under consideration, as elsewhere, constitutes a convincing interest group which constrains the regimes' ability to advance in areas other than military might, agitates for an increase in military expenditures, and associates itself with the steel and coal complexes for ever greater strengthening of the "commanding heights" of industry.[2] Furthermore, just as in many other developing states, the armies are also purposive social instruments whose roles in the transformation or maintenance of social equilibrium represent major contributions to the strength of the nation.[3] In all these traditional contributions, the armies of Eastern Europe fulfill traditional patterns that can be replicated in most societies.

Lest we forget, however, there are certain characteristics that are peculiar to the nature of communist states and which determine the relationship of the military and the polity in these systems.

The first aspect of these peculiarities lies in the nature of the allocation of power in communist states.[4] Although in many states--except those dominated by the army or by the army and party together--the military and its powers are curtailed by civilian considerations; in communist states, the role of the military--like the role of other instruments--is subordinated to the party in all its manifestations. Much has been said about the subordination of the military to the party through such traditional methods as the use of political officers, utilization of the main administration within the party apparat, or through double informing activities of ever-present political spies. At this stage, perhaps, we should try to conceptualize this relationship as functionally determined, rather than engaging in futile controversy over the party-army relationship.[5]

The concept of functional determination allows us to view the party-army relationship in a variegated light.[6] In communist polities, to use somewhat outmoded systems analysis terminology, the party controls the output, the input, and the feedback mechanisms of society. The party, in other words, determines the bases on which decisions are made, makes the decisions and creates support for the decisions reached. With respect to the army, however, the party has always had a somewhat different role: it allows--and, with some notable exceptions, has always allowed--the army to play a role in the input process. Today it is safe to assert that the input processes have been more open to army demands than to any other apparatus, with the possible exception of the political police organs. It is clear, of course, that as the modernization of the technical levels of the armed forces has increased and army's input has become ever greater; complexity has demanded technical expertise and secrecy; therefore, the party has found itself ever more reliant on the army on which, at least at the input level, it is forced to place its trust.[7]

Remarkably, as the Soviet polity developed, the party also had to open up, to some extent, even the feedback loop of support to 'spontaneous' expressions as well. Here, the army had been genuinely involved in expressing support for, or opposition to, certain measures instituted by the party that affected the performance of the military as a whole. For example, such 'minor' controversies as the percentage of recruit training time devoted to political instruction, or the use of conscripts in the physical aspects of 'building socialism', have certainly been clear instances where genuine feedback, though channelled, was used as the basis for altering decisions already set.

It is also true, however, that the output processes of decision making have remained closed to the army and have been monopolized by the party apparat. The centralism of that process is well known and the decisions rendered leave no doubt that the army must accept them. And yet, even this process has been refined during the last decades so that today there are two mechanisms that make the process of subordination more palatable to the army as a whole.

The first of these mechanisms relates to the role of the leading personalities of the military complex. The party has been exceedingly careful to promote military leaders, not merely on the basis of their technical knowledge, but also on the basis of their party loyalty. Consequently, a military decision maker, regardless of rank, is not placed in his position of authority solely because of his abilities, but also because of his party connections: loyalties coupled with military ability. While the importance of party loyalty can characterize any sphere of communist power relationships, it is especially applicable to Soviet and East European military/party power relationships. Mistakes will, of course, occur: A Zhukov, a Moczar or a Kiraly may step forward in periods of stress, but the party has been remarkably successful in judging its military cadres.[8]

The second mechanism of output, subordination-pallatibility, refers to the peculiar nature of the alliance system within which multinational units are integrated. In this instance, independent decision making within national military units, is subordinated not merely to national desiderata, but also to cross-cutting leavages within the alliance system.[9] In other words, determining what percentage of the national budget can be devoted to the armed forces is only one element of the national decision making process; also the military leadership receives additional funds or equipment, training or exercise support from the Warsaw Pact, more specifically from the U.S.S.R. Conversely, national decisions regarding the percentage of allocations for defense or army-related activities are frequently set at the Pact level rather than at the domestic level. In a sense, of course, this duality not only creates tensions within the domestic decision-making system (e.g., Romania, East Germany or Hungary), but it also lends a certain level of responsibility to the leaders of the armed forces which they would otherwise not possess.

A second aspect of this peculiarity lies in the fact that the armed forces, in general, are supposed to have emerged from the population as a whole and are supposed to represent the widest strata in the common national effort to defend the socialist fatherland(s); however, from the outset of the existence of communist power, fear of Bonapartism has plagued communist leaders.[10] Power centered in individuals--such as Trotsky, Tuklachevsky and Zhukov, who also possessed dominant personalities capable of acting against the party leadership--was viewed with alarm greater than necessary from the perspective of rationality. Nonetheless, this somewhat irrational fear of Bonapartism--based on the mistaken reading of incidents in European history from which incorrect 'laws' were deduced, feared, and generalized by people who did not really understand history, but who wished to alter that which they understood so little--has led to the peculiarity that the party simultaneously created a duopoly of power: the army and the political police. The KGB and its separate organizations, indeed, are expected to act as checks on the power of the military and, in the service of their mission to the party, they are certainly expected to exercise at least a coequal function in system and subsystem maintenance activities.[11]

Some, of course, would argue that this is not unique: Hitler's Germany was also characterized by similar dualities.[12] What is unique, however, in the Soviet and East European cases is that the KGB and its various local counterparts have (a) successfully penetrated, and to a great extent control, the various armies, and (b) that they retain a cross-national network of control that is truly integrated under Soviet direction to a far greater extent than that in existence among the communist armies in general.[13]

A third important aspect of the peculiarity of the communist alliance system stems from the nature of ideology. Marxism, before the establishment of the Soviet state--and internationally before the establishment of the communist states of the region--was a prescriptive ideology; from 1917 and 1945, respectively, it has become descriptive, a tortuous zigzag of meaningless phrases in search of justification for the existence and exercise of power. As the doctrine acquired body, the system territory, and as communist encirclement replaced enforced isolation, the presence of the new 'fraternal' states had to be justified in ideology as well.[14] The cautious justification of instilling socialist patriotism in the citizenry of the member-states of the alliance systems, as this ideology developed 'creatively', comes dangerously close to raising the specter of nationalism and that of the common enemy. Aside from the perspective of Bulgaria, such a possibility is not viewed by the U.S.S.R. as beneficial to its own existence. Consequently, the U.S.S.R. and the ruling parties have utilized two major and more controllable issues in order to insure mastering the military subsystems: fostering cynicism on the one hand, and instilling certain socialist values on the other.[15]

The fostering of cynical attitudes is unique to Soviet-type systems only insofar as the scope of cynicism is concerned. In other systems cynicism is an accepted part of the operation of society due to the comprehensive nature of communist ideology; however, cynicism--the operationalized concept of cognitive dissonance--is mandated for a whole array of human activities. It is, of course, true that for the efficient operation of the communist system, one must drift away from the prescriptive ideology that lies in 19th century history, grossly misunderstood. As the system develops, cynicism fostered by reality and prophecies that are unfulfillable, must be stressed over idealism and becomes necessary for survival and system maintenance. What _is_ unique, however, is that the adoption of cynicism becomes _expected_ in all forms of socio-political existence; behavior must conform to values already set in advance.

A concomitant desire of instilling certain values through the process of socialization as a long-term goal, however, must reinforce the instilling of cynicism mentioned above. As far as the U.S.S.R. is concerned, it is obvious that its leaders care very little about a whole array of value-socialization that takes place internally. They do not care if internal system propagate a wide array of values with differing emphasis in each of these states. The parameters of tolerance relate to two values only: the unquestioned control of the society by the party on the one hand, and the non-existence of unbridled anti-Soviet nationalism on the other. The _necessitas sine qua non_, therefore, that the Soviet elite must instill in the members of the alliance system, lies in the socializing of _attitudes that require the army to follow orders of the party and not act against the U.S.S.R. on the one hand, and to be prepared to fight "traditional enemies" other than the Russians, on the other_. The U.S.S.R. does not care if a political system in the Warsaw Pact stresses Stalinism or democracy, liberalism or centralism, private farming or state control, private initiative and profit or total socialist control; it only cares that the values of the allies not propel them toward loosening the reins held by the party or turning them away from the existing military-political alliance system. And, consequently, with the help of the party and the KGB, and through the benefits, training and elite status extended to the military, the system must insure the loyalty and reliability of the professional armed forces.

THE WARSAW PACT: SYSTEMIC PECULIARITIES

Excellent studies in the past have dealt with various aspects of the Warsaw Pact as a military alliance; both classified and unclassified studies in the United States and in the countries of the region admirably describe the physical dimensions of this impressive alliance system.[16] Based on these studies, intelligent observers certainly can delineate the physical size, organization and even performance of the Pact. Suffice it to say, here, that the Warsaw Pact is primarily composed of armies of Communist states whose physical locus is Eastern Europe, whose deployment as a force in action has only taken place in intra-systemic conflict, and whose development and deployment has been generally in accordance with the desires of the major actor of the alliance, the U.S.S.R.

And herein lies the first, major conceptual problem in the discussion of the alliance system, namely, the problem whether one can regard this system as a "genuine" alliance, or one that is "imposed upon" by the participating states. On the one hand, it should be noted that the very size of the U.S.S.R. makes its weight in the system so great as to raise serious questions about the importance of such tiny allies as Bulgaria, Hungary, or Albania. On the other hand, the dominance of the U.S.S.R. and the distribution of military global tasks among the various armies of the Pact--for example, the assignation of global political police training tasks to the East German army and UB--raises the point that it is a specific type of an alliance system with variegated missions.

History, of course, is a limited source to provide predictive values. It is contradictory at best; descriptive analyses of past events are useful only as visits of condolence. For history often demonstrates that the size of a preponderant ally renders its miniscule partners' role so subordinate that the true nature of an alliance becomes obsolete.[17] Although it assures us that such aberration as the tail wagging the dog is possible, compatible size remains one of the operational concepts for genuine alliance systems. And yet the history of this alliance system shows remarkable divergences of opinion on various issues, regardless of actual size. Witness the vehement demand of Germany and Czechoslovakia, in advance of Soviet policy shifts, for a speedy occupation of Hungary in 1956 on the one hand, versus the divergent attitudes of the variously-sized allies in 1968.

The genuineness of the alliance system has also been questioned because it has been imposed upon the member states. Certainly there is a great deal of proof that the Soviet forces, even after 35 years of presence in the region, are viewed as occupiers; 1956 and 1968 are outstanding examples to prove this point, although in the case of Czechoslovakia the true animosity toward the U.S.S.R. only occurred after August 21, 1968. Some elements of support for the alliance--aside from that of sheer imposition--however, have come from within the native military establishments and from the officer corps that has lived a continuous existence for more than a quarter of a century. The reason for their support of the system is relatively simple: they have been told that the only options to their participation would be: (a) retaliation by an angry populace; (b) at best, neutralization and abolition of the army as a potential defender of the historic nation; and (c) a corresponding end to their power, prestige and livelihood. Although we will be dealing with this subject later, it is safe to conclude that the vast majority of the professional members of the armed forces prefer their present existence to an uncertain future.

Certainly it would be remiss not to mention some aspects of the Warsaw Pact that are more positive from the communist perspective than the views implied above. Undoubtedly, from time immemorial there has been a broad spectrum in which 'alliances' tended to work; notwithstanding Machiavelli's advice to his Prince, alliances have frequently been unipolar and concentrated around a particular actor.[18] Preponderant U.S. or German strength has not brought NATO or the Axis powers' alliance into question as to its genuineness. What brought the Warsaw Pact into question has been the political reality of imposed rule upon Eastern Europe and not the nature of the military alliance that stemmed from the political imposition of occupation by the U.S.S.R. Nonetheless, the U.S.S.R. itself has generally been averse to institutionalization of the alliance system precisely because informal arrangements are more subject to manipulation by the dominant power. In this sense, though probably only in this sense, the Warsaw Pact can be and should be viewed as a victory for the non-Soviet actors of the system.[19]

Curiously, there are other aspects of the Warsaw Pact that are peculiar, though not necessarily counterproductive, from the systemic perspective. One of these is the fact that the presence of the alliance system helps psychologically to mitigate the feeling of loneliness as the "shipping boy of history" experienced by the U.S.S.R. It is a symbolic function, to be sure, but to be able to refer to an action undertaken by the 'Communist alliance system' or the Warsaw Pact, is preferable to acting alone. Hence, unlike 1956 in Hungary, the invasion of Czechoslovakia in 1968 was undertaken by the Warsaw Pact--even if Romania did not participate and Hungarian participation had to be coerced, i.e. Soviet pressures on the Hungarian leader, Kadar, who wished to avoid Hungary being labeled as an invader by the Czechoslovak population.[20] In fact, there is a great deal of evidence that Bulgaria, East Germany, and Poland had agitated for intervention <u>before</u> the Soviet Politburo had been prepared to do so.[21]

Moreover, it is important to recall that the Warsaw Pact can be regarded also as a genuine system because of the high level of interaction that takes place among the members. As mentioned previously, the military in each of the member states derives not merely prestige, but real, significant benefits from the system: from plush officers clubs and special stores, these benefits range to include the possession and use of the most modern military hardware to awe both foreigners as well as the domestic population. The more modern and extensive the hardware, the greater the prestige of the domestic controllers of the use of violence. Conversely, not possessing that hardware--for example, anti-aircraft or modern missile systems--implies a lack of prestige. In this respect, the U.S.S.R. is regarded by the military elite as the source of benefits and a source of tension as well: one gets from the U.S.S.R. as it gives, and complains about the U.S.S.R. not giving as much modern equipment to its allies as it gives to some non-member states in military aid.

Lest we forget, this alliance system is also an important contributor to the physical prowess and economic health of at least some of the member states. The allocation of responsibilities for military production--small arms, artillery, tanks, etc.--within the Pact has increased significantly the economic capabilities of such states as East Germany and Czechoslovakia. The net export of arms produced in some of these states brings hard currency influx or other external trade benefits. But there is one more export item that is as important as hardware: the export of military personnel. East Germany's 'traditional' role of supplying the developing states with security training, personnel and apparatus, for example, in some parts of the world such as Africa is certainly far more ubiquitous today than the role of the United States had been in previous times. The role played by the East German security forces makes CIA training of the SAVAK look like child's play.

In short, then, the system that exists in Eastern Europe is an alliance based on two contradictory elements: (1) imposed rule by a great power that determines both the political context of the domestic environment and the limits of its change on the one hand, and (2) a system of mutualities and mutual benefits of military-economic relations on the other. The stress and tension existing between these, not very creative, contradictions is the dynamics upon which the alliance system must operate.

THE EVOLUTION OF THE WTO: THE HISTORICAL PROCESS

At this juncture, it is useful to reconstruct the changing historical processes that have been responsible for the alteration of the goals of the Warsaw Pact. As mentioned above, on the one hand it would be simplistic and not very useful to say that Pact changes have always been the <u>result</u> of changing Soviet strategies and the pursuit of Soviet policies. It is obvious that these changes were related to or connected with Soviet shifts, but not in the sense Soviet strategists and ideologues would like to see. As the Pact matured, one could detect two sets of evolving differences: (1) between the individual armies and the parties that ran them, on the one hand, and the U.S.S.R. on the other; and (2) the Pact as a whole and Soviet desiderata on the other.[22] A brief survey of the last three decades serves, here, as a useful guide to bolster our line of reasoning.

The implications of the last sentence should serve as a take-off point to guide our tortuous path. "The last three decades" mentioned above, of course, is an imprecise statement, since formally the WTO came into being only in 1955 with the original goal of providing a common defense against the imperalist.[23] But informally, the Warsaw Pact as a defensive organization had come into being much earlier in some primitive form of cooperation against fascism: a common and coordinated organization among Polish troops under Soviet command, between Bulgarian and Romanian troops after their defection from the German cause and their switch to the Allies in August and September, 1944 respectively, and among the various Czech and Slovak 'volunteer units' operating with the Soviet army as it advanced westward--such cooperation was already in existence a long time before May 14, 1955.[24] The cooperation referred to here was enormously strengthened by the Sovietization of all the armies that took place beginning in 1948-1949 and by the creation of an East German fighting force in 1949. Although these military alliances were informal and deliberately vague to give maximum latitude to Soviet control and influence, the new "people's armies" had shown a certainly not-too-surprising proclivity toward identity of views and policies.

These common views were especially strong concerning the native military perception of a threat from the West. That threat existed in the perfectly understandable fear of the renewal of German strength, the awesome destructive potential of which, as well as its ability to wreak havoc with Eastern Europe, was shown in two preceding world wars. Coupled with the near omnipotence of the United States, that power could once again affect adversely the lives of the inhabitants of the power vacuum known as Eastern Europe. Their fear of the Allies, both in the beginning years of the Cold War and later, was not just a fear for the nation--though if one were charitable one could attribute it to that, admitting some national decency to policymakers who could otherwise be simply labelled as mere Soviet stooges--it was also a fear for themselves personally. It was a fear for what would happen if the Soviets lost and their satraps had to retreat with them back to the land where so many of them spent years filled with terror, a land from where even the hell of the Spanish Civil War seemed desirable quietude. But an even greater fear had gripped these men: the fear of losing and having to face personal retribution from within the nations on whose military thrones they now sat, ensconced there by the bayonets of a Red Army that was clearly viewed by the majority in 1949 as an <u>occupying</u> force. It was these fears, then, that compelled the military and political elites to join the U.S.S.R. in common defense against real and perceived threats from the West; in this sense the Warsaw Pact had been in existence at least six or seven years before its official inauguration.

These East European fears were reinforced by (1) the American involvement in and growing commitment to the Cold War, (2) the establishment of NATO, a formal alliance aimed at containing perceived Soviet aggression, and (3) the subsequent creation of the strategy of encirclement through such organizations as NATO, CENTO, SEATO and eventually ANZUS. As the Cold War matured and as the Soviets tried to maintain their position in Eastern Europe, the U.S.S.R. had to commit all its efforts to the maintenance of its systemic powers. The death of Stalin as well as revolts and riots in East Germany, Czechoslovakia, Hungary, and Poland, kept the Soviets preocuupied with one trouble spot after another; thus there was little opportunity for the disruptions which had threatened the West in the early years of the existence of the WTO. It is true that the doctrine of strategic encroachment--the acquisition of bases and allies on a global scale with the purpose of countering the policy of encirclement--had already been developed in Soviet military thinking, but practically, it could not be implemented as long as the West stood firm, had the strategic, materiel, and tactical capabilities and the desire to oppose Soviet aggression or encroachment wherever it took place.

All this, of course, began to change with the common possession of thermo-nuclear weapons and with the adoption of a 'more reasonable' Western attitude toward the U.S.S.R. These views, as they appear in the West, emphasized that the theory of containment and the Dullesian hardline policies placed the U.S.S.R. in a position that was 'unfair', that given enough leeway and incentives the U.S.S.R. could become a stable, status quo power with whom agreements for the maintenance of peace and spheres of influence can be made if reasonable men negotiate reasonably. Given impulse by the tragedy of 1956, the sudden break in NATO unity at Suez in the same year, and by the spirit of accommodation that led Eisenhower to Geneva, Nixon to Moscow, and Kennedy to Vienna, a new era began, the main motto of which was detente by many other names. This policy of non-containment has been pursued since the advent of John F. Kennedy's administration, despite various fluctuations such as the Cuban Missile Crisis and the war in Vietnam. The lessons drawn from Cuba and Vietnam by the U.S.S.R.--the necessity of an enormous military machine that can never again be humbled in the first example and the defeat that can indeed be inflicted upon the U.S. and its allies with relative ease and by a minimal Soviet commitment of men and prestige in the latter--were unfortunately not lessons that had served American strategic interests abroad or its domestic interests.

The strategy of globalism, the penetration of the Third World, the use of proxies, have all been tested during these years, following the perfection of Soviet expansionist opportunism as a tactic aimed at the strategy of expanding Soviet influence. It is worthwhile to repeat that, at the root of the decrease in American belligerency toward the U.S.S.R. and its goals, lay a conviction that peaceful coexistence and the subsequent policy of detente means an essential end to major conflict between the two superpowers. Unheeded and unappreciated was the constant Soviet disclaimer that detente and peaceful coexistence meant neither an end to ideological struggle nor to the termination of Soviet assistance to national liberation movements; the elixir of a peaceful world, especially in the post-Vietnam years, was too strong and it prevented the U.S. from reevaluating the global range of Soviet policy.

Soviet global strategy was a natural consequence of the fact that it faced less and less real threat from NATO. The major goals of the U.S.S.R. toward Western Europe--that of neutralization, the division of the alliance system through the encouragement of divergence within, and the potential Finlandization of the area--were assisted by decreasing Western defense expenditures, social turmoil and welfare-state policies that weakened defense, a morale and drug problem within the armies, squabbles between NATO arms manufacturers, and, not the least, the switch in recruitment strategies within the U.S. Army, a development with potentially the most damaging results. This relative demobilization on the part of NATO by 1975 created an imbalance that led to the conventional superiority of the Warsaw Pact in many different theaters, both on land and sea.[26]

Though, perhaps, all this is too well-known, it is worthwhile to stress again these points, for the policies discussed above have also led to serious mistakes on the part of the U.S.S.R. and its allies. The mistakes and miscalculations I refer to are well known: the failure of Soviet-Chinese policies, the instability of some of its allies, the inability to maintain alliances in peripheral areas, the underestimation of Western resolve and interests in other areas, miscalculation concerning Western and Third World responses to Afghanistan, and the consequent doubt cast on Soviet intentions by those who, prior to Afghanistan, were willing to view these intentions as serving the interest of "peace for mankind".

Suffice it to say, at this point, that both the few failures and the relative abundance of success, in short the very historical developmental processes, have had unintended effects in creating stresses within the Warsaw Pact *qua* an alliance system--stresses that have been responsible for a major change in the nature of the alliance system, from its totally subservient role to one where major cleavages are exhibited.

STRESSES WITHIN THE PACT

One can identify three major sets of stresses in the alliance system as it had evolved since its formal inception, although undoubtedly other aspects can also easily be added. The three major stresses were (1) the very development of the policy of detente; (2) the role of the Pact in suppressing intra-systemic violence, especially in Eastern Europe; and (3) the development of the Sino-Soviet split and its effects on the policies of the various WTO states.

Whether one calls it peaceful co-existence or detente, the simple fact is that the public embrace of that policy by the U.S. lowered the threshold of imminent danger that was previously obvious to the Eastern Europeans. As the superiority of Soviet and WTO strength in conventional weaponry--especially in the Central and Northern sectors of Europe--became clear, the political managers of the states in the alliance system began to be less and less fearful for their own success and survival. Gone were the fears of the earlier years, the specter of Western, but especially German and American, armies marching into Eastern Europe; the fears of overthrowing communists and army commanders had turned out to be a chimera, especially as Western military strength continued to decline. The German threat transposed itself into a very welcome German economic presence, the existence of the Social Democractic governments of the continent did not even imply a capitalist threat, and President Johnson's respect for the Yalta accords prior to the invasion of Czechoslovakia lessened even further any possibility of a major threat to the political systems of the WTO allies.[27]

These developments prompted the adoption of a questioning attitude among the members of the alliance system. They questioned the need and necessity for two major components of Soviet desiderata: the continued need for an offensive forward strategy by the WTO and the necessity of increasing arms expenditures.

The forward offensive strategy of the WTO is cast, of course, as a defensive one, aimed at the prevention of a potential NATO attack on the East European states. And yet, it is clear to the planning and commanding staffs of both alliance systems that offensive roles are assigned to the Czechoslovakian, Polish, and East German forces in the Northern tier as well as to those of the Bulgarian forces in the southern tier. Doubts of the need for such a strategy were raised in the middle and late 1970s by Ceausescu as the Romanian political leadership realized that the WTO posed a principal threat to the survival of its independent or autonomous policies, and hence to the survival of Ceausescu's nepotocracy.[28] These doubts were exacerbated by the 1968 crisis in Czechoslovakia. While only Romania challenged _openly_ the need for offensive strategy, the Polish and the Hungarian leadership were delighted with this challenge and privately supported Romanian concerns. As expected, the East German, the post-1968 Czechoslovakian, and the Bulgarian leadership continued to support the U.S.S.R. uncritically, as they had in the past.

The Romanian challenge was made extremely clear through a series of statements beginning with 1978. While continually insisting on their allegiance to the original WTO goals of defending any state attacked by the West, the Romanians made it clear that they would not send troops into offensive conflicts.[29] Hence the Romanians, following the Yugoslav example, developed the doctrine of the "defense of the fatherland by the entire people" and their military strategy is based on national defense that can only be undertaken _on the territory of the Romanian state_.[30] It is repeatedly stressed that Romania will not send its troops to participate in offensive action against the territory of another state, whether or not it is a member of the WTO.[31] Such questioning by an ally within the WTO, of course, intensified Soviet concerns and had led, as Christopher Jones implies, to the use of joint Soviet military exercises with other WTO allies as a means of preventing the further spread of the Romanian-Yugoslav model.[32] What is important for NATO, however, is that _the very diminution of a visible threat from the Western alliance system has led to the unintended result of causing major stress within the Warsaw Treaty Organization_.

Another unintended result of the 'successful' pursuit of detente and the subsequent weakening of NATO was the emergence of a serious challenge to the necessity of increased military-defense spending demanded by the Soviet Union following the May 1978 NATO approval of the Long-Term Defense Program. Moscow, once it had achieved conventional and strategic superiority in the European theater, sought parity: it demanded a three percent real increase in defense budgets of the WTO member states, just as the U.S. sought such increases among its allies.[33] Once again Romania, Hungary, and Poland--led by Romania's Ceausescu whose stand at the Political Consultative Committee meeting in Moscow on November 22-23, 1978 was the most provocative one as far as the U.S.S.R. was concerned--questioned the necessity for such increases. Awareness of the enormous superiority of the Pact in the Northern tier in conventional weapons and doubt cast on the West's aggressive intentions severely limited Moscow's hand.[34] Indeed, in spite of the Soviet desires, only East Germany met the goal of a three percent increase in defense spending and the U.S.S.R. learned that it must bear the cost of any major increase in the costs related to military expenditures just as the U.S. must pay for these increases in NATO. Once again, however, what is important to note is that the very success of the WTO in improving its position vis-à-vis NATO created major stress in the alliance system when further increases in defense expenditures were demanded by the U.S.S.R. from its allies in the waning days of the "era of detente".[35]

A second major cause of the stress in alliance system resulted from the use of Soviet and Pact forces to stabilize intra-systemic dysfunction. While in 1956 only Soviet forces were used in the suppression of the Hungarian revolution, troops of the entire Pact, with the exception of Romania, were ordered into action in Czechoslovakia. Opposition to that use of force, today, is well known and does not need to be reiterated. Yet, in spite of Kadar's opposition, even Hungarian troops were forced to participate, for the presence of Soviet forces on the territory of Poland, the German Democratic Republic and Hungary guaranteed that such an intervention would be coordinated.[36] It was precisely this joint intervention which prompted the Romanians to denounce the use of force against a fraternal ally, and thus creating considerable tension. Subsequently, Hungary joined Romania in very visible and vocal opposition to an adventurist policy against Poland. Moreover, there are unconfirmed reports, from usually reliable sources, that Hungarian opposition to military action against Yugoslavia immediately after the death of Tito helped mitigate potential Soviet threat to that country. In short, the use of Pact forces in action against each other or other socialist states has weakened the WTO as a defensive organization against the West, and has created opposition to the use of the Pact as an instrument to suppress 'fraternal' nations seeking to settle their internal problems along the acceptable "separate and different roads to socialism".

Finally, Soviet handling of the China question has led to major stresses within the alliance system. The Sino-Soviet dispute has long been a source of contention between the U.S.S.R. and some of its allies; Albania, of course, was the first--and the last--to change position on that issue. But in the mid-1960s Romania broke ranks with the other WTO countries and refused to subscribe to the existence of a Chinese threat to socialism. Although it has not been successful in altering the Soviet position, because general unanimity is required for WTO statements and policies, Romania has been able to soften Soviet statements on China in joint documents such as, for example, the Soviet-Romanian and the Political Consultative Committee statements of November 25 and November 27, 1976.[37] The issue of China, then, in itself is not a major issue within the alliance system; rather it is just one more area of stress that continues to surface between the alliance system, on the one hand, and some of its component parts, on the other.

ISSUES OF TENSION

While the above-mentioned areas of stress remain continuous and pervasive on the highest levels of political-military decision making, there are equally important issues of tension which aggrevate relations at less important levels. Four major issues may be identified: command, armament needs, deployment of forces, and military spending. Although other issues could be added to this admittedly skimpy list, these four represent, perhaps, the greatest potential source of tension at the micro level of policy formulation.

Command

The question of command is a nagging one which has never been solved adequately to the satisfaction of all parties. To understand it fully, a brief description of changes in the WTO institutional structure is necessary. Under the present structure, the WTO has two organizational components--one political and the other military. Overarching this bifurcated structure is the Political Consultative Committee (PCC) which consists of First Secretaries--or their deputies--of the member states and which is responsible for the overall political decision-making process.[38] Below the PCC, lines of responsibility separate sharply. On the political side, decisions are made by the Council of Foreign Ministers (CFM) of the members, and below this level, by the deputy foreign ministers who presumably deal with less important policy matters. In the period between these meetings, two bodies--the Permanent Committee of the PCC and the Secretariat of the Council of Ministers, the latter staffed by foreign policy departments of the respective party secretariats located in Moscow--are responsible for daily coordination of political matters. While Romania occasionally balks at Soviet pressure, the issue of command in the political component does not pose a problem.

In the military sphere there are altogether different considerations. Originally, the WTO had a Commander-in-Chief (always a senior Soviet officer) assisted by the Deputy Commanders-in-Chief who are also defense ministers of the various member states.[39] A joint armed forces staff, including the permanent representatives of the member joint chiefs of staff, is located in Moscow.[40] Since the Budapest meeting of March 1969, additional organs have been created to conduct military affairs. A newly created Council of Defense Ministers is at the top of the current military organization chart. Prior to 1968 these officers met three times--namely in 1961, 1962, and 1963; since 1968 the defense ministers have met once every year and twice in 1975. The Council of the Chiefs of Staff seems to have been subordinated to the Council of Defense Ministers and, in fact, has not been formally convened since 1971. It functions, apparently, have been partially assumed by the Military Council which, although subordinated to the Joint Council, remains the most significant group for contact between the military missions of member states.

With the exception of 1976, the Military Council has met twice a year and seems to have responsibility for planning and operational integration rather than either the Council of Defense Ministers or the Council of the Joint Chiefs of Staff, the latter which seems to have disintegrated. While the 1969 meeting also established a Technical Council (which was assigned the tasks of operational integration of new weapons, weapons research and delivery coordination, and military technological innovation), it remains clearly subordinated to the Military Council and functions, apparently, under the latter's guidance.[41]

The question of why the Commander of the Joint Armed Forces must be a Soviet commander and why that commander--who is not even the Defense Minister of the U.S.S.R., but his subordinate--should issue orders to the member defense ministers has been a festering problem since the early 1960s, especially with senior military men and with Romanian political leaders. The control by native commanders in some joint exercises has mitigated the situation somewhat, but Soviet domination of command continues to prevail. Between 1961 and 1979, out of 83 exercises of the WTO held on the territory of states other than the U.S.S.R. and for which commanders can be identified, there were 19 native commanders vs. 38 Soviet commanders.[42] Furthermore, out of 15 exercises of anti-aircraft troops, air force, naval or rear services held between 1961 and 1979, only one had a non-

Soviet commander.* These figures provide ample indication of potential conflict.[43]

The question of the command of joint exercises is not only one of prestige at top levels; there is considerable evidence that the subordination of native units to Soviet commanders causes resentment in the line levels as well.[44] And there is no doubt, today, that on the level of non-commissioned officers and conscripts, the problem of non-native commanders has the potential for serious dysfunction. Soviet leaders are sensitive to the problem and have consistently avoided putting non-Soviet troops into direct contact with Soviet commanders or observers, but the issue remains a festering sore. The Romanian statement of February 6, 1970 which implied in case of any conflict involving Romanian or WTO troops with Romanian participation, Romanian components would be commanded only by Romanian officers points to the seriousness of this problem.[45]

Modernization of Armaments

A second issue of tension relates to the modernization of armaments and to modernization of the various military machines. It is in the interest of the U.S.S.R. to provide its allies with the most up-to-date military equipment, if it intends to use the WTO in a projected conflict against the West. And yet, the modernization of the military of the Pact has been slow, sporadic, and never takes place until well after such weapons have been introduced into the arsenal of Soviet forces, even those of category two status. In fact, one source suggests that such equipment does not reach the front line units of even the favored Northern tier units for three to four years after these weapons are acquired by the Soviet troops located in the same theater.[46]

Even though often considered mere extensions of the Soviet forces, the WTO member militaries represent national pride in the region and they believe, correctly, that they receive modern weapons considerably later than the Soviet forces because the U.S.S.R. does not consider them to be fully reliable, and hence not fully equal, partners in a common alliance system. Moreover, the fact--presumed or real makes no

---

* The non-Soviet commander was General Martin Dzur, Czechoslovakian Minister of National Defense, who served in a 1971 exercise involving Czechoslovakian, Polish, and Soviet troops.

difference--that the Soviets frequently send some of the most modern equipment to dubious Third World allies, even before release to 'time-tested' WTO allies, is viewed as an insult. Although, such resentment is most evident among those officers below major command positions, it cannot be ignored.[47]

Deployment of WTO Forces

The third issue of tension concerns the purposive use of the WTO forces. As indicated above, the question of offensive or defensive use remains in the forefront of the debate between Romania, with Hungarian support, and the Pact as a whole. It is clear that these forces would have no complaint against deployment in case of a direct attack against the WTO by NATO; the issue of tension seems to be centered upon the question of deployment in offensive circumstances. Perhaps with the exception of the Bulgarians and the East Germans, the East Europeans are reluctant to commit troops for offensive purposes, especially when the need seems to be rather minimal. Romania, in fact, has flatly refused to commit its troops for such purposes.[48]

Moreover, offensive deployment against a fraternal ally remains an odious act; Romania and Hungary have been the most vocal opponents of such deployment. Although Czechoslovakia might be expected to join Romania and Hungary in condemning such action, revenge for Polish participation in the invasion of Czechoslovakia in 1968, might mitigate any tendency toward military non-intervention. At any rate, there is extreme doubt about the utility of the Czechoslovak forces in any major conflict, notwithstanding the findings of the otherwise excellent Johnson, Dean, Alexeiev study.[49]

WTO Defense Expenditures

In spite of Soviet pressures since 1978, the real increase in defense spending has been minimal in Hungary, reduced in Romania, and has dropped below even the minimally expected level in Poland. But the question of defense spending in toto remains a major question in the continuing national debates concerning allocation of scarce resources. For instance, the 1980 decision to reduce, by six months, the required military service in Hungary for conscripts will result in reduced costs for manpower and training, a saving which must be reinvested, especially in acquiring more up-to-date equipment and technology for military use. Debates concerning investment priorities within the military etablishment have indeed been vicious--for example, between the air defenses, on the one hand, and the military engineering services on the other--with service chiefs complaining to their liaison officers, or perhaps to friends acquired sometime before at the Moscow service academies.

Similar problems seem to occur in other areas of defense spending as well. Resentment at spending in areas that are not clearly and evidently in the interest of the national mission, or the inability to spend in areas that are clearly in the envisaged national purpose, create difficulties which cannot easily be resolved at the periodic annual meetings of the Military or Technical Council. Debates over the manufacturing of specialized materiel, such as small arms, tanks, computers, etc., or their sale, and the accruing of credits or hard currency for such sales, apparently can become acrimonious events with no end in sight; agreement, according to a usually reliable source, is reached frequently only after strong bargaining or the imposition of Soviet _fiat_; the latter rarely welcomed by any of those present. But, here, too, the Soviets are learning to pay the price of greatness, and that price, frequently, is very high indeed.

VULNERABILITIES OF THE PACT IN THE 1980s.

The causes of stress that have triggered the specific areas of tension will affect both the macro- and micro-levels of the policy process in the Warsaw Pact during the coming decade. It seems to me, then, that it might be fruitful to analyze the _specific_ vulnerabilities that the organization itself is going to exhibit as a system, in order to discern what the West can and should do to exploit them to its advantage in the years to come. The bluntness of this language is deliberate, with the intention of making it clear that the WTO is an adversary system, and that its major aim remains to provide a visible threat in the chain of Soviet global foreign interests.

The first vulnerability is produced by the very great differentiaton between the values of the East European population as a whole, including the less politically inclined portion of the officer corps, on the one hand; and the party, its related organs and those portions of the officer corps who are committed for a variety of reasons to support the WTO and most Soviet policy initiatives, on the other.[50]

Socialist societies are often characterized by the enormous differentiation between the committed believer/

professional practitioner of the policy-process, on the one hand, and the cynical population on the other. Care must be taken, of course, to exclude from this category the Russian people as a whole, although even in the Soviet Union, differentiaiton is apparent; but that differentiation is considerably less significant for a variety of historical national socialization comparability reasons. Suffice it to say, that for the average East European, the gap between the party and the people in terms of belief system is enormous and self-evident through every manifestation of daily life. As a popular Polish joke in 1981 had it, the best way of committing suicide in Poland is by throwing oneself into the abyss between the party and the people. It is an abyss of disbelief, fostered by the ever-changing party line, by constant upheaval, and by the fact that, for the vast majority of these people, the party and the rulers remain a symbol of alienation. Though there have been some attempts to identify the party with the people--such as Dubcek's honorable, decent, and extremely naive drive to create socialism with a human face--these attempts have always been crushed by weapons ready for use in the interest of preserving socialism with a different, but far more realistic human face: that of a Hobbesian nature--mean, petty, vicious, power-hungry, and used in order to maintain the power monopoly of the party.[51]

Since every success flows from the party in Communist societies--perhaps with the exception of Hungary since 1968--every issue remains a political one; thus, the communist party becomes the focus of blame for all failures, from bus delays to the current political crises; and inability to de-politicize society remains the greatest vulnerability of any communist system.

A good example is the gap which exists between the professional cadre (the political core of the army) and the conscripts. The conscripts--young men between 18 and 22 years of age who account for roughly 60 percent of the total manpower of WTO forces--possess the same cynical values as the general population. The attempts made to inculcate them with socialist values are, at best, half-hearted, at worst, unsuccessful: only when socialist values mingle with fierce nationalism can major coalescence between conscript and professional political values occur. The primitive nationalism of a Soviet, a Romanian or a Polish soldier is heightened, of course, when it exists in the defense of the fatherland; it is precisely this element that causes grevious problems for Soviet planners. The phantom of coalesced values among the Polish army of 317,500 soldiers is not one the Soviet leadership would want to materialize, if they could possibly prevent it. Similarly, Romanian desires to alter the old version of the Romanian state--from being national in form and socialist in content to socialist in form and national in content--was intended to close the gap between the people and the party. The quiet depolitization of the Hungarians through the "greyhound effect", albeit differently, was also designed to create coalescence between national and socialist values; hence, giving national legitimacy to the party leadership.[53] As a Warsaw street poster--appearing on a CBS presentation in December 1980--depicted it, the old slogan "Party Program Equals People's Program" was changed to read, "The People's Program Must Be The Party's Program".

The military elite, in particular, are torn between loyalty to Moscow and the Warsaw Pact on the one hand, and to the nation on the other.[54] The ghost of Colonel Maleter and the participation of the few Moscow-trained officers in the 1956 revolution continues to haunt Moscow.* Even Emil Zatopek's sad, slow and, in a truly human sense, pathetic condemnation of the Czechoslovakian invasion in 1968 came as a shock to those planners in Moscow who thought that title, fame and privilege lavished upon the military elite would ensure unfailing support. To be sure, there are and always will be Eastern European political and military elites who support Soviet policies. Fear of defeat and subsequent retaliation at the hands of an angry populace, fear of career failure and loss of wealth, personal value convictions, ideological blindness, or the simple recognition of geographical contraints imposed by Eastern Europe's central position: all these factors, either singly or in combination will continue to produce support for the U.S.S.R. among the military elite.

But the conscript, the lower ranks of the officer corps, most of the non-commissioned officers (NCOs) and those committed to the idea of a nation will not obey Soviet orders, especially, if that order is to fire upon the national population. Even in the interest of defending socialism, support for such invasions as, for example, against Poland, would be difficult to muster among the socialist states of Eastern Europe: Hungary and Romania would certainly refuse to participate; the Czech army would comply, but in its weakened condition

---

* Colonel Maleter was a leader in the Hungarian revolt of 1956 and was subsequently appointed Defense Minister in the Nagy government. (Ed.)

would not contribute much; and the U.S.S.R. could only depend--as always--on the obedience of East Germany and Bulgaria.

Prediction of a continuing gap between the party and the people, between the conscript and the professional military, is predicated upon the assumption that no state perceives a threat from NATO. The external defensive reliability of all these armies is very high if faced by threats from the West; specifically, if those threats envision aggressive territorial intentions that the communist leadership can parlay into national dangers. Given, however, a careful policy of minimizing threats from the West, this gap is bound to increase and cause considerable difficulty for the U.S.S.R. in the future.

The second area of vulnerabilities for the WTO system relates to the economic performance of the socialist system: its two key components are (1) the spending limits that these states can tolerate if they are to maintain existing standards of living and (2) the critical manpower shortages they will be facing in this decade. Undoubtedly, the 1970s had been the decade for one of the most dramatic advances in the economic life of Hungary and Romania, Bulgaria and East Germany. At the same time, for Czechoslovakia and Poland, especialy the latter, the second half of the decade of the 1970s had been one of economic disaster. Specifically for Poland, economic mismanagement had resulted in a 9.2 billion dollar annual debt service for an economy that, at best, is capable of returning some seven billion dollars worth of hard currency annually from its resources. East Germany and Hungary achieved the highest levels of living, with Hungary leading the way towards a well-supplied market socialism where the distribution-consumer side is favored over the planning-producer side of market economies.

What is important, however, is that all of these states face tremendous limitations on the amount which can be allocated to increase military spending; hence, Hungary, Poland and Romania have not been able to meet the three percent increase stipulated in the 1978 WTO decision to match NATO spending goals. Moreover, increases in the defense budget of Czechoslovakia have been realized at the expense of a population which remains sullen and disgruntled; and have further exacerbated the growing difference between what the party elite, on the one hand, and the people on the other, perceive as the national interest.

Finally, real limitations are also imposed by manpower shortages within the WTO as a whole. It has long been clear to those observing the economies of the WTO states that the military fulfills an inordinately large state construction role that extends from streets and roads to sport stadia and hospitals: in short, purely civilian tasks that should be completed by non-military personnel. Largely because of the demographic curve, but also because of the disasterous manpower, labor and price policies of the regimes, military involvement in construction has not been reduced.

The differences in perception between real defense needs and the needs of 'socialist construction', referring not only to buildings, but also to social services, poses the most serious vulnerability for the future. Faced with grave social problems--ranging from housing shortages to high infant mortality--the states of Eastern Europe must seek investment capital and solutions which provide more efficient use of manpower; yet defense needs negate any possibility for shifts to the civilian sector. More than ever, the adage that socialist societies are engaged in constant re-creation of scarcity holds true, and there seems to be no solution for the problem--short of a general European war which no one wants.

SOVIET CRISIS MANAGEMENT: RESPONSE TO CHALLENGES

Certainly, the question of whether the Soviets will be successful in managing the areas of stress, the issues of tension and the existing vulnerabilities is a valid subject for analysis and projection. If historical examples serve as a correct, although presumably non-predictive guide, the U.S.S.R. has been remarkably successful so far in managing differences within the alliance system. Success, of course, is a relative term and its measurement, through existing quantitative means, is a very doubtful undertaking. Nonetheless, it is quite clear that the U.S.S.R. has been successful in the following activities, despite two major intra-systemic crises in 1956 and 1968: it has prevented the alliance from disintegration; maintained political cohesiveness of the organization; created more closely integrated units for making decisions; and preserved the Warsaw Pact as a defensive organ against a projected attack from NATO.

The U.S.S.R. has been less successful in a number of areas where its *desiderata* has not been met with full support from all members of the Pact. Issues such as the need for an offensive strategy, for a Soviet central commander, for a "slow modernization" strategy, for increased defense spending, for unqualified support of anti-Chinese policies, and for subordination of national interests to Soviet interests have tended to undermine alliance cohesion. Finally, the U.S.S.R. has been unable to maintain cohesion at all with regard to intervention in other socialist states, to holding joint exercises on the territory of all member states, and to placing contingent armed forces and intelligence operations under Soviet command. Superficially, only Romania has been the focus of internal dissention; closer investigation, however, suggests that Hungarian and Polish opposition must be included. What is most important to note is that, after the 1960s, the Soviets--much to their surprise--could no longer expect automatic support from their allies: heavy bargaining on a whole array of issues was required if the U.S.S.R. wished to create a semblance of unity. It came as a rude shock to a previously dominant leader that the Warsaw Treaty Organization had become a viable international military organization, the interests of which--as perceived by its members--are far from being completely identical to those of the Soviet Union.

The mechanisms available to the U.S.S.R. to deal with these internal differences range from the very mildest requests to the extreme and crude form of an order--such as to Hungary in 1968--to follow the Soviet lead; in the 1980s, however, there is no guarantee that either of these approaches will be successful in any given situation. Negotiation for participation in a particular event may fail, just as an order may lead to disobedience by a given leader. The best opportunity for Soviet leadership to elicit compliance lies in political connection between it and the non-Soviet elites; an opportunity which is thwarted by the consultative arrangements and the cumbersome political structure of the WTO.

As discussed earlier, political decision-making mechanisms are inhibited by multiplicity of fora, duplication, and infrequency of meetings; the result is cursory and haphazard response to issues and, hence, inability to effectuate productive consultations. Consequently, crisis management of important areas of stress has to be conducted through other agents; for this purpose, the PCC Permanent Secretariat has been utilized extensively as a channel to convey Soviet wishes to political leaders. Lines of communication are also established through consultative agents and liaison officers with the secretariats of the individual communist parties and through the Soviet embassy liaison officers or specific Politburo representatives: in short, the most preferred channels, but widely differing, structure of the individual states. Communication remains, however, a one-way process which is used to elaborate and enumerate Soviet wishes. Only meetings with the full and formal political bodies of the WTO can provide two-way communication, but, ironically, they also increase the risk of non-compliance and intense bargaining for the Soviets.

Military coordination, on the other hand, does not risk direct threat and is frequently preferred. Military coordination normally takes place through formalized meetings of the Military Council of the Council of Defense Ministers; in crisis situations, however, the Joint Unified Command structure--through permanent representatives both in Moscow and in the field e.g., the respective WTO missions in each state--bears the brunt of such communications. The difficulty, however, with this type of communication is that it can take place only after the respective communist party political leadership has agreed to participation in whatever action is deemed necessary: once again, the impact of clumsy political machinery must be emphasized.

To further compound management problems for the Soviets, Warsaw Pact decisions, to be effective in a major crisis, require unanimity among the member states. Any member can sabotage a decision through lack of willingness to participate, or through deliberately leaking information--as Ceausescu did in November 1978 regarding the response to NATO's Long Term Defense Program. Likewise, a member state which opposed policy cannot be excluded from deliberations on either the political or military level. The exclusion of Romania from joint planning or joint activities on any level, for example, would not only add fuel to the fire of Romanian independence, but would also give Romanian leaders an opportunity to claim that exclusion implies the right to reneg on even the flimsiest obligations hithereto assumed. It is for this reason, of course, that Romania is always very careful to send observers to joint exercises and representatives to all WTO meetings; at the moment, the Soviets have found no effective way of thwarting these tactics.

In short, the reply to the question whether such internal differences that exist can be managed within the WTO depends on the type of differences that exist. On intra-systemic issues, Soviet leaders have found that the 'carrot' approach--e.g., large amounts of economic aid or other unlikely benefits such as the ceding of Bessarabia--works fully well with recalcitrant members; on the other hand, the threat of force does not work as well as it did a decade ago. On issues arising from direct confrontation between NATO and the WTO--especially those where the threat of an offensive war from the former against the latter is imminent, or where the environment suggests its inevitability--the WTO will pull together and its internal cohesion will be assured. In this sense, internal differences can clearly be managed by the existing alliance system.

In the case of offensive threat directed toward the West, however, internal differences within the Pact will not be easily ameliorated. Romanian and Hungarian reluctance to engage in offensive combat is clear; Czechoslovakian reliability for a military offensive is doubtful and Polish reliability, at least in the aftermath of a Soviet invasion of Poland itself, would drop dramatically. Hence, the Soviets' ability to manage reconciliation of these differences within the WTO is severely limited, if its purpose is to launch a Western offensive.

From the foregoing it seems obvious, then, that the Western alliance system has an unprecedented opportunity to exploit potential Soviet vulnerabilities: such a policy should be high on the list of priorities of any U.S. administration.

EXPLOITATION OF VULNERABILITIES: "WINDOWS FOR THE WEST"

At the outset of this concluding section, let me clarify the underlying assumptions upon which its policy prescriptions are based:

1. The U.S.S.R. remains the major, global adversary of the United States;

2. The United States must do everything within its potential to limit the use of Soviet power which can be marshalled against it and its own alliance systems;

3. The Warsaw Pact, while utilized to some extent by the non-Soviet member states to their advantage vis-à-vis the U.S.S.R., has as its dual purpose: the maintenance of an offensive threat toward NATO and Western Europe on the one hand, and the maintenance of communist states within its immediate sphere of interest and security in Eastern Europe on the other; and therefore,

4. The United States can best control Soviet global power and reduce the power of the Warsaw

Treaty Organization as an offensive threat by the adoption of a coordinated political/ military policy aimed at the exploitation of potential vulnerabilities within the Pact itself.

Given the above assumptions, it seems to be evident that the United States must adopt a policy that differentiates between the goals of the Soviet Union and those of Eastern Europe. Although differentiation has existed since Mr. Carter's "Presidential Directive Number One"--which not only officially rejected previous policy aimed at a monolithic Soviet bloc, but also illuminated the possibility of extending different treatment to the various states within the WTO--the current administration must amplify that initiative.

Heightening the differentiation between certain Eastern European states, on the one hand, and the Soviet Union and some of its allies, on the other, could be accomplished through a variety of approaches: confirming the mutuality of cordial relations with Hungary and Romania; providing support to Poland; rewarding leaders who encourage more integration with the West through various types of economic and social activities; and withholding cordiality from those who engage in greater WTO integration and greater subservience to Soviet purposes. There can be no illusions that any of these states are either going to break with the Warsaw Pact, or that they will become democratic or capitalist; geography dictates otherwise, regardless of the wishful thinking of many analysts. The adoption of these American policies, however, will make it more difficult for the Soviets to concentrate the troops of the entire alliance system, for example, against the Polish people: it will also further increase the gap between the official slogans concerning the continuous 'threat' from the West aimed at the East Europeans on the one hand, and the real value system possessed by the people of these states on the other. The rewards for deviant states could be many: credits, trade, cultural and symbolic benefits. In these instances, it is not a short-term gain of a quick change of sides that is desirable; rather a continuous and evolutionary gap between Soviet value-desiderata and real-value socialization.

At the same time, there is no reason to increase credits, trade, cordiality, or other benefits to those states that have consistently and subserviently followed Soviet directions. It is foolish to hope for a major change in the attitude of the leadership of Czechoslovakia, East Germany or Bulgaria; nor should we expect that the mechanism of rule--the use of compulsion in its various forms in these states--would allow the change.

U.S. policy toward client states could be one of neglect and refusal to be drawn into trade or credit arrangements, whereby Western creditors would be hostage to the inability of these states to repay the debts, as in the case of Poland. To accord them beneficial treatment would be interpreted, firstly, as an approval of the policies of their leadership, and secondly, as proof of Western and, especially American, weakness. On the contrary, when the behavior of these nations threaten Western interests, such as East German adventures in Africa through its security force connections, the Western alliance system must register disapproval and further restrict contact, technological trade or mutual improvements in the political climate.

The United States should, simultaneously, undertake a "peace offensive" of its own to detract from the Soviet position. Lowering the visible threat to Eastern Europe by indicating continued American willingness to negotiate--to engage in any and all deliberation reducing the threat of war--need not be coupled with actual concessions and agreements; the Soviet experience in world affairs during the last six decades ably demonstrates this point. But willingness to listen, combined with vague but repetitious declarations in favor of peace, both lowers the perceived offensive threat by the East Europeans and removes the basis for the "offensive-defensive" needs of the Warsaw Pact alliance.

Paradoxically, however, such a policy will work only if it is coupled with significant increases in conventional capabilities to repel Soviet advances, on the one hand, and a willingness to engage in that policy, on the other. Willingness alone will not suffice; neither will capability without willingness. The possession of both components will indicate to those members of the WTO who are not viewed as totally subservient to the U.S.S.R. that the risks of losing are real ones; and will heighten the fear of losing in those national leaders for whom the survival of the historic nation seems essential.

A more assertive policy in other parts of the globe would also project a firm image: for example, the deliberate and determined response of protecting American crafts from harassment in international air and naval space; swift and accurate restriction on nations and groups exporting violence against U.S. national interests, and the deliberate support of allies whose aims and policies coincide with U.S. national interests. If ever there was a need for a Reagan Doctrine, it is precisely in the above areas: a clearly delineated statement of commitment to those with an identity of views and policy, a heightened ability _cum_ desire to defend interests, and an extension of the olive branch to those interested both in stability in the international arena and decency in domestic behavior.

The above policy recommendations contradict the implications of the Sonnenfeld doctrine which suggested the recognition of an organic relation between the U.S.S.R. and Eastern Europe. That organic relation, of course, can and must exist in terms of trade between small, regional states dependent on energy or raw material, and the U.S.S.R.; unfortunately for the East Europeans, geography cannot be altered. But that organic relation does not need to take place among states that have a unitary social value system, unitary policies in the economic, social and military sphere; indeed, the West must encourage the establishment of an organic relation between the West and those WTO states that encourage openness, cooperation and a distinction between their value systems and that of the Soviet Union. It is in this sense neither the liberation of John Foster Dulles, nor the 'weaning away' of hopeful Western academics that is proposed: rather, an exercise in bridge-building among those who share common values and interests with the West and not-so-benign neglect of those who do not. U.S. policy emphasizing a lowered offensive posture toward Eastern Europe as a whole, relations based on heightened differentiation among the WTO states, and the adoption of a higher policy profile regarding American interests would not only serve Western goals, but would also exploit existing and potential vulnerabilities among the WTO states.

FOOTNOTES

1. J.C.M. Baynes, The Soldier in Modern Society (London: Eyre-Methuen, Ltd., 1972).

2. F.D. Freeman, "The Army as a Social Structure," Social Forces 27 (1948-1949); Vernon V. Aspaturian, "The Soviet Military Industrial Complex: Does It Exist?" Journal of International Affairs (Spring-Summer 1972).

3. Samuel Huntington, The Soldier and the State: Theory and Politics of Civil-Military Relations (Cambridge: Harvard University Press, 1957).

4. Dale Herspring and Ivan Volgyes, Civil-Military Relations in Communist States (Boulder, Colo.: Westview Press, 1978).

5. David E. Albright, "A Comparative Conceptualization of Civil-Military Relations", World Politics, (July 1980):553-576.

6. Timothy Colton, Commissars, Commanders and Civilian Authority: The Structure of Soviet Military Politics (Cambridge: Harvard University Press, 1979); Michael Deane, Political Control of the Soviet Armed Forces (New York: Crane, Russak, 1977); Raymond A. Garthoff, "The Marshals and the Party: Soviet Civil-Military Relations in the Postwar Period," in Harry Coles, ed., Total War and Cold War: Problems in Civilian Control of the Military (Columbus, Ohio: Ohio State University Press, 1962); Roman Kolkowicz, The Soviet Military and the Communist Party (Princeton, N.J.: Princeton University Press, 1962); William E. Odom, The Soviet Volunteers: Modernization and Bureaucracy in a Public Mass Organization (Princeton, N.J.: Princeton University Press, 1973); and Edward Warner, Military in Contemporary Soviet Politics (New York: Praeger, 1977).

7. Zbigniew Brzezinski, Political Controls in the Soviet Army (New York: Columbia, 1954); Dale Herspring, East German Civil-Military Relations: 1949-1972 (New York: Praeger, 1973); Idem, "Technology and the Changing Political Officer in the Armed Forces: The Polish and East German Cases," Studies in Comparative Communism (Autumn 1977); and David Holloway, Technology, Management and the Soviet Military Establishment (London: Institute for Strategic Studies, 1971).

8. Timothy Colton, "The Zhukov Affair Reconsidered," Soviet Studies (April 1977).

9. Lawrence Caldwell, "The Warsaw Pact: Directions of Change," Problems of Communism (Sept.-Oct. 1975); Walter Clemens, "The Changing Warsaw Pact," East Europe (June 1968); Curt Gasteyger, "Probleme und Reformen des Warschauer Pakts," Europa Archiv (January 10, 1967) Patricia Haigh, The World Today (April 1968) and Hans von Krannhals, "Command Integration within the Warsaw Pact," Military Review (May 1961).

10. Needless to say, the fear of Bonapartism or Praetorianism has not been confined to the communist militaries. For a few classical studies dealing with the topic, see S.E. Finer, The Man on Horseback (London: Pall Mall Press, 1962); Samuel Huntington, Changing Patterns in Military Politics (New York: Glencoe, 1962); and Idem, Political Order in Changing Societies (New Haven: Yale University Press, 1968), especially Chap. 4.

11. John Barron, The KGB (New York: Readers Digest, 1974); Frederick G. Barghoorn, "The Security Police," in M. Gordon Shilling and Franklyn Griffiths, eds., Interest Groups in Soviet Politics (Princeton, N.J.: Princeton University Press, 1971); Robert Conquest, The Soviet Police System (New York: Praeger, 1968); Peter Deriabin, Watchdogs of Terror (New Rochelle, N.Y.: Arlington House, 1972); and Simon Wolin and Robert M. Slusser, The Soviet Secret Police (New York: Praeger, 1957).

12. Bracher, Sauer and Schultz, Die Nationalsozialistische Machtbegreifung (Kohls: Westdeutsches Verlag, 1960).

13. Kent Brown, "Coalition Politics and Soviet Influence in Eastern Europe," in Jan F. Triska and Paul Cocks, eds., Political Development in Eastern Europe (New York: Praeger, 1977).

14. Colonel General P.I. Efimova, Boevoi Soiuz Bratskikh Armii (Moscow: Voennisdat, 1974) contains a good statement of these changes.

15. Ivan Volgyes, "The Military as an Agent of Political Socialization," in Dale Herspring and Ivan Volgyes, Civil-Military Relations in Communist Systems, op. cit. and Idem, "The Military as an Agent of Political Socialization in Eastern Europe," Armed Forces and Society (February 1977).

16. See Peter Gosztony, *Zur Geschichte der europaischen Volksarmeen* (Bonn: Hohwacht, 1977); Walter C. Clemens, "The Future of the Warsaw Pact," *Orbis* (Winter 1968); Michael Csizmas, "Das militarische Bundnissystem in Osteuropa," *Allgemeine Schweizerische Militarzeitschrift* (October-November 1967); Michael Garder, "Der Warschauer Pakt," *Europa Archiv* (December 25, 1966); and "Le Potential Militaire des Satellites de l'URSS," *Revue Militaire Generale* (June, 1965); Guedon, "Le Service Militaire dans le Pays du Bloc Sovietique," *Revue de Defense Nationale* (April 1964); Eugen Hinterhoff, "Die Potentiale des Warschauer Paktes," *Aussenpolitik*, August, 1965; and Idem., "The Warsaw Pact: Entangling Alliance," *Survey* (Winter-Spring 1969); Andrzej Korbonski, "The Warsaw Pact," *International Conciliation*, May 1969; Malcolm Mackintosh, "The Warsaw Pact Today," *Survival* (May-June 1974); J. Pergent, "Le Pacte de Varsovie et l'Inventaire des Forces de l'Est," *Est et Ouest* (July 1967); Robin Remington, *The Warsaw Pact* (Cambridge, Mass.: MIT Press, 1971); Idem., "The Warsaw Pact: Communist Coalition Politics in Action," *Yearbook of World Affairs*, 1971; Col. Paul R. Shirk, "The Warsaw Treaty Organization," *Military Review* (May 1969); Richard F. Staar, "The East European Alliance," *U.S. Naval Institute Proceedings* (September 1962); and Fritz Wiener, *Die Armeen der Warschauer Pakt-Staaten: Organisation, Taktik, Waffen und Gerate* (Wien, 1974)

17. For a good statement on the problem, see Robert O. Keohane, "Lilliputian's Dilemmas: Small States in International Politics," *International Organisation* (Summer, 1969).

18. On the general topic of alliances as "genuine" systems, see the following studies: J. Basso, "La cooperation internationale" *Annuuaire du Tiers Monde* (1965):447-462; S.J. Brams, and J.G. Heilman, "When to join a coalition, and with how many others, depends on what you expect the outcome to be". *Public Choice* 17 (Spring 74):11-25; W. Von Bredow "Intersystemare Kooperation und Abrustung," (Cooperation among systems and disarmament) *Blatter fur deutsche und internationale Politik* 19, No. 1 (1974):17-32; Theodore Caplow "A Theory of Coalitions in the Triad," *American Sociological Review* 21 (1956):489-493; Idem, "Further Development of a Theory of Coalitions in the Triad," *American Journal of Sociology* 64 (1959):488-493; H.R. Day, "The Resource Comparison Model of Coalition Formation," *Cornell Journal of Social Relations*, 10:2 (Fall 1975):209-221; R. Gordon Cassidy and Edwin Neave,

"Dynamics of Coalition Formation: Prescription versus Reality," Theory and Division 8:2 (April 1977):159-171; Jeff Chertkoff, "The Effects of Probability of Future Success on Coalition Formation," Journal of Experimental and Social Psychology 2:3 (July 1966):265-277; Terry L. Deibel, "A Guide to International Divorce," Foreign Policy 30 (Spring 78):17-35; V. Dimitrijevic, "International Relations and the Existence of Regions," International Problems (Belgrade) 14 (1973):81-88; and R.A. Kann, "Alliances versus Ententes," World Politics 28, No. 4 (July 76):611-621.

19. For a good statement of the topic, see Frigyes Puja, "Miert van szukseg a Varsoi Szerzodesre" (Why is there a need for the Warsaw Pact?) (Budapest: Zrinyi, 1970).

20. Jiri Valenta, Soviet Intervention in Czechoslovakia (Baltimore, Md.: Johns Hopkins University Press, 1979), p. 96.

21. Erwin Weit, At the Red Summit (New York: Macmillan, 1973):201.

22. For a Soviet view see I.I. Iakubovskii, Boevoe sodruzhestvo bratskii narodov i armii (Moscow: Voennizdat, 1975).

23. V.G. Kulikov, ed., Varshavskii dogovor - soiuz vo im'ia mira i sotsializ'ma (Moscow: Voennizdat, 1980). For a Hungarian view see Laszlo Serfozo, Baratok, fegyvertarsak (Budapest: Zrinyi, 1976); Vedopajzs (Budapest: Zrinyi, 1980); Rezso Dondo, Vedopajzsunk (Budapest: Zrinyi, 1980); and Idem, A varsoi szerzodes szervezete: 1955-1975 (Budapest: Kossuth and Zrinyi, 1976). A Polish perspective may be found in Marlan Jurek and Edward Skrzypowski, Tarcza pokoju (Warsaw: Wydawnictwo Ministerswa Obriny Narodowej, 1975). For an East German view see Zeittafel zur Militargeschicht der Deutschen Demokratischen Republic: 1949 bis 1968 (East Berlin: Militarverlag, 1969).

24. Zoltan Vas, Viszontagsagos eletem (Magveto: Budapest, 1980):208-210.

25. A.V. Antosiak, et al., ed., Zarozhdenie narodnikh armii stranuchastnits varshavskogo dogovora, 1941-1949 (Moscow: Voennizdat, 1975); R. Wustner, "Die Polnische Armee," Militarwesen, 9 (1973):13; Michael Checinski, "Polnischen Armee und Offiziere in der Organisation des Warschauer Pakts," Osteuropa 10 (1980):1110 ff.; and Dale Herspring, East German

Civil-Military Relations, pp. 43-55.

26. John Collins et al., United States/Soviet Military Balance (Washington: U.S. Government Printing Office, 1976).

27. For a more cautious view of the Johnson Administration's attitude see Jiri Valenta, Soviet Intervention in Czechoslovakia, 1968 (Baltimore, Md.: Johns Hopkins University Press, 1979):131-133.

28. Radio Bucharest, September 16, 1978 (1700 - 1900 hrs.).

29. "Din cuvintul participantilor," Scinteia (28 Nov., 1978):3.

30. On the Romanian defensive doctrine see Aparare National a Romaniei Socialiste (Bucharest: Editura Militara, 1974).

31. Bucharest, December 14, 1978, Agerpress release.

32. Christopher Jones, "The Warsaw Pact: Military Exercises and Military Intervention," Armed Forces and Society, 1 (1980):5.

33. For a good account see Dale R. Herspring, "The Warsaw Pact at 25," Problems of Communism (September-October 1980):10.

34. For the various statements on the subject see Pravda, December 1, 8, 1978. For example "Vremia Bol'shikh Srevshenii za Mir i Bezopastnost."

35. Radio Bucharest, December 12, 1978 (2100 hrs.).

36. Ivan Volgyes, "The Military as an Agent of Political Socialization: The Case of Hungary," in Herspring and Volgyes, Civil-Military Relations (Boulder, Colo.: Westview Press, 1978):161 and Dale Herpsring and Ivan Volgyes, "Political Reliability in the East European Warsaw Pact Armies," Armed Forces and Society, 2 (1980):274.

37. Pravda, November 25, 27, 1978 listed the statements in detail. For example "Za novii rubezhi v mezhdunarodnoi razriadke za ukreplenie bezopatnosti i razvitie sotrudnichestva v evrope."

38. See article 6 of the Warsaw Treaty.

39. A varsoi szerzodes ..., p. 14; Organizatsiita na

<u>varshavshiiat dogovora</u> (Sofia: Voennizdat, 1977):77; and A.S. Bakhov <u>Organizatsiia varshavrkovo</u>.

40. <u>A varsoi szerzodes</u> ..., p. 14; <u>dogovora</u> (Moscow: Nauka, 1971).

41. The Technical Council seems to have taken over some of the functions of the Military Council which previously was responsible for "deciding problems of military construction and expansion of the unified armed forces, their armament and equipment ..." Colonel Richard Wustner, <u>Wafferbruder-Vereingt Unbesiegbar</u> (East Berlin: Militarverlag, 1975):27.

42. Christopher Jones, "Military Exercises":13.

43. Ibid., p. 16.

44. Serfozo goes to considerable length to explain away an evident problem by listing six exercises where native commanders were in charge "even" of Soviet troops, in Baratok ..., pp. 148-150.

45. <u>Scinteia</u> (Feburary 6, 1970) statement by Nicolae Ceausescu.

46. Michael Checinski, <u>Osteuropa</u>, 3 (1977):177.

47. Ibid.

48. Bucharest, December 14, 1978, Agerpress.

49. A. Ross Johnson, Robert W. Dean, and Alexander Alexiev, <u>East European Military Establishments: The Warsaw Pact Northern Tier</u> (Santa Monica, Cal: Rand, 1980).

50. For a theoretical statement see Ivan Volgyes, <u>Political Socialization in Eastern Europe</u> (New York: Praeger, 1975) and Volgyes and Herspring, "The Military as an Agent of Political Socialization in Eastern Europe," <u>Armed Forces and Society</u>, 3 (1977):249-269.

51. Volgyes, <u>Political Socialization</u>, p. 33.

52. George Schopflin, "Rumanian Nationalism," <u>Survey</u>, 2-3 (1974):92.

53. Ivan Volgyes, "The Impact of Modernization on Political Development," in Charles Gati, ed., <u>The Politics of Modernization in Eastern Europe</u> (New York: Praeger, 1974):328-337; and Idem, "The Kadar

Years", Current History, April (1980):159-164.

54. See, for example, the Gottwald Memorandum of 1968 and General Prchlik's statement to the press: Lidova Armada, July 2, 1968; the Prchlik statement is included in Robin Remington, Winter in Prague (Cambridge: MIT Press, 1969):214-215.

55. For a detailed study see Ivan Volgyes, The Reliability of the East European Southern Tier WTO Armies (Unpublished government report, Department of Defense, 1981).

10
The Soviet Response to Poland and the Future of the Warsaw Pact

Richard Ned Lebow

THE CONTEMPORARY RELEVANCE OF SPARTA AND ATHENS

Alliances are best not described as a generic phenomenon; they differ with regard to purpose, structure, and size. These characteristics determine their strengths and weaknesses and dictate the range of policies that are both appropriate and effective. The same problem can exist in two different alliances, but may have different implications for their capabilities or survival, and may also demand quite a different set of responses from alliance leaders. Alliance management, therefore and above all else, requires an understanding of the character of the alliance to be managed.

No one understood this problem as well as Thucydides who made elaboration of the different natures of alliance systems a central focus of his history of the Peloponnesian War. The distinctions he drew between the Athenian and Spartan alliances based on their different power structures have lost none of their analytical relevance. They can offer insight into the character of both NATO and the Warsaw Pact as well as the problems their management poses for the two contemporary hegemons of the Western world.

The analogy between the cold war and the ancient rivalry between Athens and Sparta is not a novel one. For years, American intellectuals have been fond of comparing the United States to Athens--that bustling, commercially oriented, and rudely democratic parvenu of the ancient world. At the same time, they denigrated their cold war adversary as a modern-day Sparta--a centrally controlled "garrison polis" in which individual interests were subordinated to those of the state. These analogies, which certainly contain an interesting kernel of truth, have been understandably criticized as polemical and historically superficial. It is curious that those with a penchant for historical comparison have failed to make the far more apt and revealing analogy between the foreign policies of these Greek city states and those of contemporary superpowers; perhaps because such an analogy requires a disquieting reversal of roles. Sparta, that plodding authoritarian society, stood at the head of a democratic alliance system in which policy was made by consensus--often arrived at only after long and arduous negotiation--whereas Athens, the school of democracty, dominated and exploited its allies in a manner not at all dissimilar from the way in which the Soviet Union dominates the Warsaw Pact.

The Athenian alliance system developed in the course of Athens' effort to expel the Persians from Greece. As city states were liberated, they were incorporated into the alliance and compelled to contribute ships or money to sustain the campaign against Persia. The Athenians generally saw to it that the libertated states were governed by democracies and, thereby, ideologically compatible. From the Athenian perspective, the alliance provided a strong defensive position from which to block any renewed Persian aggression. It ensured that these less powerful Greek "poleis" did not submit, as they had in the past, to Persian intimidation or force of arms. For the allies, Athenian assistance was a prerequisite first of liberation and then of continued independence. In the course of time, as the threat of Persian invasion waned, most allies elected to pay tribute to Athens in lieu of sending ships and sailors to join her fleet. As most of them had trade dependent economies, they prospered under the protection of the Athenian navy and were able to pay considerable tribute without undue economic strain. The alliance became an important and expanding source of Athenian wealth and power as other city states elected to join it in return for Athenian support against their domestic rivals or regional enemies.

Hegemony of Athens, the dominant characteristic of the Athenian alliance, was made possible by her overwhelming maritime supremacy and the fact that her allies were, for the most part, either islands or coastal states with economies based on seaborne trade and thus particularly vulnerable to naval power. Athenian dominance was also facilitated by the continuing dependence of many democratic governments upon Athenian power for survival against the opposition of aristocratic foes.

Athenian leadership, exercised in an increasingly dictatorial manner, made many of her allies resentful and even rebellious. Actual rebellions were most often associated with revolutions that overthrew the democratic faction and brought aristocrats or oligarchs into power. As the size and cohesion of the alliance had become the barometer of her power, Athens did not hesitate to use force against recalcitrant allies. To the extent that Athenians felt threatened by foreign foes, they sought to establish tighter control over their allies in order to discourage any of them from harboring thoughts of independence. Nowhere was this later concern more apparent than in the Melian Dialogue which took place in the sixteenth year of the Pelopennesian war. Melos, originally a Spartan colony, was an island in the Aegean and one of the few that was not an Athenian ally. According to Thucydides, the Melians had scrupulously observed neutrality to avoid giving offense to Athens. Even so, the Athenians, at a low ebb in their fortunes, demanded that Melos join their alliance or be destroyed. The Melians tried to dissuade the Athenians from this course of action, arguing that they were of more value as a friendly neutral than as a subjugated ally. The Athenians were unmoved and replied that their empire rested on their power and the fear it inspired in others; that the very independence of Melos, located in the midst of an Athenian sea, was an affront to that power and an encouragement to disgruntled allies to challenge Athens.

The Melian Dialogue, often cited as a defense of 'realpolitik', was in fact used by Thucydides to illustrate the extent to which Athenian power depended upon other's perceptions of that power. The Athenian alliance was at its strongest when Athens was seen as strong; no ally dared contemplate rebellion in such a circumstance. When Athens was perceived as weak, the survival of the alliance was threatened as many of Athens' dependencies aspired to exploit any weakness of hers to their advantage. To guard against this prospect, it became imperative for a weakened Athens to demonstrate resolve--even if she had to look for situations in which to do so. As this concern came to dominate Athenian consciousness, it became the motivation for much of the adventurism that characterized Athenian policy in the latter years of the war.

The Spartan alliance system, based on altogether different principles, had come into being in a very different manner. Together with Athens, Sparta had offered valiant resistance to the Persian invasion and had led the ground forces that repulsed the Persians from the heart of Greece. Subsequently, Sparta withdrew into traditional isolation, despite the pleadings of other Greeks that she take the leading role in liberating those city states still under the Persian yoke. Sparta devoted herself instead to the maintenance of her peculiar domestic institutions--the survival of which required a fair degree of isolation from the commercial and intellectual currents of the outside world. Abroad, she was content to remain the dominant power and unquestioned hegemon of her immediate region, the Peloponnese.

The growing military power of Athens, her heavy-handed suppression of revolts by her allies, and her apparent willingness to use force abroad to increase her empire aroused the fear and envy of other Greek cities. They inevitably looked to Sparta for assistance as she was the only power equal to the task of challenging Athens. The Spartans themselves were divided as to their proper course of action: some wished to avoid involvement in the quarrels of other states, while others were convinced that Sparta had to challenge Athens or forfeit its position of primacy in the Greek world. The latter faction ultimately carried the day and sought to exercise Spartan influence through the Lacedaemonian Confederacy--a loose alliance of Peloponnesian states, dominated by Sparta, and of independent states outside the Peloponnes, drawn to Sparta by reason of their opposition to Athens.

The Lacedaemonian Confederacy was a democratic alliance of powers of varying strength held together, primarily, by their fear of a common enemy; for Thucydides, all the important characteristics of the alliance derived from this power relationship. Unlike Athens, Sparta--although recognized as the leader of the Confederacy--was not in a position to dictate policy to its non-Peloponnesian members. All of these states had joined the alliance in pursuit of their own particular interests, interests which not infrequently clashed with those of Sparta or of the alliance as a whole. They were jealous of their independence, resisted anything that appeared to encroach upon it, and their leaders were sensitive to the needs of their domestic constituencies which sometimes severely curtailed their own freedom of action.

When the Confederacy acted, it was because one of the allies usually one of the less powerful ones, succeeded in defining individual interests as common ones. Spartan initiatives were almost certain to be opposed by some of the allies, especially Corinth which had great power pretensions of its own. Wary of squandering power in pursuit of other's interests and frustrated by the difficulty of structuring any consensus within the alliance, Sparta pursued a leadership role which was so cautious that her allies sometimes questioned her resolve. When she did act decisively, the others--reminded of their dependence upon her--chafed at having to play a subordinate role. In the absence of a serious threat, this political dynamic dictated a policy of Spartan inaction; moreover, without external threat, the centrifugal forces of parochialism were strong enough to defeat any effort by the hegemon to coordinate and control the alliance. In face of danger or in adversity, the allies drew together and looked to Sparta for leadership--as such they constituted a formidable coalition for each city.

TABLE 10.1 THE CHARACTER OF ALLIANCES

Athens (Warsaw Pact)	Sparta (NATO)
Structure of Power	
Dominated by hegemon capable of enforcing compliance with its political-military decisions*	Democratic alliance among states of varying power.**
Nature of Decisionmaking	
All important policy decisions made by Athens	Consensual among the several allies
Sources of Cohesion	
The power of the hegemon and the dependence of some allied political elites upon Athens to sustain them in power. The cohesion of the alliance is proportional to the power of the hegemon.	Perception of acute outside threat. The cohesion of the alliance is proportional to the perceived magnitude of the outside threat.

* This did not hold true for some Peloponnesian states whose freedom of action--foreign affairs--was severely limited by their location--the orbit of Sparta.

** The Athenian alliance system also included some independent powers who associated with Athens by reason of their need to mobilize great power support against local adversaries. They retained varying degrees of freedom from Athens. This situation is analogous to the Soviet Union's alliances with Vietnam, Cuba, and Ethiopia.

cont'd on next page

Table 10.1, cont'd

Principal Threats to Cohesion	
A decline in the power or resolve of the hegemon coupled with a rise in power of an outside adversary; internal unrest or rebellion on the part of allies.	The waning of the outside threat; disputes among the allies; the involvement of the hegemon or other allies in conflicts outside of and contradictory to alliance interests; internal instability of alliance members.
Major Strengths	
A rapid decisionmaking process and response to threats; coordinated political-military strategy and doctrine; national division of labor within the alliance.	The self-interest motivating participants in the alliance; their perceptions that individual security depends upon the well-being and security of the other allies.
Major Weaknesses	
Many allies of questionable reliability; numerous forces required for garrison and policing of allies; low tolerance of political-military setbacks, offensive action limited by reliability of allies.	Slow and cumbersome decision-making process; poorly coordinated political-military strategies; inefficient use of alliance resources; tendency of allies to subordinate alliance interests to parochial interests; offensive action limited by defensive character of the alliance and the need for consensus.
Principal Strategies of Alliance Management	
Hegemon must maintain respect for his power and resolve; encourage mix of legitimacy and dependence among allied governments; influence allied policy through relationship with 'clients' within policy elite of allied states.	Hegemon must demonstrate proper mix of leadership and sensitivity to the interests and pride of the allies; act to defuse inter-allied conflicts and encourage feeling of community.

THE SOVIET UNION AND THE WARSAW PACT

The comparison between the Athenian alliance system and the Warsaw Pact is striking in almost every regard. Although they are separated by 2,400 years and are the products of societies based on different political and technological principles, they are characterized by analogous origins, power relationships and purposes, and have been managed in similar ways by their respective hegemons.

The Warsaw Pact, like its Athenian predecessor, was the outgrowth of a long war that left the victor in occupation, or at least in partial control, of numerous liberated territories.[1] As the Athenians had done previously, the Soviets bound these states in alliance and, where possible, installed governments favorably disposed to themselves; governments which remained, at least partially, dependent upon continued Soviet support for survival, as had many of the democratic governments created by Athens. In both instances, the primary motiviation behind these actions was the fear of a future challenge from the recently defeated adversary. The two hegemons were to some extent also concerned about the post-war intentions of their principal wartime ally; Athens in the case of Sparta, and the United States in the case of the Soviet Union. As "arriviste" great powers championing revolutionary ideologies, Athens and the Soviet Union aroused the suspicion and hostility of the more established powers. Victorious in war, both were also exhausted by that war and, as a result, were vulnerable.[2] They sought to enhance their capability of fending off a hostile coalition by whatever means they could; in so doing, they confirmed the suspicions of their former allies and ushered in a long period of 'cold war'. Military alliances, imposed upon liberated and dependent states, became a principal means for both hegemons to cope with conflict.

Since 1945 the overriding Soviet foreign policy objective in Europe has been to protect the western approaches to the USSR. Soviet leaders have pursued this objective in two complementary ways: by dominating Eastern Europe as a protective glacis and by attempting to keep Western Europe--especially Germany--weak, divided, and cowed by Soviet power. Moscow sought, unsuccessfully, to elicit some degree of American support for this policy. It also relied upon the domestic clout of the Western European communist parties to prevent the pursuit of anti-Soviet policies. The Warsaw Pact was only brought into being in 1955, as a counter to NATO and as a means of legitimizing the continuing Soviet occupation of Hungary and Romania.[3] For some years afterwards it languished, in the words of one Western commentator, as a "forgotten paper tiger."[4] But as Soviet influence in Western Europe declined, Moscow was increasingly forced to rely upon the military instrument as its principal means of influence. The transformation of the Warsaw Pact in the course of the last twenty years into an impressively equipped and well-integrated military alliance is indicative of this shift. It does not augur any significant change in Soviet objective but, rather, in the means by which they are to be pursued.

From its inception the Warsaw Pact was expected to play a role in maintaining Soviet influence in Eastern Europe. It was meant to legitimate that influence and to provide another institutional mechanism through which it could be exercised. Roman Kolkowicz described the Pact as "an entangling alliance by which the Soviet leaders seek to enmesh their frequently unwilling allies in the web of Soviet national interests."[5] Over the years the Soviets have indeed come to rely upon it as a means of restraining a group of turbulent and fundamentally hostile countries as well as preventing undesired domestic developments within them. Soviet interventions in Hungary in 1956 and in Czechoslovakia in 1968 provide two cases in point. In neither instance did Soviet action require the existence of the alliance; but in 1968, the Pact provided a framework for making the Czechoslovakian intervention a collective action and, thereby, giving it the facade of legitimacy that it would have lacked otherwise.

As events in Poland indicate, "fraternal bloc solidarity and cohesion" remain an important Soviet concern; however, it is questionable whether the Pact can any longer make a significant contribution to that unity. Indeed, the central thesis of this chapter is that while the Pact has served Soviet interests in Western Europe, it is becoming a less useful tool of Soviet influence in Eastern Europe because of the changing political realities of that region and because of the increased cost to Moscow of using force within it. To the extent that Soviet influence in Eastern Europe wanes, the effectiveness of the Warsaw Pact as a political-military weapon against the West also declines because of the erosion of its credibility. The deterioration of Moscow's position in Eastern Europe--a development that Soviet leaders are to some degree aware of--confronts them with some difficult choices which they may be psychologically unprepared to make. Given the repercussions which developments within Eastern Europe can be expected to have upon the Soviet Union itself, deterioration in Soviet influence, if it occurs, raises serious questions about the long-term prospects of the system as a whole.

THE COMING ECONOMIC CRISIS

At the root of the problem in Eastern Europe is the need of its communist governments to establish a modicum of popular support while at the same time remaining responsive to Moscow. Most Eastern European leaders have attempted to serve these two disparate constituencies by following Soviet guidance with respect to internal structure and foreign policy, and, at the same time, attempting to win popular support by raising living standards. Hungary, Poland, and East Germany have followed this strategy which Khrushchev derisively dubbed "Goulash Communism." Since 1968, Czechoslovakia has also moved in this direction. Romania has developed a variant consisting of ideological rigidity at home coupled with a semi-independent foreign policy designed to appeal to the national feelings of the Romanian people. Bulgaria--with no religious or national differences with Russia but, rather, a history of close relations--is a special case.

In the coming decade it will become increasingly difficult for Eastern European governments to satisfy simultaneously their two different constituencies. To begin with, most of these governments have never really succeeded in gaining acceptance of economic progress as a substitute for political freedom and meaningful national independence. Nor, as recent events in Poland demonstrate, have they been altogether successful in satisfying the economic aspirations of their citizens. While Poland is in many ways unique, even East Germans--the most prosperous of the satellite peoples--are disgruntled with the differences between their living standards and those in the West. Their awareness of these differences is heightened by West German television which 60-65 percent of all East Germans watch.[6] Discontent, not only in East Germany, but throughout Eastern Europe is almost certain to increase in coming years as the economic prospects for all these countries look rather grim.

The 'socialist community' of the Council for Mutual Economic Assistance (CMEA) has experienced a slowdown in its rate of economic growth since the mid-seventies. In 1980, the economies of Eastern Europe expanded only 0.4 percent compared to an average 4.8 percent increase in GNP in the period 1971-75. Their current Five-Year Plans (1981-1986) have set more moderate economic goals but even these are unlikely to be realized.[7] In

Poland, GNP declined by 1.9 percent in 1979 and 2.6 percent in 1980.[8] By the Poles' own admission, production has fallen off by at least 15 percent this year because of political turbulence.[9] Poland's crisis, while more immediate and pronounced than that of its neighbors, may nevertheless be indicative of a general trend as many of the factors contributing to its economic decline affect the other Eastern European states as well. Even the most efficient states--Hungary and East Germany--are shackled by centrally directed and poorly managed economies. They are further burdened by the cumbersome apparatus of the Council for Mutual Economic Assistance for planning and coordination. Devised by the Soviets as a means of integrating and nationalizing the economies of Eastern Europe, CMEA has, in practice, turned out to be another layer of stifling bureaucracy set above the already over-managed economies of its member states. The spurt of growth that Eastern Europe experienced in the early 1970s took place in spite of this effort at supra-national economic integration.

Economic growth during this period was in part the result of capital and technology imported from the West. Between 1971 and 1980, Eastern Europe's combined net debt to the West rose by $51 billion. Poland alone accounted for 43 percent of this, although Hungary and East Germany were also big borrowers.[10] The East Europeans had hoped to use foreign capital for generating sufficient productive capacity to repay their debts and to earn a sizeable profit by exporting surplus to the West. But this gamble failed to pay off. Poor planning--especially in Poland--plus generally inefficient management of capital, and a restricted Western market for Eastern European goods contributed to the negative outcome. Servicing their foreign debt has now become an increasing burden for several of the CMEA states; default could become a barrier to further loans without which these countries would find it difficult to stimulate the production necessary to meet their domestic and foreign obligations.

In the past, all of these states have profited from a cheap and plentiful source of energy. Eastern Europe imports about one-fourth of its energy; more than three-fourths--nearly 85 percent if Romania is excluded--is supplied by the Soviet Union. Soviet deliveries account for almost 80 percent of East European oil and oil products, and 99 percent of its natural gas; moreover, oil is sold at 40 percent of the world market price in accordance with an agreement which provides a five-year lag in Soviet oil pricing. But the Soviet Union is, itself, expected to become a net importer of energy during the current decade and has already notified CMEA members that they will have to seek alternative sources of supply. The Soviets can be expected to provide no more than half of Eastern Europe's imported energy by 1990, and that at spectacularly higher prices.[11] Because of their hard currency deficit, the Eastern Europeans will find it difficult, if not impossible, to meet their energy needs through purchases on the open market; instead, they will have to lower their economic goals.

Eastern Europeans will also have to pay more for raw materials. Most of their economies are geared to the importation of energy and raw materials from the Soviet Union in exchange for the export of high technology products and consumer goods to each other and the Soviet Union. The price of raw materials has been rising, and can be expected to continue to rise at a faster rate than the price of finished goods. Cotton is a case in point: seventy-five percent of CMEA cotton comes from the Soviet Union. The price of raw cotton more than doubled between 1971 and 1981, from 684 to 1,401 rubles a ton, but the price of cloth exported to the Soviet Union and other CMEA countries increased by only 30 percent.[12] A similar situation exists with regard to ore: the CMEA countries import 75 percent from the Soviet Union. The price of these ores has also been rising at a faster rate than the price of the manufactured products the Eastern Europeans sell back to the Soviet Union. Given the Soviets' own economic problems, it seems unlikely that they will agree to pay the Eastern Europeans substantially more for these products.

Former First Secretary of Poland, Edward Gierek, presciently observed in December 1979: "Some factors contributing to the high growth rates in the 1970s included a large labor reserve, the possibilities of increasing investment outlays, the obtaining of suitable loans abroad and the purchase of cheap raw materials and cheap fuels--all these have been exhausted."[13] As Gierek himself learned, the bleak economic prospects of Eastern Europe confront its leaders with the Hobson's choice of economic stagnation or cutting back on the standard of living. The latter can be accomplished by purchasing fewer consumer goods and significantly raising prices; a strategy, however, which means abolishing the long-standing policy throughout Eastern Europe of subsidizing goods and services. As the experience of Poland illustrates, either choice is fraught with danger. From 1976 onwards, the Gierek government attempted to raise prices, but backed down in the face of opposition. As a result, it experienced a 3 percent rise in the consumption of material goods at a time when national income actually declined by 2 percent. To sustain this level of consumption, economic planners were forced to reduce their investment outlay by 8.2 percent, in effect postponing but, at the same time, intensifying the ultimate economic reckoning. In 1980, the Gierek government partially reversed itself and dramatically raised prices for all oil products; it subsequently attempted to raise food prices, touching off strikes which led to its downfall and to the continuing political crisis in Poland.

THE POLISH CRISIS: CURTAIN RAISER TO AN EASTERN EUROPEAN DRAMA?

Events in Poland have made the other members of the Warsaw Pact nervous about their own domestic situations; in the short-term, however, the other communist governments in Eastern Europe are unlikely to confront organized labor opposition, even though they face similar, if somewhat less dramatic, economic problems. All of them have instituted significant consumer price increases in recent years without triggering Polish-style resistance. Three important differences exist between these countries and Poland: the gap between actual living standards and consumer expectations is narrower everywhere else in Eastern Europe than it is in Poland; workers lack the same tradition of militancy; and, unlike workers in Poland, they have failed to develop close ties to an active and cohesive core of dissident intellectuals. Even so, some of the other communist parties in Eastern Europe will in varying degrees come under pressure to share power if Solidarity succeeds in establishing itself as an independent force. For this reason, most regional communist party leaders have responded to the Polish crisis by making cautious, largely symbolic concessions to workers while cracking down on dissidents in the hope that this approach will minimize their own vulnerability to unrest.[14]

Just how successful will such efforts be in the long run? Is the situation in Poland so idiosyncratic that its neighbors have relatively little to fear? As noted above, the first important difference between Poland and the rest of Eastern Europe--the greater gap between living standards and consumer expectations--is almost certain to disappear by reason of the predicted worsening in living conditions throughout the CMEA bloc. Assuming that consumer expectations remain constant, negative changes in living conditions can be expected to trigger widespread and deep-rooted dissatisfaction, the likes of which have never before been experienced by communist governments in Eastern Europe. There is also good reason to believe that the second major difference-

-the absence of a militant labor force--has been the result of peculiar conditions which no longer apply throughout most of Eastern Europe. The late 1980s may well witness the growth of such movements in at least several of these countries.

The traditional communist strategy for keeping workers quiescent in both the Soviet Union and Eastern Europe has been to create considerable organizational distance between them and important nodes of policy-making; an attempt reflected in party-dominated trade unions, production committees, and a variety of other organs at the factory and other levels. When necessary, governments have also utilized the police apparatus, assisted by an extensive network of informers. The combined strategy of distance and suppression has worked primarily because labor militancy in Eastern Europe remained at a relatively low level. Workers have registered dissatisfaction, but have done so in episodic, unorganized outbursts which have usually been related to specific grievances and which were relatively easy to quell through a combination of coercion and concessions.

Walter D. Connor makes the case that the relative absence of worker militancy in Eastern Europe was due to the rapid economic modernization of these countries and the concomitant transformation of their working classes.[15] The working class grew in size and changed in character. At the bottom of the social pyramid, peasants--fleeing the chronic overpopulation and under-employment of the countryside--flocked into the cities and took jobs in the factories; at the top, many workers, and, even more so, their children, left the working class to become part of the new "socialist intelligentsia". They became the administrators and professionals the party relied upon to manage the economy and the state. This pattern of upward mobility which encouraged individual, as opposed to collective, solutions to workers' problems, retarded the development of any 'class consciousness'. Connor writes:

> "It made little difference that the new socialist intelligentsia of, say, 1951, did not live as well as its interwar predecessor, or that skilled workers in the Warsaw or Budapest of the same year worked longer for less than their counterparts in 1938. The frame of reference of the members of the new intelligentsia was that of the working class from which they had risen; that of the new workers, the peasant world they had left. For both, their new status yielded satisfactions, psychological and material, which gave them a "stake" in the system, a

reason to feel that what had befallen them could not have come under the old regime."[16]

Everywhere in Eastern Europe the prospect for mobility has diminished and is likely to become even less possible in the course of the coming decade. The bureaucracy is expanding at only a modest rate; those positions which do become available are likely to be filled by the sons and daughters of current incumbents who have used their privileged position to create better educations and job preference for their children. The rate of working class upward mobility has also slowed markedly as birth rates have declined; thus, causing the peasant labor supply to diminish. Today's workers will begin to view their social status--if they do not do so already--in a very different light than did their fathers. The chances are that most of these youths will be forced to remain proletarians against their will. This reality, Connor suggests, will encourage the development of class consciousness in the traditional sense of the term.[17] Heightened class identification, at a time of economic retrenchment, is almost a certain recipe for labor militancy. The Polish disturbances of 1970, 1976, and 1980 as well as the Rumanian strikes of 1977 may be seen, in retrospect, as the harbingers of this change.

The third distinctive feature of the Polish situation has been the emergence of an alliance between labor militants and intellectual dissidents; as elsewhere in Eastern Europe, dissidents and workers have tended to live in different worlds, to pursue different--if not contradictory--goals, and to harbor considerable antagonism toward one another. In 1956, 1970, and 1976, when Polish workers took to the streets to protest precipitous price increases, the intellectuals rarely followed suit; the few who did, pursued policies that were not only uncoordinated with the workers but also directed toward different ends. For their part, the workers' councils that formed during these upheavals were often critical of the goals and tactics of the intellectuals. When protest was sparked by students and dissidents in 1968, the workers remained on the sidelines because the demonstrators' demands for greater political freedom seemed irrelevant to them. The Czechoslavakian experience in 1968 told a similar story: attempts by reformist intellectuals to build support across class boundaries met a lukewarm to hostile response. It took Soviet troops to bring a worker-intellectual coalition into being and even then it was shortlived.[18]

To some extent the gulf between the two groups represents the success of long-standing efforts by communist leaders in all Eastern European countries to foster worker prejudices and dislike of intellectuals, but it also reflects the very real differences in attitudes and objectives on the part of the two groups. Workers have had little or no sympathy for the political objectives of the intellectuals. The interest of the latter in artistic and political freedom has generally been perceived as irrelevant to the plight of the working class, while dissident prescriptions for economic reforms--with their usual emphasis on performance and efficiency--have been viewed by workers as threats to their interests and security. They have particularly objected to proposals that would close unproductive factories, lay off surplus labor, and reward energetic workers at the expense of their less productive colleagues. Intellectuals, in turn, have despaired at the narrow economic focus of worker protests which are typically triggered by price increases and food shortages. To one Hungarian dissident, the Polish protests of 1970 and 1976 represented rebellions of workers as 'consumers' not as 'producers'.[19] As his analysis indicates, the bread and butter concerns of workers have been viewed with disdain by the intellectuals--many of whom attribute the economic ills of their countries, at least in part, to the self-aggrandizing "I'm all right, Jack" attitude of the working class.

The beginning of worker-intellectual cooperation in Poland goes back to the summer of 1976 when fourteen dissidents denounced government reprisals against rioting workers in an open letter to the Polish parliament. Shortly thereafter, Jacek Kuron, a leading Polish dissident, wrote to Enrico Berlinguer, head of the Italian Communist Party, soliciting Euro-communist support for the Polish workers.[20] Kuron also took a leading role in organizing a Workers' Defense Committee (KOR) among Markist intellectuals which involved them in a direct and personal way with the plight of the strikers. They also established a "samzidat" journal, <u>Robotnik (The Worker</u>) that promoted the goal of greater worker control over production through the creation of worker-dominated trade unions to replace those docile ones led by the party. In November 1977, KOR--now reconstituted as KSS-KOR--announced its success in establishing a worker 'cell' in Radom which, in the words of one Western observer, was "The first concrete evidence of institutionalized links between the workers and the intelligentsia".[21] Even so, most students of Polish affairs were not very sanguine about the prospects for such links, and were surprised by the extent of the cooperation that developed between workers and intellectuals in 1980-81.

As was true of previous labor unrest in Poland, the most recent crisis was triggered by price increases which were announced on 1 July 1980. The increases were actually miniscule in comparison to previous ones, but nevertheless, enraged workers at the Ursus Tractor Factory who took over the plant and demanded large wage hikes. With hindsight, it is apparent that the turning point in this confrontation was the decision by the Polish Presidium on the third day of the sit-in strike to grant a $6-7 (U.S.) monthly pay increase to the strikers--an increase which encouraged workers elsewhere in Poland to occupy their factories and voice similar demands. The success of these strikes set off something of a chain reaction and ultimately much of the country, including farmers and students, were pressing their demands on a harassed and divided government.

The scope of this disturbance aside, what really distinguished it from previous labor unrest in Poland were the objectives of the strikers. After 17 August 1980, the focus of the strikers shifted away from mere wage and price concessions toward the establishment and official recognition of an independent trade union movement. This goal reflected the influence of KOR which had long advocated independent workers' unions as the only means of forcing the government to honor its concessions. "Almost all the strike leaders had something to do with KSS-KOR. It prepared the way for events", observed Marcin Krol, a Polish historian.[22] During the strikes, KSS-KOR took an active part in helping workers throughout the country formulate and negotiate their demands. Solidarity in turn forced the government to release scores of dissidents who had been jailed temporarily because of their support, or suspected support, of the strikers. Severals of these dissidents, among them Jacek Kuron and Adam Michnik, became advisers to Solidarity.

At the present time (April 1981), the results of the Polish experiment are unclear. Solidarity appears to have established itself as an independent political and economic force and to have compelled a major shake-up of the Polish leadership as well as a partial transformation of the way in which the Polish state and economy are managed. However, Soviet bayonets could put an end to this experiment as they did to the Prague Spring. Soviet invasion of Czechoslovakia effectively squelched political revisionism in Eastern Europe for thirteen years. Military intervention in Poland, while it would certainly mean the demise of Solidarity, would only temporarily set back the forces of change that gave rise to it. There are several reasons for this difference.

Conditions responsible for Poland's upheaval will increasingly be found in varying degrees in other Eastern European countries as well. The gap separating actual living standards from expectations is widening in all of these countries and will continue to do so in the future. Labor militancy is also growing, fanned not only by the conditions analyzed above, but stimulated as well by the apparent success of the Polish strikes. The Polish upheaval has had reverberations in Hungary, Czechoslovakia, Romania, and in the Soviet Union itself, where Lithuanian workers in several cities walked off their jobs.[23] More importantly, the apparent success and obvious payoff of worker-intellectual collaboration in Poland are likely to provide an incentive for similar efforts at building coalitions across class lines elsewhere in Eastern Europe. It may already have begun to happen in Czechoslovakia where, in November 1980, a member of the Central Committee publicly alluded to a "kind of echo of Polish events", admitting that numerous Czechoslovaks had begun to talk with intellectuals about establishing independent trade unions.[24] No doubt, other examples of such collaboration will surface in the future; although, it will not be easy to overcome the great gulf between workers and intellectuals that exists everywhere in Eastern Europe. Nor, it should be pointed out, will other Eastern European governments look kindly upon such collaboration in light of the Polish experience.

The real lesson of Poland may be that communist governments in Eastern Europe are more vulnerable to organized popular protest on the part of workers and dissident intellectuals than the governments in question have been willing to believe. When authority ultimately rests on fear of the consequences of challenging it, only one effective challenge is required to expose its pretense. Solidarity, to some extent, did just this. While the Polish government could not really be said to have had feet of clay, neither did it reveal the kind of determination and decisiveness that would have been required to suppress the Polish workers at the very outset or to break up the strikes when they spread. Later, the government and Party also capitulated to demands for internal reform from the rank-and-file, which adamantly insisted that the leadership had lost touch with the people. The Party's temerity was, at first, probably the result of Gierek's illusion that he could retain power by buying off the strikers; later, it was due to paralyzing divisions within the Party and the army's refusal to be drawn into a domestic struggle. The inability of these communist-dominated institutions to cope with challenge from below will be duly noted by other Eastern Europeans; although, they and we, must be aware of the important differences that still distinguish the situation in Poland from that in other Warsaw Pact countries.

MOSCOW'S DILEMMA IN POLAND

Developments in Poland have called the credibility of the Brezhnev Doctrine into question. Both leaders and dissidents in Eastern Europe are asking themselves whether Moscow is really prepared, as everyone had supposed, to use force to crush revisionism. Even if the Soviets do intervene, the manner in which their response to developments in Poland evolved made very clear the variety of constraints that militate against their use of force.

Soviet leaders at first took a moderate position, hoping, no doubt, that concessions to the strikers and, later, a change in the Polish government would ease the situation. They subsequently accepted the legal registration of Solidarity, something which could hardly have pleased them. They probably viewed it as a tactically wise concession that would give new Party boss, Kania, the time he needed to defuse the workers' rebellion and restore unquestioned Party supremacy. Ambivalent Soviet press reaction to developments at the time suggests that the Kremlin leadership was by no means unanimous in its approach to the problem. As in 1968, Soviet 'hard-liners' appear to have been lobbying for a tougher policy and looking for support from Eastern Europe leaders, some of whom must have felt even more threatened than the Soviets did by the turn of events in Poland. From the very beginning, the Eastern Europeans voiced opposition to Solidarity, although only the East Germans and Czechoslovaks hinted at the need for intervention. President Ceausescu of Romania, who spoke out against any "interference in Poland's internal affairs", nevertheless referred to developments in that country as anti-socialist manifestations.[25]

There can be no doubt that Soviet leaders saw developments in Poland as threatening to some of their most vital interests. The expansion of Solidarity into a nationally organized and independent trade union claiming a membership of seven million, twice that of the Polish Communist Party, was an unprecedented challenge to the primacy of that Party. Worse still, was the fact that this happened in a country with a strong anti-Russian tradition. As early as November 1980, Moscow publicly voiced alarm at the potential threat to its rail links with Soviet forces in East Germany--almost all of these lines run through Poland. Soviet spokesmen even hinted at their fear that Solidarity would undermine the reliability of the Polish armed forces, at 317,000 strong, the largest national component of the Warsaw Pact after the forces of the Soviet Union itself.[26]

Soviet commentators also expressed concern for the economic consequences of continuing labor unrest in Poland. First quarter statistics for 1981 reveal that industrial production was down more than ten percent, and building construction had declined more than twenty. Total exports to CMEA declined by 15 percent in comparison with the same period a year before.[27] The Polish economic decline has already had an adverse impact on CMEA, but primarily on East Germany. The East German economy has experienced an even greater retraction because some of its generating plants also run on Polish coal.[28] Other CMEA members, most notably Romania, East Germany, and Czechoslovakia, are also dependent--in varying degrees--upon Poland for coking coal and have been forced to spend hard currency to buy substitutes in the West.

Economic problems notwithstanding, the greatest threat posed to the Soviet Union by events in Poland is ideological. Moscow has repeatedly condemned the concept of free trade unions, insisting that workers' organizations be subordinate to the direction and needs of the Party. To permit Solidarity to represent the workers and Rural Solidarity, the farmers threatens the monopoly of the Polish Communist Party. The transformation of that Party itself, in response to demands for 'renewal' from below, represents an even greater ideological deviation. The Party Congress in July 1981, to which delegates were elected by secret ballot from a list of competing candidates, was a revolutionary departure from communist practice; even more so were the delegates' election by secret ballot of the Party Secretary. Most frightening of all from the Soviet perspective may be the rapidly developing horizontal links at almost all levels between Solidarity and the reconstituted communist party. Soviet spokesmen have repeatedly pointed out that "democractic centralism", Lenin's own euphemism for dictatorship from above, is essential to the continuation of "Marxism-Leninism" in Poland.[29] Finally, there is the question of precedent. Poles and Soviets both know that dissidents and political leaders everywhere in Eastern Europe are carefully monitoring the Polish situation. The extent that the Soviets tolerate Polish efforts to "advance the development of socialism", as one member of the Polish leadership put it, they encourage similar efforts elsewhere in Eastern Europe.[30]

If acquiesence to Polish revisionism is costly to the Soviets, so is intervention. In Czechoslovakia, they were able to intervene and retain the support of a significant percentage of the communist party because many of the "apparatchiki" were equally fearful of the consequences of Dubcek's reforms. Moscow was also able to neutralize the Czechoslovakian Army through surprise and skillful use of Fifth Columnists; surprise seems out of the question this time. Nor will it be easy for the Soviets to paralyze the Polish Army from within, as the Polish command is certainly cognizant of the details of how this was done in Czechoslovakia and, it is reasonable to suppose, has taken precautions against its repetition.

Although seemingly simplistic, perhaps the most important difference between Poland and Czechoslovakia is the fact that Poles are not Czechs; therefore, they cannot be expected to behave as passively. Russians, moreover, have always been extremely unpopular in Poland, and it will be difficult for them to rally support--even among hardline communists. Polish deviation, unlike its Czechoslovakian predecessor, has strong nationalist overtones. Recent Western visitors to Poland have reported being struck by the intensity of anti-Russian feeling, even among party and government officials. Polish collaborators are almost certain to be shunned in a way their Czechoslovakian counterparts were not; the social pressure against acting as front men for Moscow is, accordingly, much greater. In the absence of a large anti-reform faction anxious to be returned to power by the Red Army, intervention entails the prospect of having to restructure the party, government, and economy from the bottom up. The administrative and economic burden of such an operation is certain to be staggering; it would also put the lie to any pretext of Polish independence and, thereby, undercut all the careful efforts the Soviets have made over the years to provide an aura of legitimacy to their dominion in Eastern Europe.

Nor can Moscow assume that its intervention will be unopposed. Poles have fought German and Russian invaders often enough in the past under equally unfavorable conditions to lend credibility to the warning, allegedly issued by the Polish military in Autumn 1980, that they would resist any intervention.[31] The Soviets also know that in 1956--the last time Poland faced the prospect of Soviet intervention--the leadership prepared to defend itself by mobilizing and deploying loyal army units and arming newly formed workers' battalions.[32] While the Red Army would, in the end, overcome any Polish opposition, an armed conflict of any kind would render Poland useless as an ally for some time. It would also compel the Soviets to station large numbers of occupation troops in the country; thus, reducing the percentage of their forces available for other purposes. Occupation forces would be subjected to harassment from guerrilla bands and possibly even urban terrorist groups. An even more extreme vision would see Poland, whose history and people have many parallels with Ireland and the Irish, transformed into the Northern Ireland of Eastern Europe by her people's implacable and violent opposition to Soviet rule. A lingering and bloody confrontation of that sort right in the heart of Central Europe would have incalculable consequences for Moscow.

Soviet intervention in Poland threatens the cohesion of the Warsaw Pact, given the opposition it will evoke from some of that alliance. In 1968, all of the Pact countries, except Romania, were induced to participate in the invasion of Czechoslovakia. The presence of the East Germans so aroused the Czechoslovakians that they were promptly withdrawn. Polish soldiers were reported to have been acutely embarrassed by their participation, even though the Czechoslovakians are a traditional enemy. The Hungarians apparently had even greater morale problems.[33] The Czechoslovakian experience, even though it involved no significant bloodshed, has made many Eastern European political and military leaders less than eager to participate in such an operation again, especially if it involves a very real possibility of serious fighting.

Romania has made its unwillingness to intervene clear from the outset.[34] The other members of the Pact seem to have had their threshold of intervention raised by the experience of Czechoslovakia. Well into the spring of 1981, the East German government was reported to be ambivalent about intervention, even though all of its members agreed on the need for a "physical solution" to the Polish problem. The cost of intervention was apparently perceived as so high by some that they were willing to give Kania more time in the hope that he could assert control over the situation.* One East German official confided to a Western newsman, "That people I've spoken with would like the Polish Party to pull a rabbit out of a hat." But no one seems to believe in their hearts that this will happen.[35]

---

* Mr. Kania was replaced as First Secretary in August 1981 by Gen. Wojciech Jaruzelski. (Ed.)

Even if the Soviets should eventually succeed in gaining support from the Pact for intervention, the Hungarians, at least, would be most reluctant of participants; assuming they did join in, they would probably limit their operations to token occupation of sparsely populated rural areas. The Czechoslovakian army might wish to do the same. The Romanians would refuse to participate and would be likely to condemn the invasion; their protests would be supported by the Yugoslavs, the Eurocommunists and the Chinese.

Pact opposition to intervention significantly enhances its cost to the Soviets. Dale Herspring and Ivan Volgyes observe:

> "An invasion force which omits two or three states is an open admission of Moscow's failure to gain the support of its allies. An invasion force which either refuses to fight or openly expresses support for the indigenous population is worse than no invasion force at all. From Moscow's standpoint, it may be better to do the job alone than to take a chance on the Eastern Europeans."[36]

But to do the job alone is to jettison all pretext of legitimacy which the Soviets have gone to great lengths to create in Eastern Europe. Intervention might thus create serious problems for their Eastern European client states and, perhaps, for themselves as well.

As far as anyone can determine, Soviet public opinion has been generally supportive of Soviet foreign policy. Despite the attendant economic consequences, the average Russian appears to favor high levels of defense spending to counter the threat he perceives from the West. According to most accounts, Russians--although, less so than other Soviet nationalities--have been receptive to their government's assertion that it intervened in Afghanistan to forestall counterrevolution being fostered by China and the United States. Some disenchantment with Soviet policy in Afghanistan has, nevertheless, become apparent and is not limited to the usual, narrow circle of intellectual dissidents. Opposition to Soviet policy in Afghanistan can be expected to grow to the extent that the Red Army continues to sustain the same or even higher levels of casualties. It is inconceivable that Russian opposition to the war would reach the fevered pitch of anti-war feeling in the United States during the Vietnam years, but public opinion must still be a matter of concern to the regime.

Evidence for this can be seen in Moscow's effort, begun as early as September 1980, to expand its domestic propaganda to provide a justification for possible intervention in Poland. This propaganda cited the alleged concern of "responsible Polish opinion" about the recent course of events in their country, especially their fear that "counterrevolutionaries" and even "fascists" were taking over. In April 1981 the Soviet press also began to talk about "revisionist forces in the Polish Party" who are trying "to pluck the revolutionary soul out of Marxism and undermine the belief of the working class and toiling masses in socialism".[37]

Intervention, as in Czechoslovakia, would almost certainly be justified to Soviet opinion as necessary to restore socialism. The claim would also be made that it was carried out with the support of the vast majority of the Polish people; however, to invade Poland without foreign communist support--actually, in the face of considerable communist opposition--would make this argument difficult if not impossible to sustain. If the Poles did not resist, it is likely that Soviet occupation troops would have enough casual contact with them to be exposed to their version of events. Some soldiers would almost certainly become infected by the virus of Polish revisionism. An even greater number would suffer from psychological dissonance induced by the contradiction between the Polish reaction to them and what they had been led to expect by their political officers. This particular phenomenon was reported among Soviet occupation forces in Czechoslovakia and is said to have brought on a serious morale problem.[38] Military resistance by the Poles would probably create an even greater political problem for the Soviet forces.[39] And whether the Kremlin realizes it or not, disaffection among Soviet forces arising out of their occupation of Poland is bound to fuel opposition to Soviet policy in Afghanistan as well.

Faced with high costs for intervention, some or even all of which must be apparent, Soviet leaders have tolerated the Polish experiment with democracy longer than almost anyone in the East or West would have thought likely. In part, this tolerance reflects the failure of Polish and Soviet leaders to grasp the full extent of Polish grievances and the determination of the workers and farmers to push for their redress. This is hardly surprising as neither Polish nor Soviet policymakers were cognitively disposed to recognize just how dissatisfied people were with the policies for which they were responsible. As a result, they thought the strikers could be mollified by minor concessions and, when this failed, through changes in the leadership; after all, this policy had worked in 1970 and 1971. In their willingness to replay this scenario, Polish and

Russian leaders joined a venerable list of policymakers who have learned superficial lessons from history. Robert Jervis suggests that this is a common failing because people rarely seek out or grasp the underlying causes of an outcome but instead assume that it was the result of the most salient aspects of the situation. This phenomenon gives rise to a tendency to apply a solution that worked in the past to a present problem because the two situations bear a superficial resemblance.[40]

Hardliners in both Warsaw and Moscow may have had fewer illusions about the extent of the opposition to them and for that reason favored a crackdown from the outset. This policy might have worked--although it almost certainly would have involved bloodshed--but was presumably opposed by Gierek because he knew that, even if successful, it would probably lead to his ouster. Gierek was supported in his conciliatory approach by Brezhnev, who had favored intervention early on in Czechoslovakia, but in this case was clearly among those who hoped that Polish communists would be able to contain the crisis without outside assistance.[41] Divisions among both the Warsaw and Moscow leaders was another factor favoring caution--presumably a consensus would be required, or at least advisable, before any extreme action could be initiated; however, the caution displayed by the Polish leadership permitted the situation to gain momentum which led to loss of control. One can suppose that the point was rather quickly reached where a crackdown, now seen as all the more necessary to those most opposed to Solidarity and what it stood for, was, nevertheless, seen by others in the leadership as an increasingly less viable option because of the scale of the operation and the violence it would certainly involve.

Hardliners in Warsaw, and probably in Moscow as well, continued to push for a tougher response. Some of the actions they appear to have favored were rejection of Solidarity's demands, imposition of martial law, arrest of the strike leaders, and, if necessary, the use of troops or security forces to clear striking workers out of the factories.[42] If the principle of cognitive consistency can be taken as a guide, the hardliners would have been considerably less sensitive to the adverse implications of a crackdown and, later, of intervention than those in the leadership who opposed either course of action. Overruled at home, they probably lobbied other Eastern European leaders for support of a tougher line. Generating demands from other Pact leaders is a time-honored tactic of minority opinion within Pact leaderships for forcing the hand of their own governments. However, this time the ploy, if used, seems to have backfired for it revealed just how divided the Pact was about the wisdom of putting pressure on the Poles, and later, of intervening. This division was not only national--that is between countries--but also within their policymaking elites as well.[43]

Intervention became less attractive to many Eastern European political and military leaders as they perceived it likely to induce violent opposition from the Poles. Their caution may have been an important factor in confirming for Brezhnev the correctness of the position he had taken.[44] But if intervention was premature and possibly costly, passivity in the face of the changes occurring in Poland was clearly also intolerable. So instead, Brezhnev and presumably others in the Soviet inner circle, opted for the middle ground: they would seek to strengthen the hand of those Polish leaders opposed to Solidarity by employing a version of both the carrot and the stick. The carrot would consist of some loans and food shipments to Poland to help ease the economic distress and of more latitude for Kania--who was seen as Moscow's man in Warsaw--to cope with the upheaval. The stick was the implicit threat of force, made credible by military preparations for intervention.

The threat of intervention was deliberately played up in December 1980 and again in April 1981; both episodes were part of a carefully orchestrated war of nerves calculated to shore up the position of orthodox Polish communists and moderate Solidarity's demands. This policy required well-publicized Warsaw Pact maneuvers which, coincidentally or not, occurred at times when the Polish Communist Party appeared to be on the verge of losing control of the situation. The April affair culminated in Brezhnev's trip to Prague, amid rumors of a Pact summit, where a stiff speech by Czechoslovak President Gustav Husak, followed by a somewhat milder one by Brezhnev, underscored Soviet concern for developments in Poland.[45] The symbolism of Prague as the choice of venue for Brezhnev's warning was assuredly not lost on the Poles. Continued Soviet reliance upon this strategy--even after it had become evident to most observers that it was only slowing down the pace of change in Poland, not stopping it--was probably indicative of Brezhnev's awareness of the costs of intervention. Nevertheless, he and his colleagues in the Kremlin will have to face this possibility if Polish revisionism continues to flourish.

EAST EUROPEAN LEGITIMACY AND PACT COHESION

As has been argued above, Poland is not altogether a special case; that is to say, many of the conditions responsible for unrest in Poland exist or are likely to develop in at least some of the other countries of the Warsaw Pact. The Polish experience will almost certainly serve as a catalyst in this regard. Solidarity has released the genie of reform from the bottle in which the Soviet Union sealed it over a decade ago when it invaded Czechoslovakia. Regardless of its ultimate fate, Solidarity exposed both the vulnerability of Eastern European governments to challenges from worker-intellectual coalitions and the reluctance of Moscow to use force to suppress them. For both these reasons it is unlikely that anything the Soviets now do will effectively succeed in putting that genie back into his bottle. Toleration of Solidarity for very much longer, even accompanied by a major propaganda effort to define Poland as a special case, will only encourage other Eastern Europeans to emulate the Poles. However, a Soviet or even Pact invasion of Poland, especially one that encounters resistance, might create even more constraints on the future use of Soviet power to suppress revisionism. A prolonged and violent Soviet occupation of Poland--one that consumes scarce Soviet resources and generates opposition, perhaps at home as well as abroad--would not be a situation the Soviets would seek to repeat. The only satisfactory outcome from the Soviet point of view would be the successful suppression of Solidarity by the Poles themselves or a quick, unopposed Warsaw Pact intervention in Poland that swept Solidarity aside and restored orthodox communists to power. Neither outcome is likely. The transormation of the Polish Party has gone too far to permit it to carry out a *coup de main*. If anything, those within the Party who favor such a course of action are about to be purged. A repeat of Czechoslovakia also seems implausible for reasons already discussed.

The inescapable conclusion is that events in Poland have accelerated the long-term trend toward political instability in Eastern Europe which results from the failure of most of these communist governments to manage their economies with any degree of success. Material dissatisfaction will usher in a crisis of legitimacy because political systems that have relied so openly for so long upon material progress for their main *raison d'etre* are bound to run into difficulty when their economies stagnate. To make matters worse, most of these governments have no resevoir of ideological support to draw upon in hard times. The manifestations of this crisis are already apparent. Poland aside, sporadic strikes have become more frequent in Rumania, East Germany, and Hungary. Dissident groups of intellectuals in Czechoslovakia, Hungary, and Romania are more active and overt in their protest; even juvenile delinquency has taken on political overtones as police baiting and anti-Russian demonstrations have become something of a popular sport in East Germany.[46]

Crackdowns against dissident intellectuals and workers, which certainly can be expected to intensify, cannot in the long run serve as a substitute for legitimacy. They can merely forestall the ultimate day of reckoning unless these regimes can use the breathing space to improve their economic situation or to transform the basis of their support. The former solution seems most unlikely since the governments in question have very little power to influence the economic parameters such as energy and raw material costs that constrict their growth. They also appear to lack the will to carry out the kind of internal reforms that would be required to improve economic performance.

The high watermark of economic experimentation in Eastern Europe has already been passed. It was reached in the 1960s when Pact leaders had their greatest feeling of security and independence. East Germany led the way in 1963 with the adoption of its New Economic System. Two years later, Hungary began to implement the principles that in 1968 became known as the New Economic Mechanism. Bulgaria, Poland, and Czechoslovakia subsequently introduced their own variants of reform. All of these efforts were characterized by some degree of economic decentralization and greater worker participation in decision making. Hungary and Czechoslovakia went the furthest in the direction of decentralization by introducing some market mechanisms at the factory level. Hungary and Poland implemented the greatest degree of worker participation through the device of workers' councils. The Soviet Union blessed all of these departures from economic orthodoxy and, despite intervention in Czechoslovakia, permitted the Hungarians and Poles to continue experimentation.[47]

For the most part these reform efforts have now been abandoned--East Germany has largely reversed its economic policy and Czechoslovakia returned to orthodoxy after the overthrow of Dubcek. Only Hungary, still committed to the New Economic Mechanism, is preparing to introduce new reforms. There is no evidence that any of these reversals were carried out in response to Soviet pressure; rather, they seem to have been the result of indigenous concern that decentralization, which of necessity requires some degree of democratization, courts loss of control over the political process by the Party. This was one of the lessons other Pact leaders drew from Czechoslovakia; a lesson reinforced, no doubt, by the more recent Polish experience. It has made these leaders less rather than more willing to engage in economic and political experimentation.[48]

Pact leaders must nevertheless do something to revitalize the faltering legitimacy of their regimes; one possible strategy is to make them into vehicles for the expression of national feeling. Such sentiment has always run deeply throughout Eastern Europe and, as the Romanians have demonstrated, can be tapped as an important source of support.

The Romanian experience is interesting for what it reveals about both the possibilities and the limits of national independence within the Warsaw Pact. The Romanian bid for freedom opened with a flourish: the establishment of relations with Germany, maintenance of ties with Israel during and after 1967, and then condemnation of the Soviet invasion of Czechoslovakia. However, in the aftermath of Czechoslovakia, the Soviets are rumored to have twice threatened to intervene in Romania and, at the very least, have kept steady pressure on Ceausescu. He, in turn, has been careful to avoid overstepping the boundary of what Moscow defines as acceptable. Ceausescu's more dramatic gestures of defiance, for which he still retains a flair, must be seen in this light. His friendship with China, lavish welcome of Chairman Hua to Bucharest, and well-publicized refusal to increase defense spending in accord with Warsaw Pact guidelines--all appear to have had tacit support of the other Eastern European members of the Pact which made it difficult for the Soviets to do more than protest verbally. Without such backing it is unlikely that Ceausescu would have acted.[49]

Other members of the alliance have only a limited ability to play the Romanian game. To begin with, Romania's quasi-independence in foreign policy is made possible, at least in part, by the fact that the other allies adhere to a more orthodox line. If all or even several of them attempted to follow Romania's example, the pursuit of an independent foreign policy by any ally would become less acceptable to Moscow. Most Pact leaders also remain fearful of the possible domestic consequences of a more national foreign policy. For several of them, an upsurge in nationalism could exacerbate nationality problems they have gone to some lengths to resolve or at least to diffuse. It might also involve them in conflicts with their neighbors as some of the territorial controversies that have always divided

Eastern European peoples from one another have never really been settled. The recurring tensions between Hungary and Romania over the treatment of the Hungarian minority in Romania is a case in point. For the German Democratic Republic, a revival of nationalism would damage that regime's legitimacy because it would highlight its role as the defender of the independence of a rump state. German nationalism is also unacceptable to other members of the Pact, all of whom retain vivid memories of World War II. One must suppose that Eastern Europe's leaders also have some residual ideological commitment to the principle of proletarian internationalism and would find too strong a tilt in the direction of nationalism anathema to their own political values.

These caveats aside, there are still some rewards to be reaped by a government tapping national feeling in Eastern Europe provided that such a strategy can be carefully managed and controlled. In this regard, it is important to note the shift in the focus of nationalism that has taken place in most of these countries. Past nationalism in Eastern Europe most frequently found expression in the form of hostility to neighboring peoples. In the first instance these peoples were singled out because--as in the case of the Germans, Hungarians, and Turks--they clung tenaciously to their dominion over empires that stood in the way of the independence of most of the region's nationalities. Neighboring peoples were also the object of hostility because of competing territorial claims. Finally, for reasons that varied from country to country, nationalism also took the form of anti-semitism. With the exception of the Poles and the Ukranians, the Slavic nationalities of Eastern Europe were well disposed toward Russia; they saw her as a useful ally in their struggle for independence. Today, the cast of villians has changed. The old empires are gone; so are the Jews. Even many conflicting territorial claims were rendered moot by the population transfers that took place at the end of World War II. The Soviet empire and its Russian rulers, for the most part, have taken the place of these traditional enemies for the peoples of the Warsaw Pact. Every Pact nationality, except possibly the Bulgarians, views the Soviets as a major impediment to meaningful independence. They are also resented for their heavy-handed efforts to spread their culture and language through the region. Anti-Russian feeling is a potent force throughout Eastern Europe and is strong enough to have created bonds of sympathy between traditional enemies like the Poles and Czechs.

Superficially, the rising tide of anti-Soviet sentiment lends itself to exploitation by governments anxious to improve their popular standing. At the same time, there are very real limits as to how far any of the governments can permit such feelings to be expressed or pander to them in surreptitious ways before incurring the wrath of the Soviet Union. This constraint is most obvious in East Germany and Czechoslovakia, whose leaders are particularly dependent upon Soviet support, but it may actually be greater for countries bordering the Soviet Union--such as Poland and Romania, who have restive co-nationals residing within their borders. Demonstrating national independence from the Soviet Union could be analogized to walking a tightrope. The acrobat who attempts it attracts everyone's attention and even admiration, but one false step in any direction and the act quickly comes to an end, often with tragic consequences. Nevertheless, an experienced politician, like an experienced acrobat, can still negotiate the high wire with success.

To the extent that Eastern European leaders choose, or perhaps, feel compelled to express their independence from Moscow, there are several political-military issue areas over which they might string their symbolic high wire. The first of these pertains to Soviet foreign policy outside of Europe. Eastern Europeans, like their Western counterparts, sometimes feel that their regional interests are sacrificed in favor of the global interests of their hegemon. They become concerned whenever Moscow gets involved in conflicts elsewhere in the world for fear of the variety of possible adverse consequences to themselves. Not infrequently, they resist Moscow's efforts to involve them by, at least, eliciting their verbal support. The Sino-Soviet split is a case in point. Following the Ussuri River clash in 1969, Moscow tried and failed to get its Pact allies to issue a declaration in support of its position. The next year the allies reacted negatively to Moscow's urging that the Pact recognize defensive obligations in Asia as well as in Europe. A few Eastern European officials specifically denied that they were compelled by existing arrangements to come to the Soviet Union's aid in the event of a war with China.[50]

More recently, Eastern European leaders are reported to have been displeased by Soviet intervention in Afghanistan. Eastern Europeans, in general, become alarmed whenever Soviet troops march across national borders. The Romanians are certainly the most fearful in this regard and Ceausescu has made no secret of his opposition to the invasion. Even Bulgaria, normally outspoken in favor of all Soviet initiatives, has tried to maintain the lowest possible profile on this issue.

Poland and Hungary also have been less than fully supportive and have been particularly concerned with the implications of Afghanistan for East-West relations. Both countries are sufficiently dependent upon the West for financial support that any renewal of the Cold War is viewed as a serious threat to their economies. Along with the other Eastern Europeans, they also have a political interest in continuing detente because the degree of independence they have at home and abroad expands when East-West tensions ease and contracts when they intensify.[51]

Should the war in Afghanistan lead to a further deterioration in Soviet-American relations, the Eastern Europeans would have an even greater incentive to dissociate themselves from Soviet policy. Fortunately for them, that conflict already seems to have become something of a forgotten war in the West. Unless Moscow were to attack Pakistan for providing a sanctuary for Afghan rebels, Soviet conduct of the war is unlikely to provoke a new crisis with the West. Such a crisis is more likely to come about as the result of a Soviet invasion of Poland, especially if that invasion meets enough resistance to compel the Soviets to use force in a massive or prolonged manner. Even if the Poles did not resist, some Pact leaders would still have compelling reasons for speaking out against the Soviet invasion. It would be a necessary step toward maintaining political and economic ties with the West without which their countries would become even more dependent upon the Soviet Union. In some Eastern capitals, a certain distance from the Soviet Union in the aftermath of her invasion of a 'fraternal socialist ally' might also be necessary for domestic political reasons.

The really interesting question is the long-term effect of a Soviet invasion upon the stability of the other Eastern European regimes. On the one hand, it would expose the pretense of communist leaders--even of Ceausescu and Kadar--to being heads of sovereign states but, on the other, would emphasize to disgruntled workers and dissident intellectuals the extent to which the exercise of national independence must remain circumscribed. In all likelihood, the strength of these divergent political vectors would vary from country to country, encouraging their leaders to choose a differing mix of independence from and reliance upon the Soviet Union. This, in turn, would almost certainly weaken the cohesion of the Warsaw Pact, but might conceivably facilitate Soviet control of that alliance by reason of the differences among the allies that Moscow could then exploit.

A second and less speculative way in which Eastern Europeans might be expected to stake out greater independence from Moscow is by attempting to establish their own priorities with regard to defense spending and policy. Once again Romania has led the way. As far back as 1963, Romania asserted the principle of national control over the armed forces and defense policy. In November 1964, Bucharest unilaterally reduced the term of national service and subsequently began to model her armed forces more on the Yugoslav concept of 'total national defense'. In May 1966, Ceausescu called for "the abolition of military blocs, the dismantling of foreign bases, and the withdrawal of foreign troops from the territory of other countries".[52] Since then, Romania has entered into an agreement with Yugoslavia for the co-production of a fighter-trainer and has purchased French Alouette III helicopters and eleven Chinese naval vessels.[53]

Many of Ceausescu's moves have been quietly applauded by other Eastern Europeans. His most popular initiatives, internally, are unquestionably those that have reduced Romania's defense burden which now constitutes 2.5 percent of the national income, the lowest level of expenditure in the Warsaw Pact.[54] Burden sharing has always been an issue in that alliance as Eastern Europeans haggle with Moscow over their fair share of defense expenditures, the terms of payment for the Soviet weapons with which their armed forces are equipped, and about other ways of offsetting the cost to the Soviets of stationing large numbers of troops on their territory. The financial side of defense policy can be expected to become a more acute issue between the Soviets and their Pact allies as all of these states enter into a period of economic decline.

Any efforts to reduce defense expenditures are almost certain to be opposed by the military establishments of the Eastern European countries. More importantly, they will be opposed by the Soviet union, anxious, one must assume, to match or surpass any improvement in NATO's military capabilities in the 1980s. The ability of all the Eastern European states to reduce their defense expenditures in defiance of Soviet wishes is limited because of their dependence upon Moscow for raw materials and energy supplies; but, as Eastern Europeans know, the Soviets would also pay a heavy economic and political price if they punished the Eastern Europeans for reducing their defense outlays. At the same time, most of these countries, citing the Polish experience, could justify delays in military modernization programs in order to ease the pressure for other kinds of economic sacrifices that are likely to threaten their political stability. So the entire question remains an area for negotiation. It is to be expected that the Pact allies will drive increasingly hard bargains with regard to both their level of defense expenditure and what they can expect to get from the Soviets in return. In the aftermath of a Polish invasion, this process would almost certainly become quite fractious.

The Eastern Europeans may also demand a stronger voice in alliance military policy in the coming decade. This can be viewed as yet another way for leaders to emphasize the national nature and purpose of their institutions. Here too, Romania has been something of a pioneer. In 1966, the Romanians were alleged to have circulated a document decrying Soviet domination of the Warsaw Pact.[55] Other members of the Pact have for some years allowed their military intellectuals to publish articles calling for both allied participation in the formulation of Pact doctrine and the development of national military doctrines to supplement it.[56] Not surprisingly, the Soviets have resisted these ideas and have insisted instead upon even tighter doctrinal integration. From the Soviet point of view, uniform doctrine, weapons, and command and control significantly enhance the military effectiveness of the alliance. In their efforts to achieve this goal, they have brought into being a cadre of highly professional Eastern European officers. This military elite is even less likely than its predecessors to remain satisfied with their assigned role as junior partners to the Soviets. A. Ross Johnson observes:

> "If segments of the East European military elites indeed become dissatisfied on professional grounds with their status vis-a-vis the Soviet Union, then one should expect the future development 'from below', on professional institutional grounds, of national sentiments within the East European military establishments that would reinforce the more familiar autonomous military sentiments developing on national political grounds 'from above' as manifested in Czechoslovakia and Romania."[57]

Looking ahead, it may well be the nuclear issue that will catalyze the development of divergent military doctrine 'from below' and greater concern for national military prerogatives 'from above'. Similar to NATO allies, the Pact members have always feared becoming nuclear victims in any East-West Europan war. East Germany, Poland, and Czechoslovakia are the most vulnerable in this regard as all three are forward staging areas for any Soviet offensive in the West.[58] At times, the Czechoslovaks and the Poles have quite openly voiced their concern, although the issue of nuclear weapons and their development per se has remained a muted one within the Pact. The Soviet Union, which alone possesses these weapons, has been--as far as we know--unwilling to discuss with her allies their deployment and use in any but the most general terms. This may become a source of friction in the future.

If deployment of the SS-20 has heightened Western European anxieties about nuclear devastation, NATO's deployment of the Pershing II can be expected to do the same in the East. Clearly, the two situations are not entirely analogous. For one thing, very different political systems are involved. Theater nuclear force modernization (TNF) has therefore triggered a greater controversy in Western Europe where its various modes of basing and their implications are openly debated. On the Eastern side, allied acquiesence to Soviet TNF basing is not at issue as the SS-20 is already being deployed. The Eastern Europeans nevertheless know, despite all the publicity about the capability of the Pershing II to reach targets in the western military districts of the USSR, that most of these missiles will probably be aimed at targets in their countries. Public opinion in the East cannot help but also become increasingly aware of this reality. The Soviet political offensive against the Pershing, NATO's equally vocal linkage of its deployment to that of the SS-20, and the West European left's opposition to all nuclear weapons--this at a time when Eastern Europe has become ever more permeable to information and ideas from the West--will give the nuclear question much greater salience in these countries than would have been true in the past. The anti-nuclear movement may conceivably find an echo in the East, especially in Poland and Czechoslovakia where ties to Western intellectuals are close.

Of necessity, the Pact governments must approach the nuclear question with caution. With the exception of Romania they could not oppose deployment of SS-20s on their soil. Such opposition would not only be ineffective, it would make them "bundnisunfähig" (lacking credibility as worthy allies) in the eyes of Moscow and it would undercut their efforts to gain a wider voice in alliance military policy. However, popular sentiment against nuclear weapons could prove a useful lever to pry from the Soviets some concessions with regard to their use. A reasonable objective in this regard, although hardly one likely to be well received by Moscow, would be prior consultation and approval of the use of nuclear weapons in a European conflict. In theory, this would give the Pact allies as much authority over nuclear weapons as their Western counterparts possess. Needless to say, it would be one more way in which Eastern European governments would, if they succeeded, demonstrate both their independence and concern for the welfare of their peoples.

The several political-military areas that we have examined present possibilities for exploitation as issues by Eastern European leaderships concerned with the erosion of their legitimacy and anxious to put their regimes' elites on a firmer national footing. This does not mean that all or even some of these elites will pursue such a strategy or pursue it to the extent of the preceding speculation. In all probability they will not. The reason for this has less to do with objective political realities than it does with the political rigor mortis of most of these political elites which makes them less sensitive to the problems their regimes face and less responsive to imaginative ways of coping with them. Like Poland's leaders they are likely to minimize the import, or even deny the existence, of some kinds of problems until they cause an explosion that is too loud to ignore and perhaps too powerful to control. As any serious effort to come to grips with them might lead to a purge of present leaders, denial may actually be the most appropriate strategy for them to follow. However, the present decade is likely to witness the passing of an entire generation of leaders from positions of power in these countries.[59] The generation that replaces them may be no less hidebound by bureaucratic tradition but, nevertheless, more willing to court Soviet disfavor in attempting to cope with the social, economic and political problems they inherit.

MOSCOW'S DILEMMA IN EASTERN EUROPE

The 1980s will be a turbulent time for Eastern Europe because of the crisis of legitimacy that many of its governments will confront. This crisis will threaten the cohesion of the Warsaw Pact regardless of how Eastern European leaderships choose to respond to it. As for the Soviet Union, it probably has only a marginal capability to ease the crisis, but could make matters much worse depending upon its response. Moscow's sensitivity to Eastern Europe's domestic problems and tolerance of its leader's efforts to cope with them will determine whether or not the Warsaw Pact endures as an alliance of any political and military value to the Soviet Union.

Change in Eastern Europe can come about in two ways: gradual change imposed from above, or more radical change forced from below. The former would be the most advantageous to Soviet interests but is also the least probable because Eastern Europe's leaders are unlikely to experiment with reform when they feel threatened. The experience of the seventies reveals that in such circumstances they take refuge in orthodoxy and do nothing that might risk loss of party control and, with it, their hold on power. Moscow would be well advised to prod Eastern European policymakers in the direction of reform, the same way they pushed a reluctant DDR into embracing detente and Ostpolitik. Reforms might help Eastern European governments to maintain popular support. Of necessity, Soviet toleration of internal reforms and their external counterpart--more nationally-oriented foreign and defense policies--would require restructuring the Warsaw Pact. The alliance would have to be put on a more democratic footing and Moscow would have to pay more attention to the needs of its allies. However, such a policy seems nothing short of inconceivable, for Marxist-Leninists are not known to foster pluralism willingly. Nor, does history offer examples of hegemons voluntarily relinquishing the reins of power over alliances they dominate. To the extent that the Soviet Union feels threatened, it is far more likely to seek even tighter control over its allies. This suggests that change, if and when it comes, will be forced from below as it was in Poland; as a result, it will appear even more distasteful and threatening to Moscow.

It is difficult to believe that Moscow can tolerate revisionism in Eastern Europe regardless of its source. Change from above or below ultimately threatens to lead to the same outcome: the transformation of the communist parties of those states into more democratic institutions and with it the purge from power of orthodox and pro-Soviet officials. This would not only reduce Soviet influence in Eastern Europe but would lead to much more independent foreign and defense policies by making their communist parties more responsive to public opinion. Either development would have profound and immediate repercussions throughout Eastern Europe and, possibly, in the Soviet Union as well.

For this reason the Soviets appear to subscribe to their own "domino theory", and one that makes more sense than the American fear in the 1960s of falling dominoes in southeast Asia. As did the Czars before them, Soviet leaders believe that liberalization anywhere within their Eastern European empire will lead to demands for similar freedoms within the Soviet Union itself. If one Pact ally pursues a course seen as too independent, either at home or abroad, all are endangered. If all or even one of the Soviet Union's immediate neighbors ever succeeded in establishing freedom, it would make Soviet control of the Baltic republics and the Ukraine more difficult as both regions are populated by nationalities which are resentful of Russian rule and quiescent only out of their respect for Soviet power. Thus Moscow felt the need to crush the workers' rising in East Germany in 1953, invade Hungary in 1956 and Czechoslovakia in 1968. It is why it will probably choose ultimately to invade Poland.

The alternative policy open to Moscow, that of maintaining political orthodoxy in Eastern Europe, has its superficial attractions but may result in an equally disastrous outcome. Beyond the dramatic and quite visible costs of military intervention in Poland, there are the less obvious costs of maintaining orthodoxy by more subtle means. Soviet domination of the foreign and domestic policies of her allies has seriously impaired the utility of the Warsaw Pact and is in the process of turning it into the mere shell of an alliance.

From the Soviet perspective, the Pact has functioned first and foremost as a means of ensuring the survival of pro-Soviet governments. Dale R. Herspring and Ivan Volgyes, nevertheless, point out that, in the seven cases known to them, Warsaw Pact armies have refused to come to the support of their governments when they were confronted by serious internal unrest.[60] The most recent example, Poland in 1980-1981, makes the score eight to zero. The Polish military is alleged to have been acutely sensitive to the divisions within the armed forces regarding internal developments in Poland; thus, the army has been kept out of politics in order to preserve it. The divisions within the Polish armed forces are said to reflect generational differences in outlook; that a much greater proportion of younger than older officers oppose using force against Solidarity. To the degree that this generational cleavage exists, it portends even greater military aloofness in the future from the fate of communist regimes, perhaps not only in Poland, but elsewhere in Eastern Europe as well.[61]

A second way in which the Pact forces have been useful to the Soviets in maintaining acceptable governments in Eastern Europe is through intervention, or threat of intervention, in neighboring socialists states which have succumbed to revisionism of one kind or another. However, Moscow's ability to send these armies across fraternal frontiers seems to have diminished considerably in recent years. For reasons already analyzed, the Polish situation has revealed considerable reluctance on the part of Pact armies and their governments to intervene in neighboring socialist states--especially if there is any prospect of meeting resistance. Ironically, Soviet success in mobilizing the support and participation of East German, Polish, Hungarian, and Bulgarian forces for the invasion of Czechoslovakia in 1968 would make their failure to muster Pact support for any contemplated move into Poland all the more politically consequential.

Finally, there is the question of Pact participation in any European conflict. Here too, there is a certain irony in the conclusions that must be drawn about the reliability of these forces. In the late fifties and early sixties, when Pact armies were poorly equipped and only marginally integrated within the Soviet command structure, they were generally believed to be unreliable in any war with the West. Since that time, the Soviets have made a herculean effort to upgrade and standardize Pact weapons with their own, to integrate Pact armies into a Soviet dominated, supra-national chain of command, and to train allied officers to work together with their Soviet colleagues in combined maneuvers and exercises. The end result, according to at least some observers, has been to produce far more effective but even less reliable military forces.[62]

The response of the Pact countries to any East-West war can be expected to vary from country to country--East Germany probably remains the most faithful ally and Romania the least. Pact reaction will also be a function of the nature of political situations from which such a conflict develops. Since Pact forces are geared for the offensive, any offensive that could be portrayed as a means of forestalling West German aggression would be the scenario most likely to gain support. Nothing else would quite convey the same sense of threat, especially to Poland and Czechoslovakia. Herspring and Volgyes speculate that Soviet setbacks in a war with either the West or China might even tempt some of the Eastern European states to use their armies to expel Soviet forces from their territory. Realistic or not, this scenario is certainly one that must have occurred to some Russians; it illustrates how the unreliability of their allies poses a threat to their security. Modernization of the Pact armies, originally envisaged by Khruschev as a way to reduce the number of Soviet forces in Eastern Europe, now requires an even greater number of Soviet forces to keep an eye on these highly capable armies--in wartime, this need would become greater still.

Put in the starkest terms, Moscow might be said to face a 'no win' situation in Eastern Europe. To the extent that it insists upon orthodoxy, it further undermines the reliability and hence the utility of the Warsaw Pact. But to the degree that it permits revisionism to flourish, it threatens the very cornerstone of its European policy. For psychologists, this is the classic "defensive avoidance" situation. A person, or in this instance a group of policymakers, will suffer from psychological stress when they realize there is a risk of serious loss associated with any course of action open to them. People often respond to such a situation by procrastinating, rationalizing, and denying their responsibility for a decision. If compelled to act, they will choose the least objectionable alternative, exaggerate its positive consequences, and minimize its negative ones. They will subsequently ward off anxiety by practicing selective attention and other forms of distorted information processing. Needless to say, such a pattern of coping, whose hallmark is insensitivity to critical information, is hardly conducive to good decisionmaking.[63]

Soviet policymakers give every indication of having resorted, for some years now, to defensive avoidance to cope with the problems of Eastern Europe. They have required members of the Warsaw Pact to follow their political directives with regard to both domestic and foreign policy, but have refused to recognize the costs to themselves of insisting upon such slavishness. This is apparent in every aspect of their Eastern European policy. In the economic realm they have continued to use the vehicle of CMEA to impose the very kind of central planning and cumbersome decisionmaking that has greatly contributed to Eastern Europe's economic stagnation. When discontent has erupted, they have dismissed it as the handiwork of counter-revolutionaries and have encouraged their clients to respond with a mixture of repression and cosmetic reform. Despite the questionable reliability of the Pact allies, they continue to demand the build-up of their military forces and to act as if these forces could be used as simple extensions of Soviet power. They have taken refuge in what might be called the 'snappy salute' syndrome; the illusion that pressed pants, polished buttons, and peacetime responsiveness to Moscow's doctrine and directions signifies commitment to the Soviet cause.

Soviet defensive avoidance is in the first place attributable to the absence of any acceptable alternatives to current Soviet policy in Eastern Europe. Recognition of this disturbing reality would clearly constitute an assault upon the psychological well-being of Soviet leaders. Instead, they have adhered to established policy and have sought to minimize or ignore its long-term adverse consequences. But events in Poland are threatening to Soviet leaders in an even more fundamental way--they are indicative of a more general failing of the Soviet system, not only in Eastern Europe but at home. The Soviet economy is in a shambles, with the agricultural sector being a particular disaster. Corruption is rife at every level of Soviet society. Few of its citizens give any indication of believing in Marxism-Leninism as a progressive force. Visitors to the Soviet Union report that the ordinary Russian has lost faith in what he calls his "unworkable system". One experienced and respected observer of the Soviet scene writes:

> "Millions of people feel cheated of their hopes, ideals, and self-respect, but have no idea how to regain them. There is no alternative to Soviet rule, no genuine debate, no real information; only a pervasive aimlessness from having reached a dead end from which the nation cannot extricate itself. _Bezizhodnost_, the word most people used to sum up their condition, is literally "exitlessness"."[64]

Even allowing for the usual hyperbole on the part of Soviet emigres and Western writers, the current state of affairs in the Soviet Union represents a perversion of the Communist vision of a better world. When they were young, many members of the current generation of Soviet leaders must have internalized that vision. To varying degrees, it imbued their life with a sense of ideological purpose. During their long careers it must also have provided them with a justification for, rather than merely an outward rationalization of, the many moral compromises they were forced to make--especially during the Stalin era. Now in their old age, knowledge of the progress their country has made at home and the stature it has achieved abroad, justifies their life work and vindicates the sacrifices, physical and moral, that they have made. They are emotionally unprepared to recognize the way in which they and the system they represent are actually viewed by the masses for whom, in the abstract, they have labored for so long. They must erect whatever defenses they can to preserve their illusions as they are so central to the core of their own identities.

Soviet denial of disconfiting realities at home and in Eastern Europe has assumed a variety of forms. The most apparent is suppression of dissent. Politicians in a democracy must ignore or repress criticism that is psychologically disturbing, but the leaders of a police state can indulge in the luxury of physically suppressing those who voice it. The intensified campaign against Soviet dissidents in recent years should probably be viewed in this light. A small circle of persecuted intellectuals does not constitute a political threat as much as it represents a psychological one. By most accounts, the like of Solzhenitsyn, Sakharov, and the Medvedevs have made very little headway in fostering political dissent among the Soviet masses; but, they have succeeded through their writings in confronting Soviet officialdom with its failures at home and abroad as well as warning of some possible consequences. Soviet leaders have been so harsh with dissidents precisely because dissent forces them to acknowledge some of the realities they want so desperately to ignore. Certainly, the Soviet response of heavy-handed suppression has otherwise been counterproductive; it has caused them unnecessary embarrassment abroad--even some real political problems--by widely publicizing the evils of the Soviet system in the West. Surely, a policy of surveillance, censorship, and harassments carried out by more subtle means than expulsion and incarceration in mental institutions would have accomplished the same goal at less cost. To the extent that campaigns against dissidents are as much a response to psychological as to political needs, we should expect them to intensify in the future as the domestic and foreign policy dilemmas of the Soviet Union become more acute.

For the same reason, criticism within the Soviet bureaucracy has not been well received and may become even less so in the future. Selective attention, denial, and almost any other psychological tactic used by policymakers to cope with threatening information can be institutionalized. Merely by making their expectations and preferences known, policymakers can encourage their subordinates to report or emphasize information supportive of those expectations and preferences. By actually punishing those who dissent or criticize, they can, in effect, rig intelligence channels so that they receive only the kind of information and analyses they want to hear. Such a process may conceivably be underway or have already affected those elements of the foreign ministry, the military, and the intelligence agencies concerned with Eastern Europe; indeed, it may help to explain why they were so unprepared for the upheaval in Poland and so belated in recognizing its magnitude.[65]

Personal and institutional defenses are not always effective in protecting policymakers from threatening information. Fresh evidence of an unambiguous kind may break through these defenses and confront them with the reality they seek to deny. Such breakthroughs can encourage adaptive behavior; it can also compel policymakers to adopt even more extreme defense mechanisms to cope with the anxiety the information generates. The upheaval in Poland probably constitutes such an event; it has been dramatic enough to have shattered whatever defenses the Soviets had erected to protect themselves from the disquieting realities of Eastern Europe.

In this sense, Poland constitutes a crisis on two levels. Politically, it confronts Soviet leaders with a challenge to their hegemony in Eastern Europe. One, moreoever, that forces them to choose between the evils of orthodoxy imposed and maintained from the outside and the evils of revisionism generated from within. Psychologically, it can be said to constitute a challenge to the political mental health of the Soviet leadership. Poland presents them with the 'opportunity' to recognize that the political realities of Eastern Europe are quite different from what they have been pretending, and that any attempt they make to maintain their faltering hegemony is fraught with serious implications.

Will the Soviets rise to this cognitive challenge? Or, will they resort to even more elaborate defenses to shield themselves from the import of the Polish upheaval and to allow them to maintain the illusion that Poland is somehow a special case? The answer to this question is critical because it will probably determine the Soviet response to events in Poland. If Soviet leaders are prepared to face the hard truths of their situation, they are more likely to accept the need for some degree of political change in Poland as a necessary step towards putting their relations with all of Eastern Europe on a surer and more realistic footing. To the extent that they are unprepared to face reality, they are likely to insist upon greater ideological orthodoxy throughout their realm as a necessary defense against future political challenges.

Insistence upon orthodoxy, the more likely of the two responses, will only succeed in postponing the inevitable upheaval. It is also likely to make it more cataclysmic when it comes. A fault in the earth where the stresses built up by two opposing plates are unrelieved by occasional slippage ultimately results in an earthquake. These events are characterized by a sudden spike or fracture which generates waves of spreading destruction outward from the epicenter. Soviet rigidity in Eastern Europe would prevent the kinds of political and economic adjustments that are necessary to relieve the fast-building pressures in that region. In the end, this would result in a political earthquake whose reverberations across the European continent might rival the worst natural disaster in their destructiveness.

CONCLUSIONS

The Soviet dilemma in Eastern Europe has disturbing implications for East-West relations, regardless of which course Moscow ultimately chooses to follow. For reasons already discussed, Soviet leaders are not cognitively prepared to recognize the revolution in Poland as representing the failure of Marxism-Leninism. Whether or not they intervene in that country, they still have a real need to explain away the causes of the Polish revolution.

It is interesting to observe that almost from the beginning, Soviet leaders charged the West with abetting and even fomenting the Polish troubles. Early on, there was a hue and outcry from Moscow when American labor leaders offered their moral support and some financial backing to Solidarity. Subsequently, Soviet spokesmen have accused the United States and Western Europe of waging a campaign of "counter-revolution" and "radio aggression".[66] It would probably be a mistake to dismiss these charges as mere propaganda aimed at preparing domestic public opinion for Soviet intervention in Poland. While this may well be their avowed objective, it is likely that Soviet leaders themselves give some credence to those charges which provide a far more comforting explanation of what is happening in Poland than does the truth. For attributing it all to capitalist and fascist or, worse still, Zionist machinations permits them to continue to believe that the system they have imposed upon Eastern Europe is really in the best interest of its peoples. If this argument seems to strain credulity, the reader is reminded of the well-documented and even more far-fetched rationalizations that American officials devised to explain the "loss" of China in 1949 and to preserve their self-image as China's long-time admired friend and big brother in the face of acute Chinese hostility.[67]

To the extent that Soviet officials seek refuge in their own propaganda, it is bound to confirm their convictions about Western hostility. It is also likely to heighten their sense of the vulnerability of Eastern Europe to Western penetration and subversion. The insecurity that this engenders must be understood in reference to the other developments that will shape the Soviet's assessment of their world position in the course of the coming decade.

The 1980s do not promise a bright future for the Soviet Union. At home, a lower growth rate, or even economic stagnation, is certain to require greater civilian sacrifices in order to maintain high levels of defense spending. This may or may not intensify popular disaffection from the regime. Nationality problems, especially in Central Asia, but perhaps in the Baltic republics as well, are likely to become more acute and may confront the system with serious challenges. Abroad, the Soviet position will deteriorate, especially with regard to the military balance. In the Far East, Chinese hostility, which is unlikely to abate, will be more dangerous because of Peking's growing nuclear arsenal. For the first time, China will deploy systems capable of devastating the Soviet heartland. In Europe, NATO's continuing modernization of both nuclear and conventional forces will significantly improve its position vis-à-vis the Warsaw Pact. If these military developments are paralleled by closer political collaboration among Moscow's many enemies, Soviet leaders may begin to feel that a global noose is tightening around them. To some extent, they may be right. At the very least, Sino-American military cooperation can be expected to increase. Japan and Western Europe may also draw closer to Washington and Peking if they are made to feel more insecure by reason of Soviet belligerence or adventurism.[68]

For all of these reasons, Soviet leaders are certain to see themselves on the defensive. Historically, policymakers in such situations have exaggerated, not minimized, the extent of their own weakness. As Thucydides documented in the Melian Dialogue, they also exhibit an exaggerated concern for their credibility, convinced that any sign of weakness of their part will only elicit more aggressive behavior from their adversaries and less loyalty from their allies. American policymakers have currently been displaying such a neurotic response to their decline in the aftermath of Indochina, the Soviet strategic buildup and, more recently, events in Iran and Afghanistan. The Soviet dilemma, which objectively is much greater in magnitude and more enduring in its consequences, can be expected to engender an even more irrational and pessimistic outlook among Soviet leaders. Such fear for the future on their part does not bode well for the security of either superpower.

In this context, it is well to remember history's first well-documented clash between rival hegemons: the conflict that pitted the Athenian alliance against the Lacaedemonian Confederacy. The increasingly desperate actions of Athenian leaders, very much on the defensive and concerned for their survival and that of their empire, helped to bring on the Peloponnesian War. The reader can use his own imagination to conjure up Soviet analogs to the Megarian Decree, the Corcyrean Alliance or later the Melian Expedition. Be it an intervention in Poland or Romania or a demarche in the Far East, Soviet spokesmen would undoubtedly find the words put by the Athenian envoys to the Spartan Assembly on the eve of the Peloponnesian war a sufficient and compelling justification of their own behavior:

> "And the nature of the case first compelled us to advance our empire to its present height; fear being our principal motive, though honour and interest afterwards came in. And at last, when almost all hated us, when some had already revolted and had been subdued, when you had ceased to be the friends that you once were, and had become objects of suspicion and dislike, it appeared no longer safe to give up our empire; especially as all who left us would fall to you. And no one can quarrel with a people for making, in matters of tremendous risk, the best provision that it can for its interest."[69]

FOOTNOTES

1. The two alliances differ in that the Athenian alliance developed in the course of the war with Persia whereas the Warsaw Pact was brought into being ten years after the war against Germany. It was organized to replace the bilateral alliances between the Soviet Union and its members which had been imposed during, or right after, the war.

2. Certain parallels are notable also with regard to Athenian and Spartan vulnerabilities. The war having been fought on their territories, both hegemons were physically devastated and economically exhausted while their principal post-war adversaries had emerged from that conflict unscathed. The Athenians were vulnerable to Spartan power because their city and port were unprotected by a wall. Under the leadership of Thermistocles, they made the hasty and furtive construction of fortifications their first priority. The Soviets were vulnerable because of American possession of nuclear weapons; hence, Stalin made the development of these weapons a top post-war priority.

3. On the origins and evolution of the Warsaw Pact, see Thomas W. Wolfe, Soviet Power and Europe, 1945-1970. (Baltimore: Johns Hopkins University Press, 1970); Malcolm Makintosh, The Evolution of the Warsaw Pact. Adelphi Paper No. 58 (London: Institute for Strategic Studies, 1969); Robin Remington, "The Changing Soviet Perception of the Warsaw Pact," (Cambridge: MIT Center for International Studies, 1967); idem, The Warsaw Pact: Case Studies in Communist Conflict Resolution. (Cambridge: MIT Press, 1971); and Stephan Tiedtke, Die Warschauer Vertragsorganisation (Munich: Oldenbourg, 1978).

4. Roman Kolkowicz, Continuity and Change in the Warsaw Pact, (Santa Monica: The RAND Corporation), p. 22.

5. Idem, "The Warsaw Pact: Entangling Alliance," Survey No. 70/71 (1969), p. 101.

6. Central Intelligence Agency, Handbook of Economic Statistics, 1980. (Washington, D.C., Government Printing Office, 1980), p.11

7. Ibid., p. 28.

8. Ibid.; Figures of 2 percent for 1979 and 4.3 percent for 1980 are given by the Economist (London), 14

February 1981, citing a report presented to the Polish Politburo by Tadeusz Grabski on 9 February 1981; Warsaw PAP English language broadcasts, 8 and 11 February 1980. _FBIS-EEU_, pp. G/-10; _The Washington Post_ (3 Jul. 81), reporting a speech by Zbniew Madej, Poland's Minister of Planning, made to the Sejm on 2 July.

9. _The New York Times_ (12 April and 2 June 1981).

10. _Handbook of Economic Statistics_, p. 39

11. For a discussion of the Soviet energy problem and its impact upon Eastern Europe, see: United States Central Intelligence Agency, _Soviet Prospects for Oil Production_, and, _The International Energy Situation--The Outlook to 1985_. (Washington, D.C.: Government Printing Office, 1977); Marshall I. Goldman, "Is there a Russian Energy Crisis?" _Atlantic_, 246 (September 1980), pp. 55-64; Edward A. Hewett, "Soviet Energy: Supply vs. Demand," _Problems of Communism_, 29 (January-February 1980), pp. 53-60; John M. Dramer, "Between Scylla and Charybis: The Politics of Eastern Europe's Energy Problem," _Orbis_ 22 (Winter 1979), pp. 929-50.

12. On this subject, see Ernst Kux, "Growing Tensions in Eastern Europe," _Problems of Communism_ 29 (March-April 1980), pp. 21-37; Robert R. King and James F. Brown eds., _Eastern Europe's Uncertain Future: A Selection of Radio Free Europe Research Reports_. (New York: Praeger, 1977).

13. Speech at Katowice, 10 December 1979, in _FBIS-EEU_, 13 December 1979, p. G/6.

14. Dusko Doder, _The Washington Post_ (19 September and 14 October 1980); _Le Figaro_, Paris, (1 September 1980). On Moscow's efforts to improve the image of Soviet labor unions, see _The Washington Post_ (4 January 1981).

15. Walter D. Connor, "Dissent in Eastern Europe: A New Coalition," _Problems of Communism_ 29 (January-February 1980), pp. 1-17; Philip Windsor, "Change in Eastern Europe," _Chatham House Papers_ (London: Royal Institute of International Affairs, 1980).

16. Connor, p. 2.

17. Ibid., pp. 2-4.

18. See Connor, pp. 4-7; David Lane, _The Socialist_

Industrialist State (London: Allen and Unwin, 1976), pp. 97-101; H. Gordon Skilling, Czechoslovakia's Interrupted Revolution (Princeton: Princeton University Press, 1976); Galia Golan, The Czechoslovak Reform Movement: Communism in Crisis (Cambridge: Cambridge University Press, 1971); Vladimir Fisera, (ed.), Workers Councils in Czechoslovakia; Documents and Essays, 1968-69 (New York: Columbia University Press, 1979); Alexander Matejko, Social Change and Stratification in Eastern Europe (New York: Praeger, 1974).

19. The Hungarian press has recently begun to admit the existence of broadly based social and political opposition to economic reforms that try to introduce a market environment. For a discussion of this attempt, see Peter Pogany, "Hungarian Press Reveals Resistance to Economic Reform," FBIS, Press Note No. 53, 19 June 1981; Andras Hegedus, "The Main Characteristics of the Social Structure of East European Societies, and the Alternatives of Democratic Development of their Power Structures," paper presented to the 1978 Annual Meeting of the National Association for Soviet and East European Studies, Cambridge University. Cited in Connor, p.3.

20. Connor, pp. 7-9; Adam Michnik, "The New Evolutionism," Survey (Summer-Autumn 1976), pp. 271-80.

21. Connor, pp. 7-9, citing documents published by the Association of Polish Students and Graduates in Exile, Dissent in Poland 1976-1977. (London, 1977), pp. 11-24; Windsor, pp. 24-26.

22. Cited by Jonathan Spivak, Asian Wall Street Journal, Hong Kong, (25 September 1980).

23. The Baltimore Sun (23 October 1980); The Washington Post (19 September and 16 October 1980 and January 4, 1981); Windsor, pp. 22-30.

24. T. Frojtik, Tribuna, Prague, (3 December 1980).

25. The New York Times (8 September, 17 October 1980 and 9 April 1981); Le Figaro (15 September 1980); The Wall Street Journal, New York (24 September 1980).

26. The New York Times (9, 16, 26 April 1981).

27. Trybuna Ludu, Warsaw (11 April 1981) cited in The Washington Post (12 April 1981).

28. Los Angeles Times (8 October 1980); The Washington

Post (12 April 1981).

29. *The New York Times* (16, 24, 26 April 1981).

30. *The Washington Post* (13 April 1981), quoting a speech by Polish Politburo member, Kazimierz Barcikowski, before the 10th Congress of the East German Communist Party in Berlin.

31. Jiri Valenta, "Soviet Options in Poland," *Survival* (March-April 1981), p. 53

32. Richard Hiscocks, *Poland: Bridge for the Abyss?* (London: Oxford University Press, 1963), p. 213 Idem, *Krushchev Remembers: The Last Testament* (Boston: Little, Brown, 1974), pp. 203-204.

33. Dale R. Herspring and Ivan Volgyes, "Political Reliability in the Eastern European Warsaw Pact Armies," *Armed Forces and Society* 6 (Winter 1980), p. 285.

34. *The New York Times* (18 December 1980); Valenta, p. 55.

35. *The New York Times* (8 April 1981).

36. Herspring and Volgyes, p. 285.

37. *The New York Times* (8, 16, 22, 24, 26 April 1981) citing *Tass*, *Pravda* and *Radio Moscow*.

38. Herspring and Volgyes, p. 285.

39. A case can be made for the reverse argument as well. Widespread opposition to intervention, perhaps even organized by the Polish Army or elements of it, would certainly put the lie to any Soviet claim to be intervening with the support of the majority of the Polish Party and people. On the other hand, it would be less likely to result in meaningful contacts between Russians and Poles and also might provide Soviet military leaders with an effective means of maintaining troop morale, i.e. through combat and the sense of group solidarity it usually engenders. In this regard, the most effective Polish strategy for sowing disarray within the Soviet ranks might be that of massive non-violent resistance to occupation, a strategy certain to maximize both the exposure of Soviet forces to Polish views and perhaps their receptivity to them.

40. Robert Jervis, *Perception and Misperception in*

International Politics (Princeton: Princeton University Press, 1976), pp. 227-28.

41. Dusko Doder in The Washington Post (16 April 1981); Valenta, pp. 51-53.

42. See Valenta, pp. 52-53, 55-57 for an attempt to reconstruct the policy debate in Moscow and other East European capitals; also Dusko Doder in The Washington Post (16 April 1981).

43. On intra-Pact coalition building, see Kent N. Brown, "Coalition Politics and Soviet influence in Eastern Europe," in Jan. F. Triska and Pal M. Cocks, eds., Political Development in Eastern Europe. (New York: Praeger, 1977), pp. 241-55; A. Ross Johnson, "Soviet - East European Military Relations: An Overview," in Dale R. Herspring and Ivan Volgyes, Civil-Military Relations in Communist Systems. (Boulder, Co.: Westview Press, 1978), pp. 243-57.

44. The Washington Post (16 April 1981) reported that Brezhnev was alleged to have cast the decisive vote against intervention in December 1980.

45. Excerpts from these speeches appear in The New York Times (8 April 1981).

46. Le Figaro, 1 September 1980; see Windsor, pp. 17-20 on juvenile delinquency and police baiting.

47. See Morris Bernstein, "Economic Reform in Eastern Europe", in U.S. Congress Joint Economic Committee, East European Economies Post-Helsinki. (Washington D.C.: Government Printing Office, 1977), pp. 102-34; Windsor, pp. 37-42, for a discussion of the problems associated with economic reforms.

48. Another point to be considered in this regard is the possible adverse consequences of the success of economic reforms. Philip Windsor, p.38, observes that the introduction of market mechanisms would mean that enterprises might be allowed to fail, something that would contradict the commitment of all of the East European countries to full employment. And full employment "is a most important instrument in the attempt of any Eastern European regime to maintain the acquiesence of the masses. The knowledge that, however inefficient one is, or however fictitious one's employment, one cannot be sacked, is a powerful argument for the acceptance of the system. The fact that one can only be sacked for political reasons only seems to emphasize the

political importance of full employment. In this way, government can be assured of a passive acceptance by most of the population; and such passivity, while economically harmful, is still politically necessary".

49. David Binder, "The Challenge of the Romanians," The New York Times (8 December 1978); David A. Andelman in The New York Times (30 November and 2 December 1978); A. Ross Johnson, pp. 259-60; Windsor, pp. 28-29.

50. The New York Times (8 December 1978); Dale R. Herspring, "The Warsaw Pact at 25," Problems of Communism 29 (September-October 1980), pp. 6-7, 10; Mackintosh, pp. 9-10; A. Ross Johnson, pp. 260-61.

51. Murray Seeger in The Los Angeles Times (8 October 1980); Le Matin, Paris (17 February 1981).

52. Scanteia, Bucharest, (8 May 1966); Mackintosh, pp. 9-10.

53. Aviation Week and Space Technology (6 March and 22 August 1971); The Military Balance, 1976-77. (London: International Institute of Strategic Studies, 1977), p. 14; Remington, p. 130; A. Ross Johnson, pp. 259-60.

54. The Military Balance, 1979-80. (London: International Institute of Strategic Studies, 1980), p. 94; Strategic Survey 1978. (London: International Institute of Strategic Studies, 1979), p.114; A. Ross Johnson, pp. 252-53, 261; Herspring, p. 7.

55. The Times, London (17 May 1966), Mackintosh, pp. 9-10.

56. A. Ross Johnson, p. 260.

57. Ibid., p. 262.

58. The Pact can be divided de facto into a northern tier composed of Poland, East Germany, and Czechoslovakia and a southern tier made up of its Balkan members. The northern tier constitutes by far the more important strategic area for the Soviet Union. In evidence may be cited the fact that the Soviets have carried out over 80 percent of the Pact's training exercises over the last ten years within the northern area. Mackintosh, p. 10, and A. Ross Johnson, p. 261.

59. Excluding Poland, whose leadership is in a state of flux, all Pact leaders were born between 1892 and 1918. Their average age is 72 years. They have been party chiefs for an average of 18 years, the doyen being Todar Zhivkov of Bulgaria who has been in power since 1954.

60. Herspring and Volgyes, pp. 277-79.

61. Such generational cleavages have also become apparent within the party according to West German academic observers of the Polish scene.

62. For some views on the question of reliability, see Wolfe, pp. 44-45; Herspring and Volgyes, pp. 270-96; A. Ross Johnson, pp. 7-8.

63. For a discussion of the concept of defensive avoidance, see Irving L. Janis and Leon Mann, Decision Making: A Psychological Analysis of Conflict, Choice and Commitment. (New York: The Free Press, 1977), pp. 57-58, 74, 107-33.

64. George Feifer, "Russian Disorders: The Sick Man of Europe," Harper's (February 1981), p.55.

65. For an analysis of the ways in which leaders can rig their information channels to confirm the preconceptions and the detrimental impact of this upon decisionmaking, see Richard Ned Lebow, Between Peace and War: The Nature of International Crisis. (Baltimore: Johns Hopkins University Press, 1981), pp. 153-69.

66. The New York Times (9, 16, 22, 26 April 1981) quoting from Literaturnaya Gazeta, Pravda, Tass and Trud, all of which emphasized the theme of outside provocation during the month of April.

67. See, Lebow, pp. 192-216, 222-28, for documentation.

68. I have elaborated upon this theme in "Clear and Future Danger: Managing Relations with the Soviet Union in the 1980s," in Robert J. O'Neill and D.M. Horner, ed., New Directions in Strategic Thought. (London: Allen and Unwin, 1981):221-45. A condensed version of this chapter appears in The Bulletin of the Atomic Scientists, (May 1981), pp. 1-19.

69. Thucydides, The History of the Peloponnesian War. (Philadelphia: The Franklin Library, 1980), p. 38.

11 The Warsaw Pact as an Instrument for Inducing Political and Military Integration and Interdependency

Lawrence L. Whetten

INTEGRATIVE PROCESSES OF THE WARSAW PACT

The purpose of this essay is to review the growing, although still scanty, literature on the issue of Warsaw Pact integration. Until the Polish events, the Soviets repeatedly claimed that the integrative process in economic, political and military fields had reached the highest level of any region and that interdependency had progressed to a degree of mutual satisfaction. The unpredictability of the Polish developments, however, necessarily renders any conclusions about Pact cohesion, the nature of the constraints on Soviet policy options in Eastern Europe, and the degree of national autonomy within the alliance highly tentative. This new dimension, however, does not invalidate the need to analyse Pact political-military integration; indeed, the Polish question adds a new sense of urgency to the study of these phenomena. A brief description of Pact integrative processes will be followed by analyses of the major political and military developments that have influenced the East Europeans' interpretations of Pact cohesion and national autonomy.

The Warsaw Treaty Organization was not founded in 1955, as is sometimes presumed, as a countermeasure to the Western initiative in 1949 creating NATO. Rather it was a deliberate manifestation of Soviet dissatisfaction over the rearmament of West Germany and its entry into the Atlantic Alliance. Yet West Germany had no armed forces at the time and could not be viewed as a military threat. (Indeed, to reduce embarrassment on the issue of German militarism, the seven existing East German

---

I am grateful to my colleague, Douglas Stuart, for commenting on the initial draft.

divisions were excluded for the time being from the Warsaw defence force.) Initially the Pact was a political gesture intended for non-military ends. The 11 May Pact communique announcing the Joint Command was noteworthy for the laudatory praise of the new Soviet disarmament proposal introduced the previous day at the communist-sponsored Helsinki World Peace Council. The Pact also served as a bargaining chip for the subsequent Soviet plan for a Pact/NATO bilateral non-aggression treaty.[1]

During its formative period the Pact remained largely a paper organization. The Joint Command was an integral component of Department 10 of the Soviet General Staff. Soviet officers assigned to the Joint Command remained in place and a newly created Resident Representative, a senior Colonel General Soviet General Staff officer, was posted to each East European capital. The apparent purpose of these minor reorganizations was to insure the thorough education of the East European military forces about the new doctrinal changes occurring in the Soviet Union, which emphasized strategic warfighting capabilities.[2] The WTO did not initially enhance significantly the military strength of the non-Soviet Pact Forces (NSPF); indeed, it increased their Sovietization without correspondingly guaranteeing their political reliability.

Thus the Pact was perceived by the Soviets primarily as a political instrument for bargaining with the West and for implementing East European integration in lieu of the unsatisfactory performance to date of the Council for Mutual Economic Assistance.[3] At a time of major changes within the Soviet Union itself and in its East European policy modulated by Khrushchev's flirtation with national communism, the Pact was intended to serve as an additional component in an entire series of multilateral institutional ties that could gradually provide new political guidelines as alternatives to the personalized Stalinist form of governance.[4] As James Brown has observed, since Stalin's death

> "Cohesion and viability have been the main Soviet aims in Eastern Europe....Cohesion is a situation where, in spite of local differences caused by variation in local conditions, there is a general conformity on ideological, political and economic policy, both domestic and foreign, as laid down by the Soviet Union in any particular period. By viability is meant a degree of confidence and efficiency, especially economic, in East European states that would increasingly legitimize communist rule and correspondingly reduce the Soviet need for

a preventive preoccupation with this region."[5]

Over time, cohesion and viability have tended to become rival priorities. The recurring examples of public unrest have all stemmed initially from economic grievances that have been translated into other demands, suggesting that viability remains a continuing source of Soviet concern--for which integrative innovations have been inadequately applied (Moscow's position), or excessively restrictive (notably the Polish stand).[6] In the area of political-military cohesion the Pact appears to have an equally spotty record, and the Soviet claim of attaining the highest level of regional integration appears to be seriously exaggerated.[7]

The political developments in 1956 and 1957 revealed the contradictions at that time between the Khrushchevian notion of the compatibility between strengthening regional cohesion and accepting national autonomy on the one hand, and "separate roads to communism" on the other. While massive economic investments were diverted from China and the Third World to shore up the viability of Eastern Europe, Moscow exhibited little confidence in the military reliability of the NSPFs. The Hungarian military establishment was thoroughly reorganized, yet elsewhere fence mending was required. Ostensibly, the Pact as an institution was used to conduct discussions about economic concessions, withdrawal of Soviet troops from Rumania, recall of Soviet officers, renationalization of NSPFs, and agreements on the stationing of Soviet troops in Eastern Europe under negotiated "status of forces" accords.[8] The latter agreements provided the semblance of greater East European exercise of sovereign authority, but in reality they insured a heavy East European contribution to stationing costs of Soviet garrisons. Thus for the first five years, the Pact was employed only marginally to promote military proficiency and political integration. Indeed, the leading organ of the Pact, the Political Consultative Committee (PCC), was convened only four times between 1955 and 1961, rather than its statutory semi-annual requirement, suggesting that the Pact was not yet empowered with crisis management prerogatives.[9]

Significant improvements in the political and military status of the Pact were made in 1960-61 and coincided with a variety of other international developments. Khrushchev had formally announced that wars of national liberation were "just" and would receive Moscow's full support; as evidence, the USSR was heavily involved in the Congo and elsewhere. The Sino-Soviet dispute had reached the breaking point, and tensions over Berlin had brought East-West relations to a new low. The Kremlin apparently felt compelled to integrate the East Europeans more fully, which would permit them to assume greater responsibility for regional affairs without becoming involved in Soviet global aspirations. Accordingly, the Soviets sought acceptance of the concept of supranational planning and division of labor in national economic production. Likewise, at the March 1961 PCC meeting, the Berlin situation was reportedly candidly discussed, as was the Soviet decision to create a separate military service--the Strategic Rocket Forces--in order to achieve strategic parity with the United States. Equally important from the East European perception, it was agreed to convene the PCC on a regular semi-annual basis.[10]

At the same time the Soviet doctrinal debate between the "modernists" (those seeking maximum deterrence through strategic missile procurement) and the "traditionalists" (who advocated strengthening conventional forces in Europe) resulted in rapid modernization, first of Soviet stationed forces and then the East European national units. SAM-2 air defense missiles were first deployed in 1960 with the Group of Soviet Forces Germany (GSFG), followed by SAM-3, and were fully integrated into the Soviet air defence system PVO Strany (which, with the Joint Baltic Fleet Command, are the only integrated Pact military services because their missions are a vital strategic Soviet interest). The national forces began receiving advanced weapons: T-55 tanks and MIG-21 and SU-7 tactical aircraft.[11] Regular large-scale maneuvers were conducted, generally in the Forward Area of Central Europe (DNIEPER in 1967 and DVINA in 1970 were conducted in the USSR reportedly because of Russian language deficiencies and lack of adequate automation among NSPFs).[12] Pact training emphasized the new Soviet doctrine of combined forces in a blitzkrieg attack, rather than reliance on Soviet mobilization capabilities. "Using Soviet figures", for example, a motorized rifle division "committed to high-intensity operations would be completely expended in five days". Total loss rates of "30 percent over some seven days as average", including armored divisions, are indicated.[13] By the mid-1960's most NSPF divisions were assigned first and second echelon missions and expected commensurate losses.[14]

While the military proficiency of all Pact forces had improved significantly in the decade before the Prague Spring, institutional integration had stagnated with the exception of air defense and the Baltic Fleet. There was no analogy to NATO's unified command structure. National forces were subordinated directly to the designated Soviet commander during contingencies and conflict; in the case of the invasion of Czechoslovakia, this commander was General Pavlovsky, CINC Soviet Ground Forces. Less is known about the degree of logistical support required by NSPFs, except for nuclear weapons, which remain entirely under Soviet control. Thus until 1968, the Pact's military functions were confined to training and mobilization;[15] even equipment procurement was largely a function of the Soviet General Staff.

The Czechoslovak invasion was a benchmark in Pact military political integration. Cohesion during crisis or under duress, short of violation of national territory, could no longer be guaranteed. Since the mid-1960s Rumania had sought both greater East European involvement in Pact decisionmaking and constraints against Soviet hegemony. Its refusal to participate in Pact discussions evaluating the Czechoslovakian reforms or the invasion meant that even partial or cosmetic cohesion would require endorsement through negotiation within the context of coalition politics. The invasion strengthened the Pact militarily through the garrisoning of five Soviet divisions and tactical air forces in Czechoslovakia. But the primary objective of the invasion was to insure the political reliability of the Prague regime which reemphasized the political mission of Soviet stationed forces, compounded inexorably the question of military disengagement at the Vienna MBFR talks, and undermined the political quality of cohesion and integration.

Despite the setback to cohesion and integration and the compromise of the reliability of Czechoslovakian armed forces since 1968, NSPFs have been maintained at a relatively constant level of readiness and weapons modernization has progressed--including T-62 tanks, SAM-4, 6, 7, MIG-23 and SU-29--but with important gaps (discussed below).[16] More importantly, Moscow acted politically both abroad and within the Pact to offset the impact of the invasion. After a status of forces agreement was signed in October with Prague, providing the legal basis for an indefinite Soviet military presence, Soviet Foreign Minister Andrei Gromyko convinced West German Foreign Minister Willy Brandt to reopen Bonn's Ostpolitik. Washington also agreed to renew the SALT I negotiations. By reducing Western apprehensions and intensifying Rumanian isolation, the Soviets successfully introduced, only six months after the invasion, the first major changes in Pact institutions.

The structural improvements presumably were raised after preliminary discussions with the East Europeans at the December 1965 PCC meeting when the new Soviet regime sought support for initiatives against Chinese obstructionism, against the U.S. in Vietnam, reactivation of the Soviet Middle East policy, and a renewal of its pan-European security proposal. But these reforms coincided with confidential disclosure that the USSR had achieved a breakthrough in the massive production of liquid missile propellants that would allow it theoretically to achieve strategic parity with the United States. The implications for long-range planning and enhanced Soviet hegemony through an accelerated arms race raised Rumanian reservations to the point of a veto, paralyzing the modifications that Bucharest had sought through increased East European participation in Pact decision-making. By March 1969 Bucharest tactically withheld its reservations, presumably to keep its more important initiatives open, such as with West Germany, and also to participate in Pact modifications that might provide greater equity between the USSR and Eastern Europe.

The March 1969 institutional reforms included establishing a Committee of Defense Ministers that meets annually and acts as the supreme military consultative organ. It reportedly develops broad joint policy recommendations. A Military Council was created, which meets semi-annually, is apparently subordinated to the Pact's Joint Command, and seems to have responsibility for standardization of quality control norms and procedures, and possibly the coordination of training operations. The actual organization and implementation of training, however, is conducted by the Staff of the Joint Command, i.e., apparently still Department 10 of the Soviet General Staff. The Joint Command and its Staff were expanded substantially in size with fixed ratios for national representation at the Command level. Finally, a Technical Council was formed that evidently provides continuity in various aspects of modernization and technical developments. It may even create guidelines or coordinate national military research and development programs. Later in November 1976 a permanent Council of Foreign Ministers was established with an independent secretariat and is subordinated directly to the PCC. This new body enhances the stature of the former standing consultative organ that provided support for the PCC since 1956.[17]

The importance of these reorganizations is that they provide the East Europeans considerably greater voice in Pact decisionmaking. There are many more positions now available at the working level for senior East European military and political officers. The enhanced continuity these institutions apparently provide, however, has only marginally raised consultations to the level of genuine coalition politics in either routine or crisis management decision making among all Pact members. But interviews reveal that posting to an East European country is highly desirable for senior Soviet officers and an assignment to Moscow is important for career advancement for East Europeans.[18] At least at the working level, the Pact reforms have had the positive benefit of increasing both the extent and quality of personal contacts. But what is the degree of integration at the national policy level? Is even limited integration now regarded by Pact members as authentically indispensable interdependency? The policies and behavior of several individual countries should be examined to determine the degree to which they comply or deviate from assumed or announced Pact norms or cohesion on specific issues.

THE ROLE OF THE NVA IN EAST GERMAN LEGITIMIZATION

Ever since 1978 official United States defense posture statements have been based on the assumption that NATO forces in Europe could be attacked conventionally with little or no warning by Warsaw forces in place and amounting to 500,000 men or more. That is, without mobilization or reinforcement from the USSR, some 58 divisions, including 31 non-Soviet, could be launched along the Central Front.[19] But the political reliability of the NSPFs dictates their assigned mission and the general concept of cohesion and integration in both peacetime and hostilities. East Germany offers a unique example.

The National People's Army (NVA) is a highly trained, well-equipped army without a nation. Its military traditions and _esprit d'corps_ are based largely on those of Prussia, as evidenced by the massive public exhibition on Prussia held in 1981 in East Berlin. But these thinly veiled militant traditions do not mask the tight symbiotic relation between the Communist Party and the NVA. The Party remains synthetic, hypersensitive to criticism, and an effective practitioner of _Abgrenzung_ or demarcation on issues with the West. It is vulnerable to penetration by West German media and can be manipulated by Western values and its own latent cultural refrains. After 200,000 East German citizens applied in 1978 for legal immigration to the West, East Germany reimposed some of the harshest measures against its people of any Pact government.[20]

Denied genuine legitimacy and an authentic national self-image, the GDR employed the classical instrument of securing its authority: organization, socialization, indoctrination, coercion, incentives, and ideology. In the early 1960s the Party sought an _Ersatz_ form of legitimacy based on future achievement to be accomplished by economic reforms. The reforms partially succeeded, but they did not necessarily enhance the Party's authority. Indeed, while achieving the highest Pact standards of living in the early 1970s, it was caught in a traditional dilemma of many authoritarian parties: either abuse its hegemonistic power, on the one hand, and risk further social alienation, or grant concessions necessary to gain public confidence, on the other, and thereby nourish rising expectations. In 1978 Honecker chose to impose repression with the expulsion of leading intellectual dissidents, curtailment of travel from the West, and introduction of currency constraint--without making any concessions.

On balance, it is clear that the East German party elites place greater political priorities on social stability and party security; legitimization is an important but necessarily secondary interest. Legitimization cannot be abandoned or even ignored, especially in a divided, constantly challenged nation. But denied genuine 'indigenous' legitimacy by its mass constituency, the Party is compelled to rely on 'derived' legitimacy enjoyed by its loyal participation as the "forward edge" of the Soviet collective security system.[21] Thus more than any other Pact government, the very size of the Soviet garrison in the GDR provides first stability, then security, and finally a form of legitimacy.

Therefore, the NVA is in a unique position among the NSPFs. "The uncertain political legitimacy in the GDR tends to reinforce military loyalty to the Party. This strong identity of interests would logically tend to generate an urge toward subordination in the officer corps".[22] While there may be some questions about the attitude of some other NSPFs toward the USSR and their role in Soviet planning, there appears to be little doubt about the loyalty of the NVA officers to the Soviet Union and its surrogate legitimizing function for the state and Party. NVA dependence on the Party and, thereby, the USSR severely constrains its freedom of action in either participating in political factionalism or creating an independent national military doctrine, as in the case of Czechoslovakia in 1968.[23] These strong institutional self-interests of the NVA have given the Party a high degree of self-confidence in conducting its own intra-Pact policies. The East Germany Party (SED) became on more than one occasion the leading edge against disruptive influences by Rumania, Czechoslavakia, and Poland without apparent objections from its own military establishment.

DEVIANT RUMANIA

While it can be argued that the GDR is the most politically and militarily integrated state into the Pact, Rumania, by contrast, is probably the least. The military and party establishments in Rumania are not knit into such acute dependency as in the GDR; both have developed their respective doctrine and policies based on mutually perceived nationalistic motivations. This does not mean that the Rumanian military is independent of Party control, but it has demonstrated a high degree of initiative and imagination in devising its own national military doctrine, which necessarily stems from the Party's political autonomy.[24]

The most significant initial indication of Rumania's quest for greater political latitude occurred in 1958, when it successfully negotiated the withdrawal of Soviet garrisons and the termination of the last of the onerous economic joint stock companies. Soviet largess probably resulted more from a desire to ease tensions with Hungary than to satisfy Rumanian concerns; but this was only the beginning of a long, defiant policy. In 1960-62 the Kremlin's efforts to rejuvenate its East European policy, drifting since 1956, culminated in a plan for economic divisions of labor, based on comparative advantages. Bucharest rejected the proposal on the grounds that it would be relegated to permanent ruralization and insisted instead on the Leninist concept of rapid industrialization. Rumania's rejection created a stalemate with the Northern Tier countries, primarily East Germany, which expected that the division would accelerate its own industrial growth.

While Rumania's stand in CMEA was based on primarily economic rationale, its decision to appoint itself mediator in 1964 in the Sino-Soviet dispute was purely political. This self-anointed intervention was intended to demonstrate several points that became increasingly important for the Rumanian Party. First, any party had the right and responsibility to assist in resolving disputes within the International Workers' Movement. Second, conflicts among fraternal parties must be settled without the threat of duress or expulsion which only contribute to factionalism and weakening the Movement. Finally, all parties must endorse and practice the basic principles of equality, independence and non-interference in domestic affairs. Thus acceptance of new anti-hegemonic rules of behavior would hopefully "rectify" inter-party relations.[25]

Before his demise Khrushchev had attempted to convene a World Communist Conference, not to 'excommunicate' the Chinese but to demonstrate that, unfortunately, they had cut themselves off from the international communist community. After boycotts and repeated delays by Rumania and like-minded parties, the Conference was finally convened in June 1969 in a diluted form. The former rules of secrecy and unanimity were abandoned, allowing for dissent and 'leaks'. Even so, of the original 81 parties only 62 attended, 14 publicly expressed opposition to the final document and five, including Rumania, refused to sign it. Finally, Rumania denounced Brezhnev's condemnation of China as a breach of conference rules. Later, after two years and fifteen planning sessions, the June 1976 Berlin Conference marked the high point of voluntary cooperation between equal and autonomous parties. The abruptly convened and abbreviated attendance at the 1980 Paris Conference signalled a return to hegemonic practices but not a serious defeat for Rumania's and others' efforts to secure new party behavior.[26]

On security policy matters Rumania took vociferous objection to Brezhnev's March 1965 Party Congress proposal for a pan-European Security Conference in the fear that it would be a means for extending Soviet hegemony. Ceausescu's position was so determined that Moscow was compelled to convene unprecedented defense and foreign ministers meetings--two weeks each--to dilute Rumanian opposition. Bucharest demanded and won the right of veto or abstention on the Soviet policy to gain Pact cohesion and solidarity on security negotiations, which were to be based on attaining strategic parity with the U.S. The compromise in the 1966 Bucharest Declaration was ill-fated when Rumania opened full diplomatic relations with West Germany in January 1967. At issue was the classical standoff: whether first to achieve a political settlement and then disengage militarily or first to draw down military postures in order to create the necessary climate for political negotiations. Rumania's adoption of a two Germanys policy was a demonstration that both could be attempted simultaneously.

The immediate consequences for Pact cohesion were severe. With Soviet support, East Berlin received endorsement at the Karlovy Vary Conference of the Ulbricht Doctrine, which prohibited further FRG diplomatic inroads in Eastern Europe until Bonn recognized East Germany.[27] East Berlin also demanded negotiation of a series of bilateral friendship and mutual assistance treaties with all Pact members. The new network of treaties would provide each member multilateral assistance and continued garrisoning of Soviet forces if the Warsaw Pact Treaty should ever be dissolved through negotiations. It also assured a framework for joint actions and operations in the event that complete unanimity and cohesion could not be reached. Rumania signed its bilateral treaty with the USSR after more than two years delay in July 1970 and after winning provisions for consultations, i.e., to preclude Soviet unilateralism as in the Cuban crisis. With the conclusion of the Ostvertrage, normalizing relations between Bonn and the Pact countries, Bucharest's independent two Germany policy was belatedly and begrudgingly exhonerated.[28]

Rumania's autonomous political policies can be summarized to include advocacy of party equality, refusal to participate in Pact meetings that might denounce China, Israel or West Germany, condemnation of the invasion of Czechoslovakia and interference in Poland (but rejection of the 1980 reforms), objection to numerous Soviet arms control proposals, such as the Non-Proliferation Treaty, expansion of economic relations with the West through membership in IMF and GATT and credits from EEC, and finally, frequent posturing as a semi-nonaligned state.

While such expediencies as the Polish events and its own domestic economic crisis moved Rumania in 1980 into greater conformity with Pact interests and problems, the above composite demonstrations of autonomy were compounded by initiatives in the military sphere, which ultimately led to an independent military doctrine. In 1974 Rumania cut its conscription term from 24 to 16 months, reducing 40,000 men, which was followed by a unilateral reduction in the joint costs of collective security and a call for slices in burden-sharing funds for all Soviet garrisoned forces. Bucharest announced a unilateral reduction in its participation in Pact exercises and a curtailment in the rate of modernization for its diminished armed forces. To achieve these drastic goals, Rumania strenuously sought greater East European authority in Pact affairs that could correspondingly constrain Soviet hegemony. In May 1966 Ceausescu called for the simultaneous abrogration of both military blocs and for the withdrawal of Soviet troops from Eastern Europe. Bucharest proposed that the position of the Commander-in-Chief of Warsaw Pact forces be placed on a rotation basis; to underscore its seriousness, it delayed for several months in 1967 the appointment of Ivan Yakubovsky as Marshal Grechko's replacement as CINC of the Warsaw Pact forces. The Soviet Resident Representative Liaison Mission was sent home for over six months and subsequently reduced in size. Finally, Bucharest refused to allow Pact troop exercises on Rumanian territory.[29]

Gradually a doctrine of territorial defense based on the Yugoslav model began to dictate the training, equipment, and deployment of the Rumanian army. It was smaller in size and budgetarily easier to maintain. It had little strategic logistical support and could not sustain operations beyond national borders for any period. During the Czechoslovakian crisis, Ceausescu reiterated that Rumanian armed forces could not legally be deployed outside Rumanian territory without the explicit approval of the National Assembly. After the invasion, militia and reservists were deployed to frontier and defensive positions in the first live exercise of the new doctrine. Thus there is greater similarity between the military doctrines and postures of Rumania and Yugoslavia than between Rumania and any other Pact member.[30] Indeed, there is greater affinity in the foreign policies of the two Balkan states, with the exception of the principle of collective security and wide differences on domestic policies, than there is between Bucharest and its allies. Rumania has not always stood alone on all issues, but its willingness to do so has occasionally polarized the Pact, e.g. the Czechoslovakian crisis in 1968, and more often encouraged other East Europeans to follow more flexible policies themselves.

TRUCULENT POLAND

While stability, security and legitimization have governed East German policy, and nationalism has dominated Rumanian search for an autonomous stature, the refinement and improvement of socialism have been recurring demands in Poland. The developments in Poland in 1980-81 were the most significant in Eastern Europe since World War II and, some analysists argue,[31] were the most perplexing for the Soviet leadership since the end of the Soviet Civil War in 1921. Unity between the party and people is the principal manifestation of political legitimacy in a single, minority party system. When public unrest stemming from popular grievances against the government erupted in 1956, 1970, 1976 and 1980, the Polish Party often at the explicit disapproval of the CPSU and other hard-line parties--publicly acknowledged that the complaints represented a breakdown in the bonds between the Party and the masses and introduced corrective reforms. Before 1980 the reforms were largely pursued within the purview of the Communist Party, and it was able to restore its authority, if not the full measure of legitimacy. In the wake of each set of reforms was the oppressive weight of party and government inertia and the genuine reservations of conservative elements about the risks of reforms versus improvements in traditional models. Each set of reforms failed to achieve its expected goals, although there was no complete reversion to the *status quo ante*; some changes were actually sustained. Yet the failures triggered renewed challenges to governmental performance and the Party's authority. By 1982 Solidarity, the free trade union, represented ten million workers (one-third of the total population) and Rural Solidarity claimed support of two million farmers. Both enjoyed the strong support of most intellectuals and the Church in what appeared to be a genuine national protest.

Solidarity's initial success stemmed from its demands for moral resuscitation and rectitude, whereby it usurped the moral authority of the Party and reinforced its alliance with the Church. The Party's leading role within the society was seriously undermined by the workers' demands for moral reforms at all levels. Receiving wide national endorsement for its assumption of the role of guardian of public morality, Solidarity had complicated Soviet intervention options and thereby the preservation of detente, upon which Polish national survival depended. In other words, it would be difficult for a Soviet invasion force to counter a worker's moral crusade demanding the restoration of integrity and efficiency in the Party, government and factory.

In assessing the potential implications of the Polish events for various communist parties, it should be noted that facile comparisons between the Prague Spring and the Polish developments could overlook important dissimilarities, which reflected positions on both Soviet policies.[32] First, the Czechoslovakian experiment was led by a communist party that was becoming a reformist body. The nature and extent of the reforms remained largely within party controls, despite Soviet charges to the contrary, but did not receive extensive worker support. The 1980 reforms in Poland were introduced from outside and in defiance of the Party. Indeed, popular pressure from below was the sustaining element of the reforms. In both cases Party cadre were purged, though more extensively in 1980 than 1968, and a sharp decline in Party morale occurred in Poland. The Soviets apparently concluded that the Polish leadership, like Gomulka, could eventually turn the reforms around. They had lost that confidence in Dubcek.

Secondly, and as a corollary to the first point, the momentum behind the Polish developments was sustained not only by proletarian grievances, but by those of virtually all segments of society except the ruling elite. The 1980 events assumed the dimensions of a national crusade for the restoration of public morality. The Prague experiment was the enterprise of the intellectual and non-proletarian strata of society. The Soviets could move with greater impunity against largely centralized, elitist factions, while appealing to those who would be aggrieved by the reforms, than they could against the workers, the Church and the intellectuals with established channels for promoting their respective reforms which coalesced around mutual interests.

Thirdly, the Polish economy was on the verge of bankruptcy, which could only be exacerbated by intervention. The introduction of food rationing is commentary enough. With increasing economic demands from friends and allies, the USSR could ill afford the additional burden of Polish dependency. This was not the case in 1968. The Czechoslovak reform movement began in the 1962-63 economic slump. But by 1968 the economy had rebounded to the point that it could even sustain the shock of a Soviet invasion.

Fourthly, there were also strategic differences. Poland's geography controls the accessibility of the Soviet Union to East Germany. The logistical lines necessary to preserve vital Soviet interests in the German problem are governed by the Poles and cannot be readily and efficiently replaced. (The Poles recognize these geopolitical realities; until the beginning of 1982 the railway workers did not strike the international trunk lines, only local commuter connections.) The main reason for the 1968 invasion was to insure political control over a local constituency. There were, of course, important military advantages of positioning five additional Soviet divisions closer to Bavaria. But they do not play as critical a role for the protection of Soviet vital strategic interests in Central Europe as do the two divisions garrisoned in Poland.

Fifthly, there were sharp asymmetries in factors extraneous to the immediate crises. Soviet economic growth was lower and the strains more visible than twelve years earlier. China was no longer in the throes of the debilitating Cultural Revolution and has since normalized relations with the U.S. and Japan. Soviet overseas dependencies (Vietnam, Cambodia, Afghanistan, South Yemen, Ethiopia, Angola, Mozambique and Cuba) required the expenditure of money and resources not anticipated in the 1960s. Furthermore, the attainment of even the immediate Soviet planned objectives necessitated the continuation of the present level of Western technology transfer and trade, which depended largely on the political atmosphere. (In 1970 the EEC imported only $4.8 billion in goods from the Soviet bloc and exported $4.8 billion in products. In 1979 the Community bought $20.3 billion from COMECON countries, while selling them $18.5 billion in goods. In 1980 West German exports to the USSR rose 30 percent to over $4 billion and Franch exports by 31 percent to over $2 billion.)

Finally, in 1968 Moscow was just exploring the opportunities and advantages of detente, which were only temporarily impaired by the invasion. By 1981 it was seeking ways to keep remnants of detente viable, which would undoubtedly be quashed by intervention in Poland. Thus the 1956 Polish reformist movement is a closer analytical parallel because of the broader public support, despite the fact the Poles then had less experience in national communism. Yet even 1956 does not provide accurate analogs for Soviet tolerance levels for national deviations in 1982.

Pressures from virtually every facet of Polish society forced the emergence of the most drastic political reforms ever practiced by a Marxist-Leninist party. Exposure of corruption, the development of "horizontal" rather than "vertical" communictions among various organizational levels, open nominations and secret balloting resulted in purges of the leadership and the solidification of the Party 'renewal' process. Only 90 percent of the 1955 delegates to the July 1981 Extraordinary Party Congress had attended previous congresses and, in turn, reelected only 16 members to the 200 member Central Committee, only four to the Politburo and ousted virtually every district first secretary. Extremists among the hardliners and reformers lost heavily, while moderates rallied around Party leader Stanislaw Kania. Preliminary analyses suggest that the Polish Party accepted standards of limited democratization that will be difficult for any Marxist-Leninist party advocating democratic centralism to evaluate.

The presumed response by orthodox communist parties (CPs) will be to strengthen vertical discipline to preclude the degree of horizontalization that occurred in Poland. Yet it was this process that overcame the demoralization of the Polish Party and generated the renewal movement within the rank and file. And it was this renewal effort that effectively restored the Party's leading role at Solidarity's expense. The Party was able to initiate and survive the degree of cathartic self-criticism for it to reestablish its claims to be the moral leader of the society. In the course of events, Solidarity's moral suasion diminished, leaving it in the difficult position of having to introduce and possibly enforce the government's inevitably harsh economic reforms. Speculatively, this could create a genuine partnership between labor and government, as Solidarity had advocated. Alternatively, it could produce an impossible situation of the present labor leaders to demand reforms without causing factionalism, its demise and the undermining of the free trade union movement. Without its former excessive claims to moral leadership, Solidarity may become an embattled trade union in a 'no-win' situation as economic imperatives freeze it into immobility between the workers and the government. The outcome will depend heavily upon the nature of the economic reforms that can now be predicated on the revitalization of the Party.

Finally, in the near term, Solidarity's credibility within the society is likely to depend upon its ability to reduce its own factionalism, organize labor and civic self-help operations for the needy during the 1981-82 winter, collaborate effectively in the emergency tripartite Party, Church and labor coalition to resolve the crisis, to eliminate wild-cat strikes--the "English disease"--and to resotre worker attention on first productivity and then reform. Recent Polish interviewees claim that the Party has been deliberately reluctant to resolve localized disputes and strikes that center mainly on personalities and minor problems despite the loss of production because they diffuse focus on more critical issues and undermine the authority of Solidarity. However programmed the Party's policy may be, the challenge Solidarity has accepted for refining and improving socialism is to insure that public concern remains directed toward fundamental reforms.

What role has the Polish military played in the integrative process throughout this repeated domestic turmoil? Because of Poland's troublesome history for Russia and its crucial geopolitical location, Moscow placed much higher interest in the "Sovietization" of the Polish armed forces after 1948 when the remnants of the pro-Western Home Army were finally eliminated. Many senior and General Staff officers and the Minister of Defense, Marshal Rokossowski, were Soviet officers. With the recall of Soviet officers after 1956, the military became a more authentic national force. The officer corps, however, remained factionalized between the so-called Partisans, or "native Communist" officers, led by then Interior Minister Mieczyslaw Moczar and the "Moscovite Communists", many of whom were Jewish and had served with Soviet-officered units during World War II. The confrontation was not resolved by Gomulka, who sought balance without aggravation. The anti-Semitic purges in the aftermath of the 1967 Arab-Israeli War cost most of the latter faction their posts, and Gomulka's demise was accompanied by the eclipse of the Partisans and formation of a non-political officer corps.[33]

According to emigré officers, the rivalry was not sufficiently intense to disrupt the growing elan fostered by the acknowledgement of the need to raise a national army to serve national interests. Yet the controversy generated enough resentment that the officer corps remained aloof from the recurring political strife. Only two major units with Polish officers accepted mobilization orders in October 1956. The military were embarrassed by their participation in the 1968 invasion and, despite national animosities, conducted themselves discreetly. In 1970 the Army ignored orders to use force in Gdansk and refused to side in the Gomulka-Gierek struggle. They were not employed during the 1976 riots and remained strictly disciplined during the 1980-1981 challenges to the Party and regime. (Soldiers were used periodically to assist in the coal mines and civil assistance capacities--both non-military functions.) Only when Defense Minister, General Wojciech Jaruzelski, was appointed Premier in 1981 and then replaced Kania as head of the Party, did the military cautiously assert itself into the political dispute. But this move should be seen as a political deterrent rather than military intervention.

The Polish military establishment has taken pride in its professionalism.[34] Recently interviewed Polish youth have generally anticipated conscription with enthusiasm seldom reflected elsewhere. Senior officers have gradually introduced educational reforms that have blended the technological and administrative requirements of both military and civilian sectors of the society to one of the most successful levels of domestic integration of any Pact member. Military education is now a respected component of higher civilian education, and graduating officers, upon retirement or resignation from military service, move readily into civilian industries.[35] While the Polish Army's combat mission commits it to the doctrine of coalition warfare, the concept of no-warning attack means that Polish forces can only be committed to third echelon advances. A sense of realism and nationalism has motivated the military elite to focus on national survival in the event of nuclear war and to adopt the role of national guardian in the event of political upheaval.[36] Short of such emergencies, the Polish Party has placed the highest priority on tailoring military education, motivation and discipline to perfecting its unique model of socialism.

CZECHOSLOVAKIAN DESIGNERS AND ENGINEERS

There is little doubt that the designers and engineers of the Prague Spring also sought basic reforms in socialism. But with the economy already recovering (from a GNP growth rate of -2.2 in 1963 to over 3 percent in 1966), the demands for economic remodeling were less urgent than in other East European protest movement. This does not deprecate the intellectual rigour or personal courage of the reformers. Indeed, they sought the most dramatic modifications of socialism that were conceivable at the time within the tolerance levels of the conservative Pact members. As an intellectual, elitist, economic, and political movement, it found a strong resonance within the military elite. Unlike the Polish armed forces, the Czechoslovakian military became deeply involved in political reformism, partly for doctrinal and institutional reasons, but mainly on political grounds. Party reformers envisioned a new national model of socialism, but important segments of the military sought regional realignments that would serve to bolster national communism throughout Eastern Europe and thereby reinsure the survivability of the reforms.

The Czechoslovakian People's Army (CPA) had been heavily Sovietized during the 1950s by the posting of Soviet officers throughout the General Staff and down to the regimental level and it became one of the best trained and equipped NSPFs. By the mid-1960s its training reflected the new Soviet doctrine of a possible conventional opening phase of a European war. Yet by 1966 the officer corps was seriously split over the military and political consequences of the new doctrine for several reasons: 1) rising disillusionment with Soviet control of the Pact and the exclusion of East Europeans from virtually all serious decisionmaking, 2) growing awareness of a potential disparity between Soviet and Czechoslovakian security interests and the need for the development of a national defense doctrine that would maximize security and minimize losses, 3) questioning at the same time by Rumania of Soviet strategy and hegemony (at the 1966 meeting of the PCC Czechoslovakia supported Rumania's rejection of the Soviet call for greater integration and discipline and endorsed Bucharest's appeal for more East European participation in the policy process), and 4) changing threat perceptions about German revanchism and the challenge of the German problem to Czechoslovakian national security.[37]

The Klement Gottwald Military-Political Academy, emulating the long Czech tradition and history of academic excellence, created in 1965 an inter-departmental study group to program a computer model for analyzing the implications of the Soviet doctrine and the discrepencies with CSSR capabilities and national interests. The general conclusions were that without an international composition of the Joint Command or the formation of a collective consultative body, no consensus could be reached on a collective military doctrine which could incorporate CSSR specific national interests. This same group was then commissioned to develop a plan for national alternatives (interviewees vary on who authorized the plan--the Academy or the military department of the Party Central Committee).[38]

The subsequent proposal, the so-called "Klement Gottwald Memorandum"[39] rejected neutrality and nonalignment proclaimed by the Imre Nagy government in Hungary in 1956 but envisioned a broader collective security concept than that of the Warsaw Treaty that would reflect CSSR sovereignty and national interests. The central feature was theater arms control: the creation of a nuclear free zone in Europe and the withdrawal of all foreign troops. Individual countries would be encouraged to conclude nonaggression treaties, especially across bloc lines, such as a CSSR-FRG pact. The main thrust was to guarantee Soviet strategic interest in Central Europe without the requirement of Soviet troops and political hegemony. The traditional glacis into European Russia must be neutralized through the formation of a corridor sanitaire based upon interlocking nonaggression agreements that would eliminate military threats and provide security perceptions, in which the Soviets and other European states could trust. One implicit implication that may have stimulated Czechoslovakian thinking was the expected simultaneous dissolution of both military blocs. But the Memorandum does not explicitly state this option. Indeed, the Warsaw Treaty was to be retained as the ultimate guarantee for the Soviets, should an unexpected threat emerge in Western Europe.

The political implications were severe; a modified Finlandization, whereby East European states would assure their own and Soviet security requirements and refrain from interfering in Moscow's foreign policy interests elsewhere in return for Soviet nonintervention in their domestic affairs.[40] The consequences for the application of the Soviet model of socialism were explicitly revealed in the reforms in the April 1968 Action Program. The Memorandum and supporting documents clearly implied a distinct separation between the re-Westernization of Marx and the Eastern sanctification of Lenin.

The members of the study group were commended for their work, implying that the plan had received some degree of Central Committee approval. The precise timing and form of endorsement remain confused among interviewees and probably was even then due to the state internal Party strife. But as evidence of the seriousness with which the Czechoslovaks considered their proposal, one member of the study group testified that it was submitted to the General Staffs of all Pact members. The Polish and Hungarian military responded favorably, and the Rumanians accepted it in principle, but were suspicious about Soviet reactions. An apparently limited sampling of Soviet General Staff officers, upon whom the idea was tested, produced mixed responses--some supporting it on the grounds of military efficiency and the possibility of reallocating resources for other priorities, others rejecting it for political reasons. The East Germans denounced the plan unequivocably. For East Berlin there were no alternative scenarios that would permit the withdrawal of Soviet troops; even a token one-third reduction could jeopardize its legitimacy. There is no evidence that the plan was ever formally discussed at the Central Committee level in any Party, but it is inconceivable that senior staff officers would not have informally consulted appropriate Party authorities. There is also no evidence of any intra-Pact consultation or of a formal Pact response.[41]

Nonetheless, Czechoslovak interviewees were convinced that East German obduracy prevented formal consideration of the plan for regional security (obviously based on GDR self-interests rather than those of other fraternal parties) and that this factor ultimately contributed to the decision to invade.

It can be argued that this sense of rejection and frustration was an underlying reason for the unprecedentedly outspoken 15 July 1968 press conference by General Prchlik (then head of the military department of the Central Committee and reportedly one of the sponsors of the Memorandum), in which he levied the broadest indictment in the Pact's history against Soviet manipulation of the alliance and its failure to seek alternatives in either concepts or procedures.[42] (He was fired after the Cierna conference with the Soviet Politburo as evidence that the CPCS retained its leading role and loyalty to the USSR.) Nonetheless, the initial ideas of national defense embodied in the April Action Program, the Memorandum and its supporting documents, and Prchlik's complaints were incorporated into the draft Statutes of the 14th CPCS Party Congress, scheduled to be convened on 14 September 1968. In retrospect it is remarkable that the Czechoslovaks had the self-confidence to approach their allies and solicit endorsement of such a sweeping security rearrangement, even if at the most informal level, and then to persist in making it part of the formal Party Statutes. Yet the plan could have eventually only succeeded with full alliance cooperation.[43]

It was largely Rumanian and Czechoslovak complaints about Soviet domination of the Pact, the revolutionary alternative security proposal presented by Prague, and Bucharest's relatively endangered and isolated position after the invasion which permitted passage of the modest March 1969 Pact institutional reforms. But what do these examples of national idiosyncrasies demonstrate in terms of alliance cohesion and viability, legitimization and integration, or interdependency?[44]

CONCLUSIONS

Dale Herspring contends that the Pact is highly integrated based on the frequency and quality of consultations, and that the socio-political institutions of its members would probably not survive without the Pact structure.[45] Living without the Pact is "essentially inconceivable", and the chief value of the alliance is that it tends to diffuse Soviet pressure on East Europeans. Yet he also posits that for external military offensive operations all NSPFs, except Bulgaria, could be expected to perform relatively ineffectively.[46] This suggests that if East European military forces are more determined to defend national interests but much less so those of the hegemonistic power they can hardly be regarded as integrated into a collective security arrangement. Furthermore, the above discussion of selected cases of national deviation and dissent indicates uneven identification with many Soviet interests and even perceptions. A refinement of terminology about the interactions among Pact members may more adequately explain these phenomena.

Economic viability is diminishing disproportionately to rising expectations in prosperity. The continuation of the world economic recession, trade discrepancies within CMEA, and growing foreign indebtedness suggest that several East European states may soon suffer a severe case of _dependencia_. (For example, East Germany is no longer a net exporter of technology to the USSR, but a net importer.) The social and economic development within Eastern Europe accelerated by CMEA's "integrative division of labor" in the 1960s and early 1970s may now further exacerbate differences rather than standardize collective norms for socialism.

Political cohesion within the Pact is less a function of coalition politics than the perception of projectable military power. The aim of "cohesion" remains as before: the preservation of regional stability and the relegation of East Europeans to "Little European status". (There is no evidence for claims, for example, that Moscow consulted its allies on the invasion of Afghanistan, despite the impact the decision was likely to have on detente and the international communist movement.) The repeated demonstrations of quests for national communism or autonomy is adequate evidence that cohesion cannot be construed to mean consensus, even on such routine issues as appropriate inter-party behavior.

Soviet goals of viability and cohesion have been only partially attained; indeed, at times military force and economic reprisals have been employed to demonstrate Soviet tolerance levels for deviation. Integration has also been evasive for Moscow. The term implies a partial surrender of national sovereignty, which, of course, exists under the application of Soviet hegemony. But the recurring assertion of national identification and self-image by East Europeans refutes periodic Soviet aspirations of establishing a collective, socialized society throughout the alliance.

The concept that appears to be more relative for future research is interdependence.[47] In future analyses interdependency should be extrapolated from economic dependency theory and enriched to include the entire spectrum of regional interactions. Military and political involvements are only two examples of the range of total behavior that should be examined and the levels of mutual penetration and manipulation that are exercised. At the same time the discontinuities within regional structures and institutions should be assessed and the relevance of extra-regional options determined for individual members (for example, how has the West German card been played by East Berlin and to what advantages and disadvantages?). In another vein, how strong is the "cobwebbing" effect of interlacing national interests to the point that incentives to remain within the system outweigh the impact of abandonment? Interdependency theory appears to be a more flexible approach than cobwebbing for analyses of a system that has become increasingly complex and yet retains its muted hierarchial characteristics. Based on only limited evidence, it appears that East Europeans will remain interdependent upon the existing system, whereby individual members can exchange emphasis on particular national interests and priorities in return for compliance with prescribed collective norms that will not jeopardize the system's stability or security.

FOOTNOTES

1. Malcolm Mackintosh, Strategy and Tactics of Soviet Foreign Policy (London: Oxford University Press, 1963), pp. 97-103.

2. Zbigniew Brzezinski, "The Organization of the Communist Camp," World Politics, (January 1961), pp. 198-199 and Richard F. Starr, "The East European Alliance System", U.S. Naval Institute Proceedings, (September 1964), pp. 36-37. Both authors contend that what coordination occurred was primarily in weapons standardization and decisions on local weapons production.

3. Michael Kaser, COMECON: Integration Problems on Planned Economics (New York, N.Y.: Oxford University Press, 1965), pp. 77-107.

4. Zbigniew Brzezinski, The Soviet Bloc, (Cambridge, Ma.: Harvard University Press, 1967), pp. 456-459.

5. James F. Brown, "Detente and Soviet Policy in Eastern Europe", Survey (Summer 1974), p. 46.

6. The degree of economic integration is difficult to measure in light of world inflation, trading priorities, fiscal policies, political preferences and inadequate information. Despite these technical difficulties, public dissatisfaction with the degree of economic viability has been demonstrated in the streets. Polish protests over food in July and August 1980 created the most acute political crisis in the Soviet system since 1919. While statistics indicate a growing recession in Eastern Europe in the early 1980s, the impact will be uneven in labor productivity, industrial growth, agricultural production, capital investment and foreign trade. As an acute example, the Polish foreign debt was conservatively estimated at over $21 billion, more than one-third of the CMEA debt, requiring 70 percent of convertible currency receipts for debt-servicing in 1980. See The European Economy in 1980: Recent Economic Developments in Eastern Europe and the Soviet Union, UN Doc. ECE (XXXVI)/1. Add. March 1981, pp. 145-147. For harbinger statements see Paul Marer, "Prospects for Integration in Eastern Europe: CMEA," in Jan F. Triska and Paul M. Cocks, eds., Political Development in Eastern Europe (Praeger, 1977), pp. 256-277; Nora Beloff, "Comecon Blues," Foreign Policy (Summer 1978), pp. 159-179; and Archie Brown, "Eastern Europe: 1968, 1978,

1998," Daedalus (Winter 1979), pp. 151-174. For a more positive assessment see East European Economic Assessment, Part 2 - Regional Assessments, Joint Economic Committee, Congress of the United States, USGPO, 1981: "Although the economies of Eastern Europe are small, have insufficient raw materials and human resources, suffer from a technology lag compared with their Western neighbors, and must satisfy a revolution of rising expectations, they do have assets. Many of the current leaders and planners are pragmatic and flexible, ... ingenious and highly professional. ... In spite of its precarious position between the economic colossuses the Soviet Union in the East, with its raw material monopoly, and the Common Market, Japan and the United States in the industrial West, with their formidable technological leadership, East Europe may not only survive, but prosper." p. 18. Paul Marer and John Michael Montias, East European Integration and East-West Trade (Bloomington, Ind.: Indiana University Press, 1980); and Eugene Zaleski and Helgard Wienert, Technology Transfer between East and West, OECD, (Paris, 1980) are two up-to-date and thorough studies. For signs of Soviet reactions against the imports of Western technology, see Philip Hanson, Trade and Technology in Soviet-Western Relations (New York, N.Y.: Columbia University Press, 1981).

7. Soviet assertions about levels of integration have been made in interviews with the author. Some officials claim they feel more closely integrated with their East European allies than with their own Asian Republics. Generally East Europeans interviewed are less emphatic.

8. Thomas E. Wolfe, Soviet Power and Europe: 1945-1970 (Baltimore, Md.: Johns Hopkins University Press, 1970), p. 82.

9. Ross A. Johnson, Robert W. Dean and Alexander Alexiev, East European Military Establishments: The Warsaw Pact Northern Tier, RAND Corp., R-2417/1-AF/FF (December 1980), p.11.

10. For a list of the PCC meetings, see Lawrence T. Caldwell, "The Warsaw Pact: Direction and Change," Problems of Communism, (September/October 1975), pp. 1-19; also Dale R. Herspring, "The Warsaw Pact at 25," Ibid., (September/October, 1980) pp. 2, 6, 7. The latter includes listings of meetings of military organs and major field exercises.

11. There are discrepancies on how modern this equipment

actually was. Wiener and Lewis list the the T-55 as first produced in 1958, SU-7 in 1959/60, MIG-21 C in 1959/60, SAM-2 in 1957 and SAM-3 in 1964. Friedrich Wiener and William J. Lewis, The Warsaw Pact Armies, (Vienna: Carl Ueberreuter Co., 1977). John M. Collins lists the T-55 as first produced in 1961, SU-7 in 1960, MIG-21 (first model) 1956, SAM-2 in 1958, and SAM-3 in 1961. American and Soviet Military Trends since the Cuban Missile Crisis (The Center for Strategic and International Studies, Georgetown University, 1978).

12. John Erickson, "The Soviet Military System: Doctrine, Technology and Style," in John Erickson and E.J. Feuchtwanger, eds., Soviet Military Power and Performance (London: Macmillan, 1979), p.23.

13. Cited by Collins, op.cit. p. 173.

14. According to emigré reports before 1968, Czechoslovakian units in the Southwest Front estimated losses at between 60 to 70 percent. On the third to fifth day the Soviet Carpathian Army would pass through the remains of the Czechoslovakian Front. These casualty rates were expected because forward units were on thirty minute alert and would have to move out under strength. This scenario had a strong negative impact on Czechoslovak officers.

15. Malcolm Mackintosh, The Evolution of the Warsaw Pact, Adelphi Papers, No. 58 (June 1969), pp. 11-15.

16. For longitudinal analyses on the various components of Pact force postures, see The Military Balance, International Institute for Strategic Studies, IISS, since 1975; see also John M. Collins and Anthony Cordesman, Imbalance of Power, (Ignacio, Ca.: Presidio Press), 1978.

17. On the nature of the reforms, see Malcolm Mackintosh, "The Warsaw Pact Today," Survival, (May/June 1974), pp. 122-126; and General Sergei Shtemenko, Za Rubezhom (7 May 1976) reprinted in Survival (July/August 1976), pp. 169-170.

18. Interviews conducted by the author over the past ten years.

19. See the annual U.S. Defense Department fiscal reports and posture statements, including the Annual Defense Department Report for Fiscal Year 1978.

20. For immigration statistics see Bundesausgleichsamt,

Bad Homburg, or Lawrence L. Whetten, *Germany East and West: Conflicts, Collaboration and Confrontation* (New York University Press, 1981), pp. 149-156; or Hans Jurgen Schierbaum, *Intra-German Relations*, (Tuduv, 1979).

21. On GDR legitimacy see Gebhard Schweigler, *National Consciousness in Divided Germany* (Beverly Hills, Ca.: Sage Publications, 1975); Andrew C. Janos, *Authoritarian Politics in Communist Europe: Uniformity and Diversity in One- Party States* (Berkeley, Ca.: niversity of California Press, 1976); Peter C. Ludz, *Two Germanys in One World* (Cambridge, Ma.: Harvard University Press, 1975); and Jens Hacker, *Deutsche unter sich* (Seewald, 1977).

22. Dean Johnson and Alexiev, op.cit., p. 75

23. Dale Herspring argues that the rising technological training in the NVA did not produce a counter-elite that operated beyond the institutional and political circumventions, "Technology and the Changing Political Officer in the Armed Forces: The Polish and East German Cases", *Studies of Comparative Communism* (Autumn 1977), p. 391.

24. Dale Herspring and Ivan Volgyes, *Civil-Military Relations in Communist States* (Boulder, Colo.: Westview Press, 1978).

25. Robin Remington, *The Warsaw Pact: Case Studies in Communist Conflict Resolution* (Cambridge, Ma.: MIT Press, 1971), pp. 56-93.

26. For details see Chapter IX in Lawrence L. Whetten, *New International Communism: The Foreign and Defense Policies of the Latin Communist Parties* (Lexington, Ma.: Lexington Books, 1982).

27. Edwina N. Moreton, *East Germany and the Warsaw Alliance: The Politics of Detente* (Boulder, Colo.: Westview Press, 1978), p. 67.

28. For details on Rumania's autonomous initiatives, see Lawrence L. Whetten, Chapter 3, *Germany's Ostpolitik: Relations between the Federal Republic and the Warsaw Pact Countries* (New York, N.Y.: Oxford University Press, 1971).

29. Emigré interviews conducted by Lawrence Whetten.

30. Alex Alexiev, *Party-Military Relations in Eastern Europe: The Case of Rumania* (Center for Inter-

national and Strategic Affairs, University of California, Los Angeles, 1979).

31. Uri Ra'anan, "Soviet Decision-Making in International Affairs," Problems of Communism (November-December 1980), p. 44.

32. Vladimir V. Kusin, "The Moscow Bloc Summit on Poland: A Look Back to 1968" (Radio Free Europe: RAD Background Report/294, 10 December 1980).

33. Johnson, Dean and Alexiev, op.cit. pp. 48-55. Two hundred military officers were purged in 1967, while fourteen generals and two hundred colonels (most of whom were Jewish) followed.

34. Herspring argues that even in political training the Polish military is more advanced than the East German, Studies of Comparative Communism, op.cit. p. 390.

35. Ninety percent of the chairs at Polish military academies (institutions of higher education) are held by full professors appointed by the Polish State Council for overall scientific achievement. One hundred percent of all lecturers are military officers. The academics include not only technical and engineering faculties, but also medicine and pharmacology. For details see Lawrence L. Whetten and James I. Waddell, "Military Education in the Polish Armed Forces", Royal United Services Journal (September 1980), pp. 51-57.

36. Johnson, et al., emphasize the importance of the concept of Defense of National Territory (OTK) formally issued in 1965, pp. 33-36.

37. See Josef Hodic, "Military-Political Views Prevalent in the Czechoslovak Army 1948-1968", Research Project, The Experience of the Prague Spring 1968, Study No. 5, (Vienna 1979).

38. Johnson, et al., provide the most extensive interview material on the subject that has yet been released.

39. "Memorandum: The Formulation and Codification of Czechoslovak National Interests in the Military Field." Lidova Armada, (2 July 1968).

40. This concept has been subsequently radicalized (complete neutrality) and publicized by East European dissidents, such as Rudolf Bahro, Die Alternative:

Zur Kritik des real existierenden Sozialismus (Europaische Verlagsanstalt, 1977), pp. 400-401.

41. Interviews conducted by the author. It is generally agreed among the interviewees that there was a split among the reformers about the pace of change. Eventually it was agreed between the economic and politico-military reformers that to safeguard the existing and planned reforms, the conservative personnel within the leadershiup would have to be removed at the September Party Congress. Dubcek would be sacrificed and a Politburo composed largely of technocrats elected as a first step toward diminishing the role of ideology in the government and the Party.

42. Text published in Robin Remington, Winter in Prague, (Cambridge, Ma.: MIT Press, 1969), pp. 214-220.

43. The plan was obviously not the only reason for the invasion. The provisions in the draft Statutes of the right to minority opinion and the implied renunciation of the principle of democratic centralism were even more dangerous to conservative Communist rationale. See Jiri Valenta, Soviet Intervention in Czechoslovakia 1968: The Autonomy of a Decision (Baltimore, Md.: Johns Hopkins University Press, 1979), pp. 93-122.

44. Hungary and Bulgaria cannot be omitted in even a limited analysis of Pact cohesion. Bulgaria, a faithful Soviet protegé, has avoided adventures in foreign and defense policies and is probably the most militarily reliable NSPF because of its traditional animosity towards Turkey. It has concentrated on economic development and has achieved one of the highest CMEA growth rates in the last two Five-Year Plans: 1971-1975, 7.9 percent and 1976-1980, 6.2 percent with roughly 5 percent planned for 1981-1985.

    After 1956 Hungary concentrated on national consolidation. It has introduced a mixed economy and intensified agricultural investment. The results are that Hungary probably has the soundest economy in Eastern Europe and the party chief, Janos Kadar, would probably be the only popularly elected leader in free elections in the Pact countries. This favorable situation has developed partially because of Kadar's policy of moderation on foreign and security issues and his active mediation in recurring Pact disputes.

45. Herspring, "The Warsaw Pact at 25", op.cit., pp. 11-13.

46. Herspring, Dale and Ivan Volgyes, "How Reliable are East European Armies", Survival (September-October 1980), pp. 217-18. It should be noted that a major source of disaffection among at least the Polish military after the 1967 June War was the severe decrease in its aircraft inventory to replenish Arab losses. After the October War the modest increases of advanced T-62 tanks were suddenly withdrawn and apparently shipped to Arab states. There was apparently a five-year depletion in advanced armour. The remodernization of NSPFs only recommenced in 1980. Syria alone had 1100 T-62s and 400 T-72s. By 1982 Algeria, Egypt, Iraq, Libya and Syria each had more T-62s and T-72s than the combined NSPFs, apparently without East European complaints. Indeed, priority was apparently higher for the Middle East for East European manufactured armour, suggesting that Moscow expected higher political dividends from selected Arab states than from its own allies. Soviet forces, of course, continued to modernize conventionally throughout the 1970s. For longitudinal comparisons refer to Military Balance, 1968-82, IISS.

    One apparent reason for the disproportional Soviet-NSPFs military build-up was to achieve Moscow's high priority aim of influencing other states' security policies to its advantage, mainly in Western Europe, where its Guards Armies would sustain the shock of any military contingency.

47. William Zimmerman touches only briefly on the utility of the concept, "Dependence Theory and the Soviet-East European Hierarchial Regional System: Initial Tests," in Ronald H. Linden, The Foreign Policies of East Europe: New Approaches (Praeger, 1980), p. 182; see also Peter Summerscale, "Is Eastern Europe a Liability to the Soviet Union?" International Affairs (Autumn 1981), p. 585.

Part IV

Economics and Defence

12
Resource Allocation for Defence in NATO and WTO

Rainer Rupp

REVIVAL OF AN EAST-WEST ARMS RACE?

Two decades ago, U.S. superiority was unquestioned and the Soviets were well behind in terms of military capability. Determined to overcome that inferiority, the Soviets have been steadily increasing their hardware inventories, building up the capability of their weaponry, and adding to the numbers of their forces. Two unrelated crises in the early 1960s impelled the Soviets to increase their defence expenditures. According to a senior specialist in national defence for the U.S. Congressional Research Service, the belligerence of China served as the catalyst and the embarrassment caused by the U.S. over Cuba served as the capstone for a new Soviet assessment which convinced Moscow that military improvements should proceed at far higher rates than previously planned.[1]

U.S. General Alexander Haig, during his Senate confirmation hearings, called it "the most complete reversal of global power relationships ever seen in a period of relative peace". "If unchecked," he added, "this growth of Soviet military power must eventually paralyse Western foreign policy and to a certain extent it already has".[2] U.S. Senator, Charles Percy, argues that the massive build-up, however, does not mean that the Soviets have any desire to go to war; and, in a recent interview, the British Prime Minister, Margaret Thatcher, explained that the real danger was that the Soviets "hoped eventually to be able to get their own way just by threat because no one dared to stand up to them".[3] These comments by public officials focus on the Soviet Union which is certainly the West's most dangerous adversary--one requiring unremitting attention; but the many dangers arising from other sources, sources with little or not Soviet connections, must not be overlooked.[4]

Indeed what we are witnessing today is an historic transformation process from the former bipolar world into a multipolar complex--a complex with increasingly antagonistic centers of political, economic, and military power, overlapped in many cases by the global competition of the two superpowers. Indeed, the more familiar East-West differences are increasingly influenced by friction between the developed and the developing nations; by a new militant Third World nationalism, sometimes mixed with religious fanatism; by the spread of nuclear weapons technology; and by competition for dwindling natural resources--all of which add to a lengthening list of potential menace to peace and stability. But there are also increasing threats to our domestic stability: international terrorism; new groups outside parliament effectively blocking the implementation of vital government decisions; and new economic problems that, if unsolved, could easily develop into real threats to our existing social, economic, and political foundations.[5]

This general transformation process has also affected the internal relationship of the North Atlantic Alliance, which has led to certain recognised transatlantic dissonances. In this context, the political and economic emancipation of Europe vis-à-vis the United States is of crucial importance. Whilst this enamcipation has given the Europeans a new sense of confidence in their own strength which, by the way, has been translated into certain economic and political solo acts, the development affecting the U.S. was just the opposite and is commonly felt and described as the American decline.[6] Already marked by the defeat in Vietnam and the political disaster of Watergate, traditional American confidence was dealt another serious blow by the deep-rooted economic crisis which is taking the "classic heartland of American capitalism" into a "self-reinforcing downward spiral".[7] A whole series of other events have added further to the growing public perception of American weakness: the successful expansion of the Soviet sphere of influence to Angola, Mozambique, Ethiopia; the SALT II debate which emphasised American vulnerability for the first time; repeated energy crises, high inflation, high unemployment, low growth with the expectation of probably more of the same to come; the fall of the Shah of Iran, the hostage drama, and the feeling of American powerlessness in the face of arbitrary actions of a third-rate nation; and, last but not least, Afghanistan which seemed the straw that broke the camel's back--in this case, American patience.

As a result, the American public was no longer prepared to acquiesce quietly in the erosion of U.S. power.

Conscious of the basic fact that America remains by far the world's strongest free nation--economically and militarily, to say nothing of its profound belief in the dignity and wealth of the individual and his freedom of choice--the American people decided to attempt the reversal of adverse political, economic, and military trends confronting the nation.

Long before the 1980 U.S. presidential elections, the desire to restore American power went like a ground-wave through the American society. By the end of 1980, 56 percent of Americans believed that "too little" was being spent on defence; the highest percentage since 1950. In 1950, 40 percent of the population still believed that the United States was militarily stronger than the Soviet Union, and only 19 percent viewed the U.S.S.R. as more powerful. Now those proportions have been reversed.[8]

It is not surprising that President Reagan's election promise to scrap SALT and to restore U.S. military superiority was enthusiastically received. The Europeans, also, welcomed this new American resolve insofar as it is designed to preserve the balance of power or to restore it in those areas where it has slipped in favour of the Soviet Union. On the whole, however, the Europeans prefer to think in terms of equilibria.[9] Consequently, the European reaction to American intention to restore overall superiority has been rather reserved, particularly as the Europeans fear both the dangers and the enormous cost of a new, intensive round in the arms race. The Soviet reaction, on the other hand, was as expected: "the U.S. administration would be naive to believe that the Soviet Union would permit the U.S. to regain military superiority".[10]

At this point, we are confronted with a number of important questions. Will a new arms race between superpowers occur? If so, who will emerge the winner? How much more can the weaker Soviet economy spend on military programmes? Can the U.S. afford guns and butter simultaneously in a time of economic decline? What will the Europeans do, faced with growing economic difficulties and little public enthusiasm to support an American drive for superiority? Will they adopt a bystander's role? If so, the Americans may feel isolated and left to carry a disproportionate share of the defence burden. It does not need much imagination to foresee serious transatlantic problems, if such a scenario develops.

Whatever the future may bring, at the moment the mood of many Americans is such that they are prepared, if necessary, to 'go it alone'. After all, the argument goes, the U.S. economy is so much richer and the U.S. Gross Domestic Product (GDP) is about 40% larger than that of the Soviet Union. Professor Georgy Arbatov, head of the Institute of U.S. and Canadian Studies of the Soviet Academy of Sciences, has replied to this argument recently on German television: "yes, the Americans may have a higher GDP, but the Russians have a greater capacity to suffer".[11]

Whatever the arguments, a revival of the arms race will seriously strain the resources of both countries. High economic growth, as it was experienced in previous decades, is not likely--either in the East or the West. A new arms race will, therefore, mean serious and prolonged economic sacrifices in both countries. The winner, if there is one, will not be the bigger spender, but the smarter one--the one who uses scarce resources most efficiently, and in accordance with a clear concept. Thus a nation's capacity to endure a new arms race, not just to begin one, depends essentially on the following factors: the ability to use scarce resources for defence most efficiently; the basic economic/war-making capability of the nation; and the public's capacity to sacrifice: i.e., continued public support and national political consensus to give priority to defence in the face of growing economic difficulties.

EFFICIENT UTILIZATION OF RESOURCES

The West seems quite convinced of its technological superiority and industrial efficiency, and it automatically assumes that scarce resources spent on defence are efficiently used. Unfortunately, this is not always the case; there are countless examples of waste: duplication of research and development, lack of standardisation, interoperability, and, most importantly, much greater waste in the procurement system. Only too often some laboratory scientist invents a new, more lethal, or more accurate device for which no operational need exists, but which after a sales talk with military experts, becomes a need and then a necessity. If the device indicates a problem for which there is at present no solution, so much the better; it must be investigated and funds are needed (the 'too-soon-to-know' stage). Soon other problems emerge and more funds are necessary (the 'too-late-to-stop' stage). Thus the miracle aircraft, Tornado, was originally scheduled to cost DM 15 million each; a price which has now reached about DM 70 million--each more than four times the original cost estimate. A German defence engineer who worked on the Tornado programme and who studied in depth the functioning of the European and, specifically, the German defence industry, concluded that, "there is more competition in the Soviet than in the West German arms industry".[12] Western ability to use scarce resources for defence efficiently certainly merits further such study.

ECONOMIC STRENGTH AND WAR CAPABILITY

Western methods of evaluating the economic strength of different nations usually concentrates on measuring the gross domestic product (GDP), i.e., comparing one nation's output of goods and services with that of another. The Soviet Union and other COMECON countries use the Marxist concept of Net Material Product (NMP), a method which eliminates most services as well as other elements contained in the Western calculation. In addition, there is a totally different valuation system, with prices of goods often having no relation to their scarcity and true market value. Thus, even if there were no data problems, straight forward GDP-NMP comparisons are worth very little--even less if the war-making capability is to be compared. Detailed studies are needed to translate the individual elements of NMP into a more or less equivalent element of GDP. With much of the Soviet data incomplete, Western studies to convert NMP into GDP require an enormous effort, and consequently, are only done infrequently. The latest such intensive study, which is an authoritative work, was conducted for the year 1976 and was presented in 1979 to the Joint Economic Committee of the United States Congress.[13] (See Table 12.1). By accident, or perhaps by design, a Soviet study which translates U.S. GNP into Soviet style NMP was also made for the same year, 1976. (Table 12.2). Although the actual figures of the two studies are quite different, the resulting overall proportions are surprisingly similar. The most interesting aspects, however, can be found in the composition of the totals and in the fact that the Soviet study looks at how NMP is produced in the U.S. and the U.S.S.R., while the American study looks at how GNP is distributed in both countries.

Clearly there are some inconsistencies in these two graphs; but, at the moment, they are the best available to compare the two economies. On the whole, the most striking aspect with regard to the United States is the consumption figure--almost 70%. (Table 12.2). The U.S. consumes, on the whole, more than it is producing. Consumption in the Soviet Union, on the other hand, is relatively lower, but an enormous amount is allocated to investment and to defence and space--almost double that

TABLE 12.1

US AND SOVIET NMP* IN 1976
IN BILLION US $

(SOVIET CALCULATIONS, USING SOVIET METHODOLOGY)

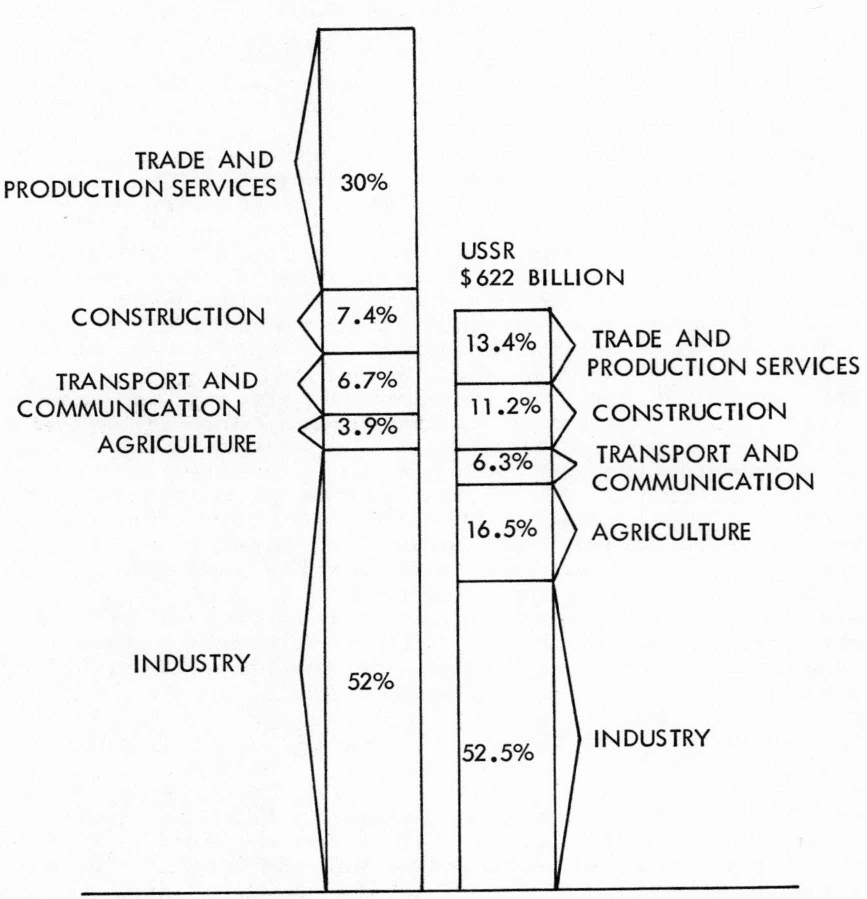

SOURCE : SOVIET NATIONAL STATISTICS
*: NATIONAL MATERIAL PRODUCT (NET)

TABLE 12.2

PERCENTAGE DISTRIBUTION OF GNP 1976

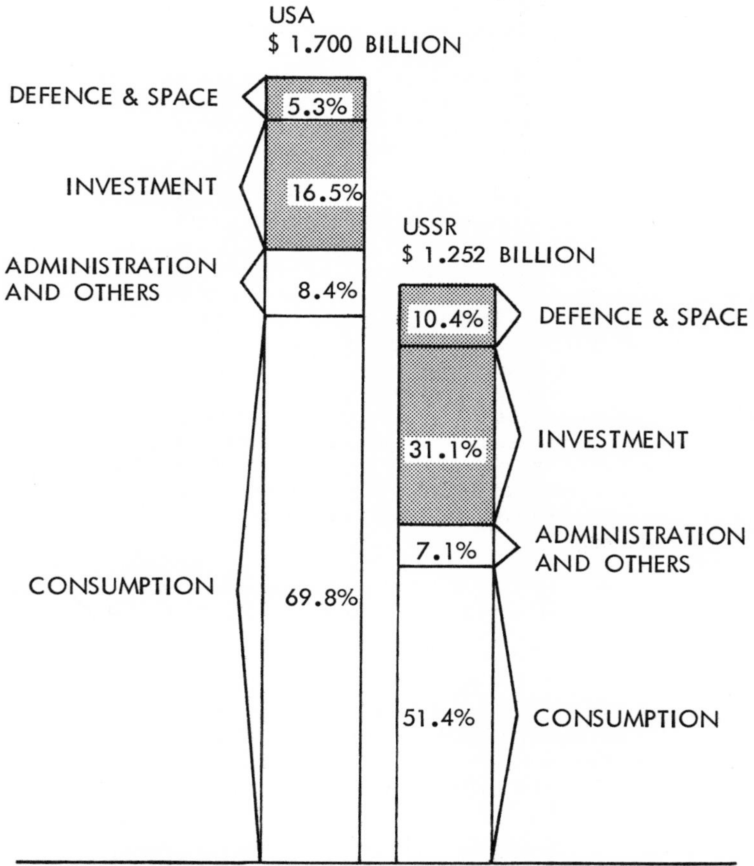

SOURCES: Joint Economic Committee, U.S. Congress, "The Soviet Economy in a Time of Change" - compendium of papers, Oct. 1979 - paper by Edwards, Hughes and Noren; "US and USSR: Comparison of GNP"; see also "CIA Handbook of Economic Statistics 1980" and "OECD National Accounts ofOECD Countries 1952-1977" Paris 1979.

of the United States. Obviously, the Soviets have the capacity to transfer resources from this investment sector into defence; although, in the long run, this capacity is related to consumption. The primary conclusion which can be drawn from these graphs is that the U.S. economy is larger than that of the Soviet, without regard to measurement in GNP or NMP. The Soviets, however, devote not only a larger share, but also a considerably larger volume of the national budget to defence and investment industries. Thus the Soviets have an industrial capacity comparable in war-making capability to that of the United States, if not even larger.[14]

In the United States, the largest percentage of GNP is produced in the non-industrial sectors of the economy which have little or no relation to the country's ability to wage war. With regard to the use of the gross national product, Western economies respond primarily to market forces which, under democratic political systems, tend to give priority to consumer demands, whilst communist systems are based on centralised control, and strongly oriented towards industrial and military investments. A report to the Joint Economic Committee of the U.S. Congress noted that "Perhaps the most noteworthy aspect of the Soviet economic history over the past twenty-five years has been the U.S.S.R.'s success in supporting both military and civilian investment so lavishly".[15] In other words, while Western consumer societies believe in butter before guns (which may be butter <u>and</u> guns, if the society is rich enough), the Soviet Union stresses basic capacity to undergird its power.[16]

Another way of comparing U.S. and Soviet economies as related to defence expenditures and war-making capability is to examine not what the Soviet Union actually spends, but rather what the United States would have to spend to duplicate the Soviet defence effort. (Tables 12.3 and 12.4)

This kind of comparison is useful for the American administration as it shows how much it would cost to support an army of four and one-half million paid in U.S. salaries, to produce as many tanks and aircraft as the Soviet Union, but at U.S. prices. According to this dollar-costing methodology, the CIA calculated that in 1980 the U.S. would have had to spend $175 billion to reproduce the Soviet military effort. It would, however, be utterly wrong to conclude that the Soviets actually spent $175 billion for their military. The official Soviet figures are far too low to be credible, but even if the actual rouble figure they spent on

TABLE 12.3

TOTAL US AND SOVIET DEFENCE ACTIVITIES

(A COMPARISON OF US OUTLAYS WITH ESTIMATED DOLLAR COSTS OF SOVIET ACTIVITIES IF DUPLICATED IN THE UNITED STATES)

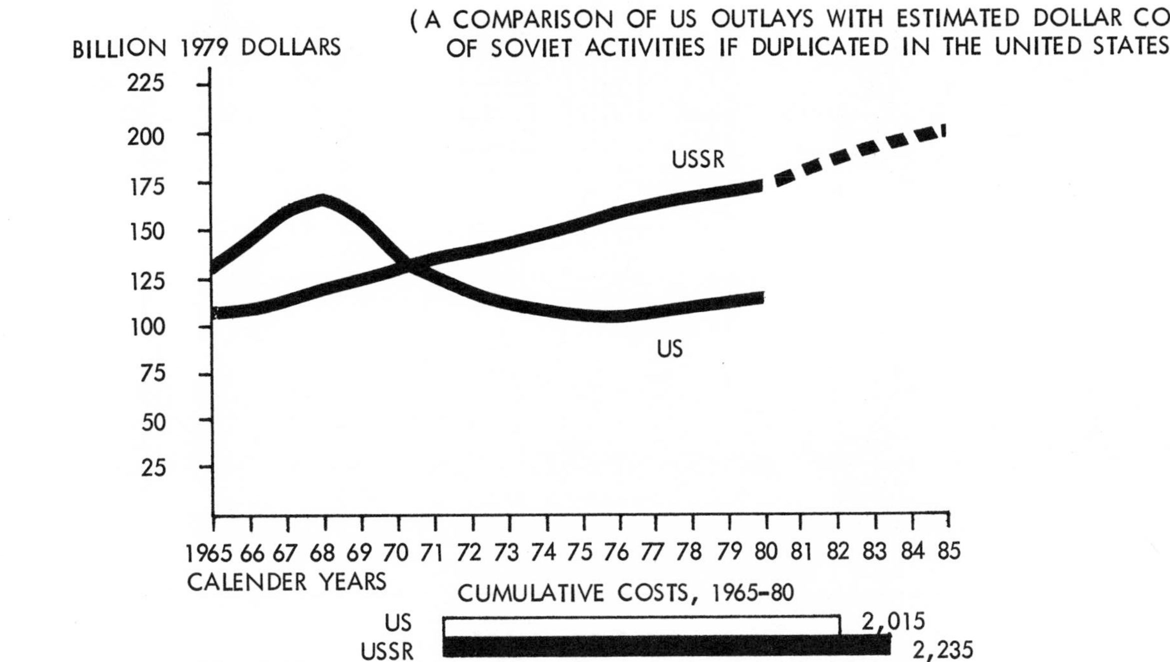

Source: Edward, Hughes and Noren, "US and USSR: Comparisons of GNP" in Soviet Economy in Time of Change. Joint Economic Committee, U.S. Congress, Vol. 1 (GPO 1979) pp. 369-394

TABLE 12.4

DOLLAR COST OF SOVIET ACTIVITIES AND US DEFENSE OUTLAYS
(IN BILLION 1979 $)

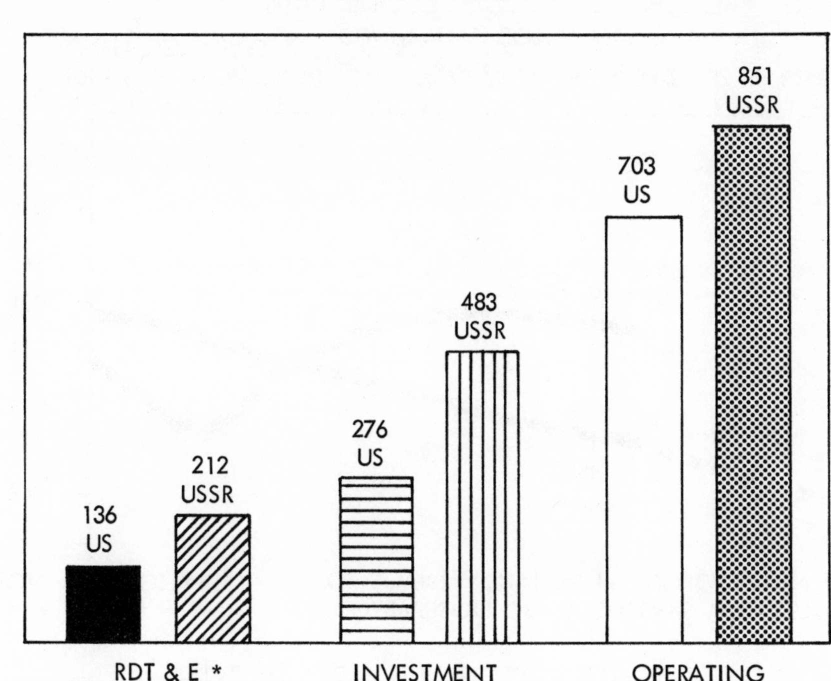

TABLE 12.4, CONT'D

CUMULATIVE COST, 1971 - 1980 (in billion 1979 $)

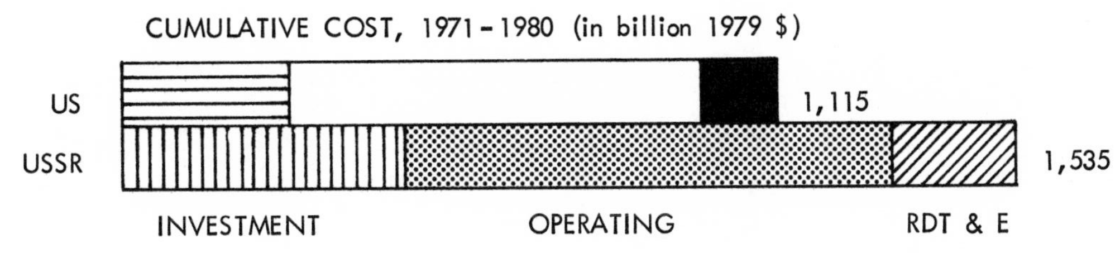

Investment includes all costs for the procurement of military hardware and the construction of facilities. Operating includes all personnel-related costs (with the exception of pensions) and all costs associated with the operation and maintenance of weapons systems and facilities. RDT & E includes the costs of exploring new technologies, developing advanced weapon systems, and improving existing systems.

* Reasearch, Development, Testing and Evaluation
Source: See Table 12.3

defence were known, it could not be translated into dollars.

The appraisal of Soviet military spending is hindered partly by extreme Soviet secrecy and partly by technical problems and complexities. The official Soviet budget figure for military expenditure rose from 12.8 billion roubles in 1965 to 14.5 billion by 1967 and peaked in 1970 at 17.9 billion. The yearly figures remained at that level until 1973, declined slightly to 17.4 billion roubles by 1974, and fell to 17.1 billion in 1979.

As mentioned above, this rise in spending gave ground for scepticism since the Soviet Union, in terms of military capabilities, overtook the United States in some areas and closed the gap in many others during the last decade.

A number of intelligence services of NATO member countries, using similar approaches, also estimate the Soviet military expenditure in rouble terms on the basis of Soviet data. The findings of these various calculations and estimates are recorded in a detailed report. The most recent unclassified version of this report stated that in 1979, Soviet military expenditure had grown to 58-63 billion roubles, up from 40-44 billion roubles in 1970 (all figures are in 1970 prices). This means that "defence expenditure in 1970 represented between 11 and 12 percent of the gross national product, but had risen to between 12 and 13 percent by the end of the decade". The evidence presented in the report points to a continuation of past trends in the production of new weapons and it forecasts that "Soviet defence outlays will grow at least through 1985 at an annual average rate of over 4 percent in real terms. If so, the defence share of Soviet GNP would rise to about 15 percent by 1985 as growth in the economy declines."[17]

THE ECONOMIES OF THE WARSAW PACT COUNTRIES

The Soviet Union is the world's largest producer of steel, oil, cement, tractors, and tanks. Moreover, the Soviet Union is a net exporter for most important raw materials and, only in a few areas, does it have to rely on imports. Nevertheless, over recent years the Soviet economy has faced increasing constraints which led to deceleration of previously high growth rates. These constraints--reflected in continued low productivity increases, a decrease in energy production, accentuated problems in infrastructure, planning rigidities, and potential labour shortages--are likely to exert a further downward pressure on Soviet economic performance in the 1980s. Despite this negative outlook, however, annual increases in GNP will probably average 2-3 percent throughout the 1980s, a level which could compare favourably with the likely performance of the West. Soviet leaders may also succeed in stimulating greater economic growth through certain reforms which have been introduced successfully in other CMEA countries. If successful in the Soviet Union as well, these reforms could enhance productivity and provide for quicker dissemination of new technology, other than in the military sphere where this is already being done.

Furthermore, as the Soviet economy becomes increasingly complex, it will need more flexibility and greater decentralisation in decision making. Recognizing the need for change, the Soviet Union may consider economic reforms recently implemented in various Eastern European countries. In these economies, which are dominated by Soviet economic strength, growth will be more uncertain, primarily because both dependence on imported raw materials is growing and demands from consumers are increasing. The combination of economic, national, religious, and political developments that led to the current crisis in Poland is, however, less likely to repeat itself in another Warsaw Pact nation. As for the Soviet Union, consumer demand has always had very little leverage on decisions concerning allocation of resources, but it may exert increasing pressure on decision making in the 1980s.

Whatever the uncertainties of the future, the Soviet economy, at least with regard to the allocation of resources for defence, has maintained many aspects of a war economy: namely, the high degree of centralisation of the decision-making process in all phases of economic activity--planning, investment, materials allocation, and planned management; and the centralized allocation of resources on the basis of administratively established priorities. Unburdened by the cumbersome process in the West for defining national priorities (and where demands for resources for defence compete with highly politicised civilian claims), the Soviet government enjoys unquestioned authority for decisions to allocate its best resources to defence. Unlike those in the West, Soviet military needs can be met with little regard for civilian claims to scarce raw materials, skilled manpower, and production capacities. In sum, whatever the final outcome of the Soviet economic growth may be in the 1980s, the Soviets have the economic capacity to maintain and expand their military capabilities. Indeed, judging by more than twenty major current and planned Soviet armaments programmes, a continued expansion of Soviet military capabilities can be expected at least until 1985. As a result, defence expenditures are expected to increase along past trends; that is to say, 3-4 percent in real terms per annum.[18] This anticipated rise would increase the share of defence expenditure in the GDP from an estimated 12-13 percent at present to approximately 15 percent in 1985. Economic difficulties, however, could give the Soviets an incentive to moderate growth in military outlays, and it is possible that they will alter their weapons production goals. Thus, economic constraints could give the Soviets added incentive to seek arms control negotiations.

ECONOMIC GROWTH IN NATO COUNTRIES

Since the beginning of the 1970s, reduced economic growth rates, rising unemployment and high rates of inflation have proved to be intractable problems facing all Alliance countries. These problems have created circumstances in which conventional economic strategies have been ineffective. The oil crisis compounded and aggravated these problems, leading to substantial transfers of real income to OPEC nations and causing serious balance of payments problems that are likely to persist. Inflation, to which most member countries have reacted with policies of fiscal and monetary constraints, is also likely to remain at high levels throughout the 1980s, seriously reducing the prospects of sustained economic growth as well as implying that unemployment may reach critical levels during the first half of the 1980s, with adverse political and economic repercussions. To meet new and changing economic and social requirements, there will be an increasing demand for more public funds. Low economic growth, however, will seriously reduce budgetary receipts, creating pressures in most countries to contain the rise of public spending. Amidst this general spending restraint, defence budgets will come under growing pressure from different social groups trying to preserve their own share of the cake. Thus increasing social discontent may pose a very serious challenge to the ability of NATO countries to give the necessary political and economic priority to defence.

On balance, however, and in view of the overall industrial, technological and economic capacities of the Alliance, total available resources in NATO are considerable and the potential to match the Warsaw Pact and, in particular, the Soviet military effort cannot be questioned. Today, the impact of defence on the Western economies is, on the whole, much lower than in the 1960s and 1970s. A considerably higher defence effort could be supported in NATO countries without intolerable economic strain. In view of the likely slow economic growth, resulting social and political strain is much more difficult to calculate, particularly in Europe. Unlike the United States, which plans to finance its military expansion by sharp cuts in social programmes, there is simply no political consensus in Western Europe for such a radical shift in priorities.

Even in the United States, it remains to be seen how the economy and the nation will react to a combination of high increases in defence expenditure, tax cuts, and continued high budget deficits. Whatever the effect, they will not be immediately felt: the sacrifices required of the nation will only begin to hurt in a year's time, at the earliest. The capacity to make sacrifices, then, emerges as a critical factor in assessing relative East-West capabilities.

DEMOCRACIES AND SELF-SACRIFICE: NATO DEFENCE EXPENDITURES

What is the capacity of free and democratic societies to endure sacrifices in the absence of war? In the case of the United States, how strong and how lasting is the national consensus to give priority to defence in the face of growing economic difficulties? At a recent meeting of the NATO Nuclear Planning Group (NPG), U.S. officials pointed out that the new pro-defence mood in the United States is "fragile" and would not endure "if there is not support within the Alliance as a whole".[19] Mr. Weinberger, U.S. Secretary of Defence, also made it clear that "the American people will not want to march alone" and "if our effort is not joined by all who are threatened ... we ... could lose at home the critical public support for which we have laboured long and hard".[20] Similar concerns are increasingly echoed from the U.S. Congress.

The United States wants a higher military contribution from the European allies, particularly as NATO Europe's GNP now exceeds that of the U.S. In 1956 NATO Europe's combined GNP/GDP, excluding Greece and Turkey) was $217 million; the US figure was $423 million. By 1970 these figures had changed to $664 million for NATO Europe and $981 million for the U.S., and last year, the figures were $2.8 trillion and $2.5 trillion respectively.* The American argument that NATO Europe's

* Corresponding ratios are as follows: 1950 - .51 to 1; 1970 - .65 to 1; 1980 - 1.11 to 1.

defence contribution is not commensurate with its economic strength is based on these changing ratios.

Many Europeans, however, see the problem quite differently. The European perspective was probably explained most comprehensively by a leading member of the West German Social Democratic Party when he rejected American attempts to persuade European nations to increase defence spending.[21] He argued that if shortcomings exist in NATO defences, it is the fault of the United States because it has failed to match Russia's arms increases over the past few years. From 1963 to 1980, defence spending in the Soviet Union doubled, while it decreased 8% in the United States. During the same period, Western Europe increased its defence spending in real terms by 30%. Perceptions of burden sharing seem to differ substantially from one side of the Atlantic to another: who is correct? The graphs on pages 285-288 illustrate some aspects of these controversies.

A cursory glance at Table 12.5 gives the impression of a tremendous rise in NATO expenditures from 1970 to 1980. It is a deceptive picture, which shifts dramatically when these expenditures are deflated, as illustrated in Table 12.6, expressed in constant 1978 prices. In the latter table, an overall decrease in expenditures is apparent, some of which can be explained by the U.S. disengagement in Southeast Asia. On the whole, however, American defense expenditure in real terms decreased, while NATO European expenditures showed a slight increase.

For some time now the question of burden sharing of Alliance defence has been a focal point of the transatlantic public debate. The development of the defence share in GDP, which is only another term for the economic burden of the defence effort, in North America and in NATO Europe is shown in Table 12.7. During the 1970s the defence burden, which decreased considerably in North America, remained well above that of NATO Europe, which remained more or less unchanged. (Table 12.10 reflects the large differences among individual nations' willingness to divert economic resources to defence.) The defence burden, which is nothing else but the opportunity cost of defence, reflects the degree of national

TABLE 12.5

DEFENCE EXPENDITURES OF NATO COUNTRIES 1970–1980

(CURRENT PRICES – BILLION US $ AT 1978 EXCHANGE RATES)

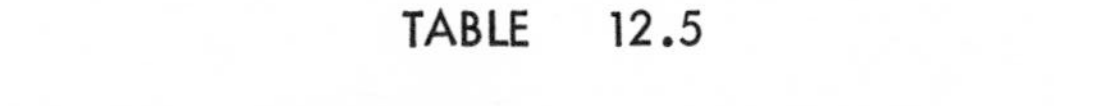

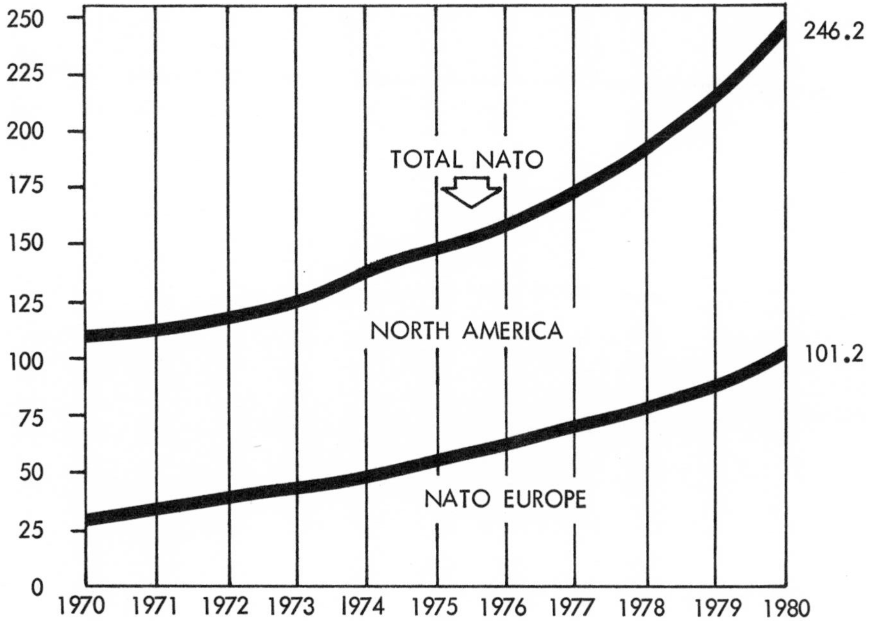

SOURCE: NATO

TABLE 12.6

DEFENCE EXPENDITURES OF NATO COUNTRIES 1970-1980
(1978 CONSTANT PRICES - BILLION US $ AT 1978 EXCHANGE RATES)

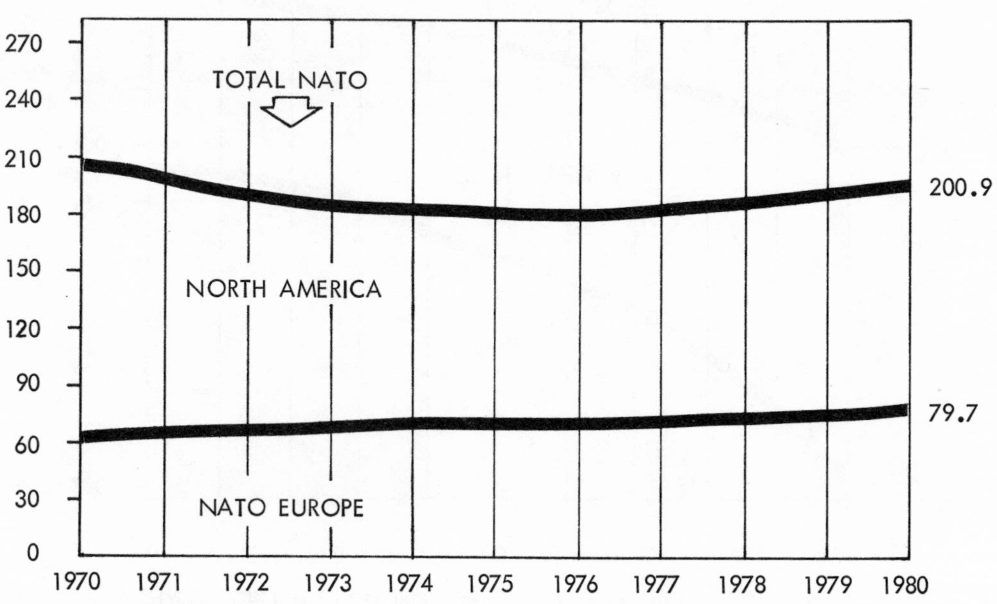

SOURCE: NATO

TABLE 12.7

DEFENCE SHARE OF GROSS DOMESTIC PRODUCT 1970-1980
(Current Prices . Calender Years)

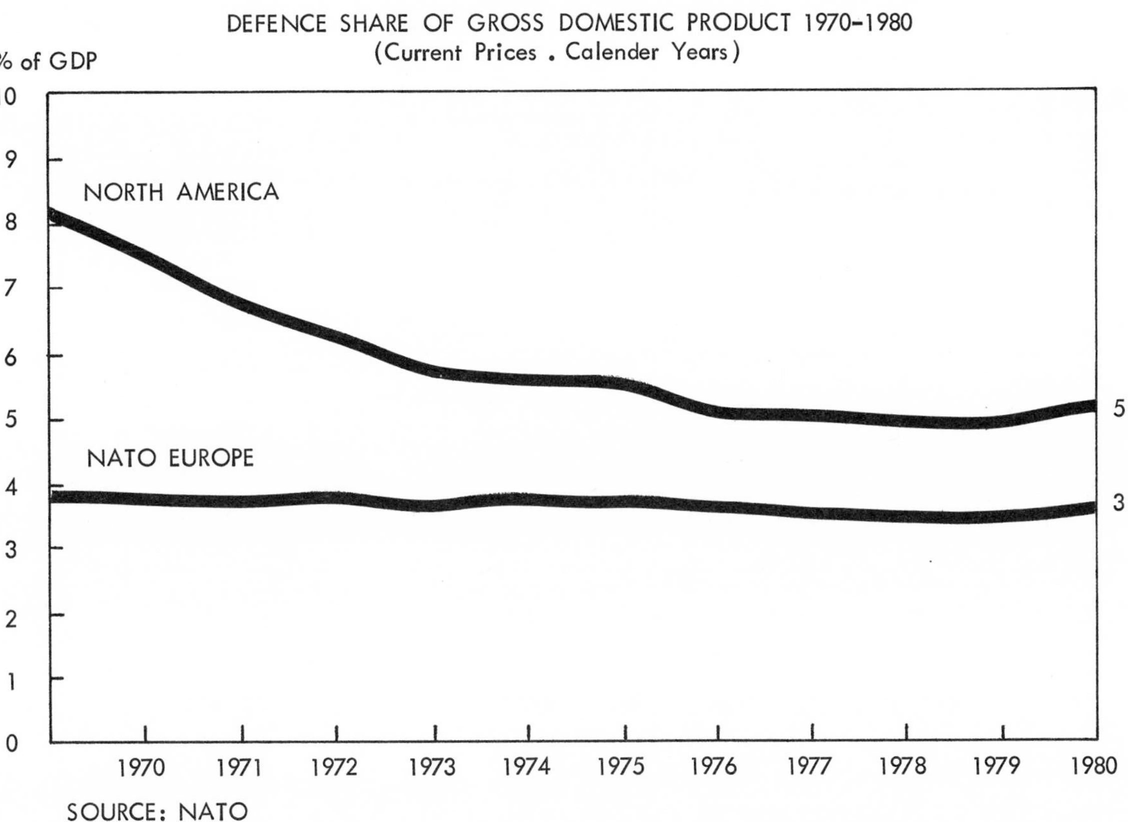

SOURCE: NATO

TABLE 12.8

DEFENSE EXPENDITURES AS % OF GROSS DOMESTIC PRODUCT 1980

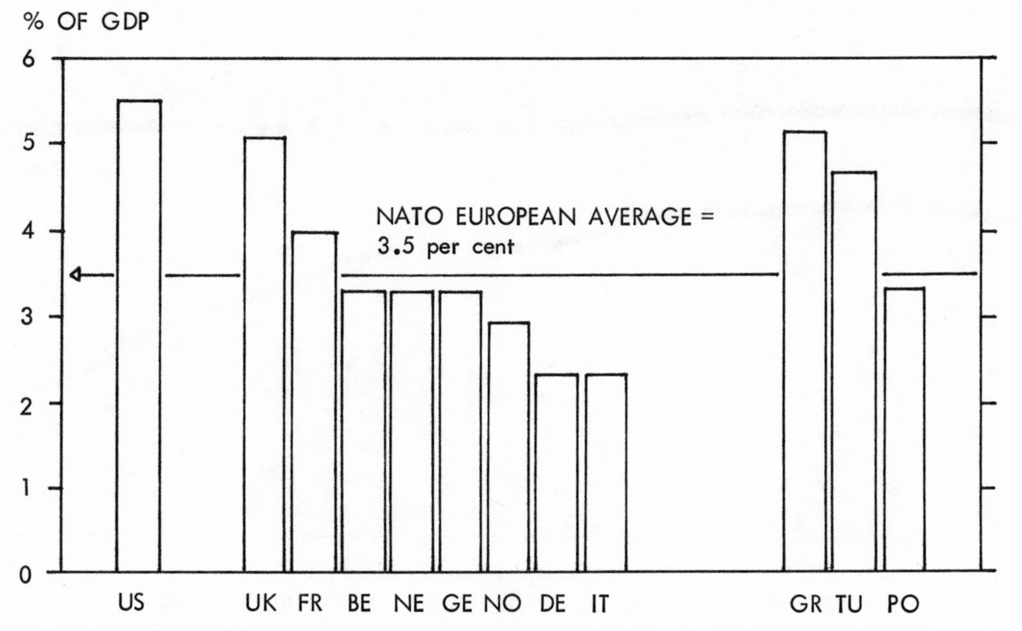

SOURCE: NATO PRESS RELEASE AND OECD

priority given to defence. By far the highest burden continues to be carried by the United States followed by the United Kingdom. Compared with the relatively rich industrialised nations of Northern Europe, the less prosperous member countries such as Turkey, Greece and Portugal are also carrying a much higher defence burden.

The question of how much each nation contributes to the totality of NATO's defence spending, is addressed by Table 12.8. In 1980, total NATO spending amounted to $246.2 billion. Taken as 100 percent, the North American contribution amounts to about 57.6 percent of which Canada accounts for 1.7 percent. NATO Europe contributes the remaining 42.4 percent of which 10.8 percent is accounted for by the Federal Republic of Germany, followed by France (10.6 percent) and the United Kingdom (10.3 percent). The other smaller European nations contribute another 10.7 percent.

Comparisons of GDP per capital and defence expenditure per capita also play an important role in the burden sharing debate. GDP per capita comparisons provide a useful, although far from ideal, indication of the relative wealth and standard of living of nations. Table 12.9 shows the large discrepancy between the less prosperous nations of the South and the rich industrialised nations of the North. The second noteworthy point is that the United States and Canada are located in the middle-range of the table. This is partially a reflection of the growth of European prosperity, but mostly a result of the depreciation of the U.S. dollar versus most European currencies during 1980. For example in 1980 one US dollar could be bought for as little as DM 1.75. In 1981, however, the dollar rallied again to more than DM 2.25. Consequently, if Table 12.9 were recalculated with this higher dollar exchange rate, the U.S. would be in quite a different position. A similar caution must be observed if defence expenditure per capita is compared (Table 12.10). Reviewing the burden sharing debate, it can be said that over most of the 1970s, defence expenditure in the United States decreased in real terms as well as in terms of burden on the economy i.e. share of defence in GDP. However, even at its lowest level the U.S. defence effort was still well above the efforts of the European nations. Most of the latter, however, quite rightfully point out that their defence expenditure increased quite substantially in real terms as illustrated by the following three tables.

Using official NATO figures as a base, these graphs present defence expenditures of NATO countries <u>in constant prices</u> in which 1970 is taken as an index and is

TABLE 12.9

GROSS DOMESTIC PRODUCT PER HEAD IN NATO COUNTRIES 1980

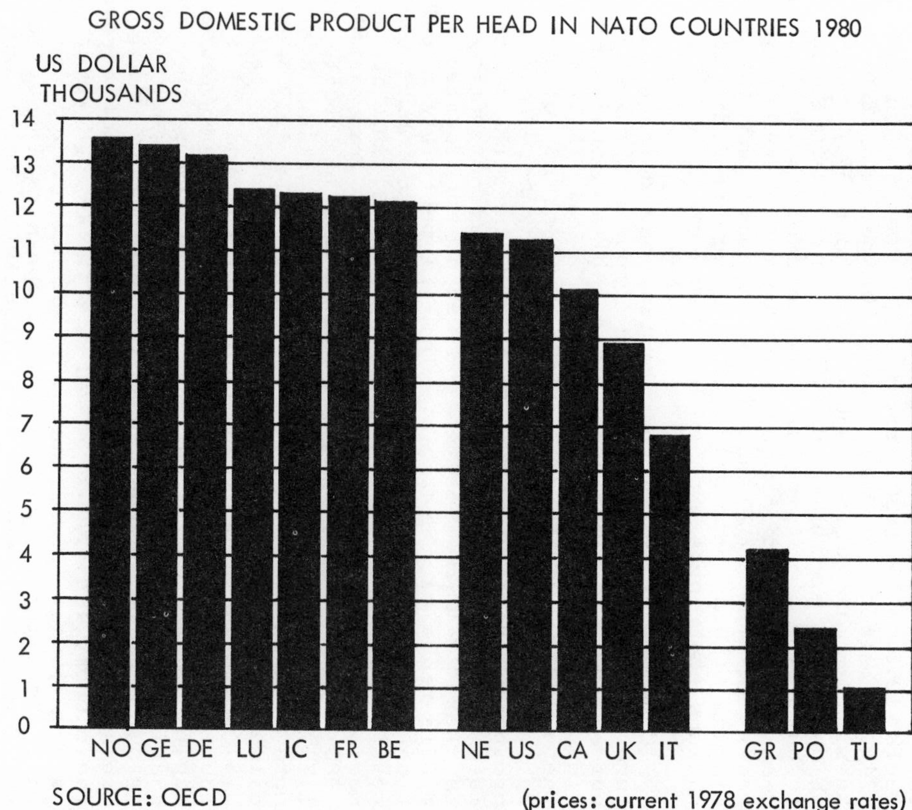

SOURCE: OECD

(prices: current 1978 exchange rates)

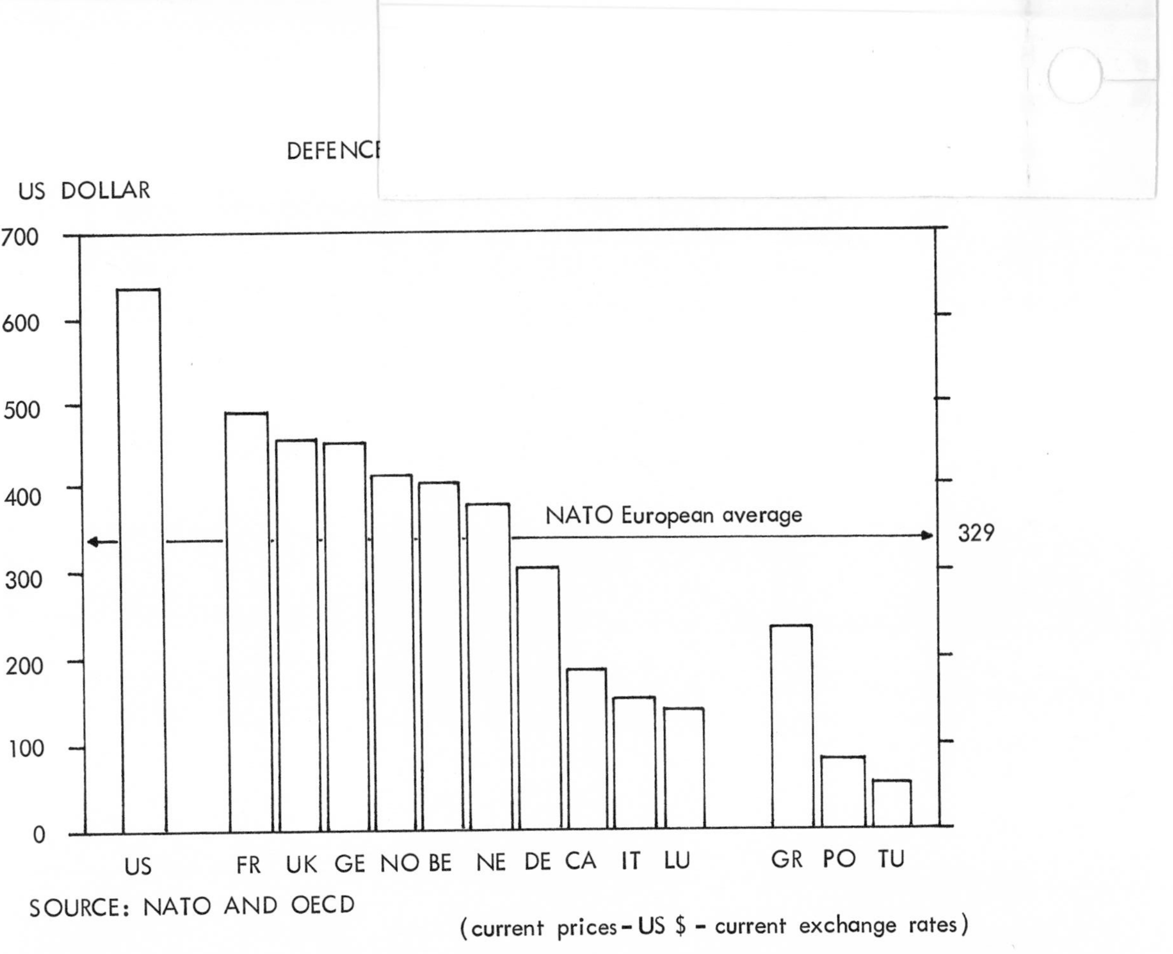
DEFENC
US DOLLAR
700
600
500
400
300
200
100
0
NATO European average
329
US FR UK GE NO BE NE DE CA IT LU GR PO TU
SOURCE: NATO AND OECD
(current prices - US $ - current exchange rates)

TABLE 12.11

DEFENCE EXPENDITURE IN CONSTANT PRICES

(GDP DEFLATORS)

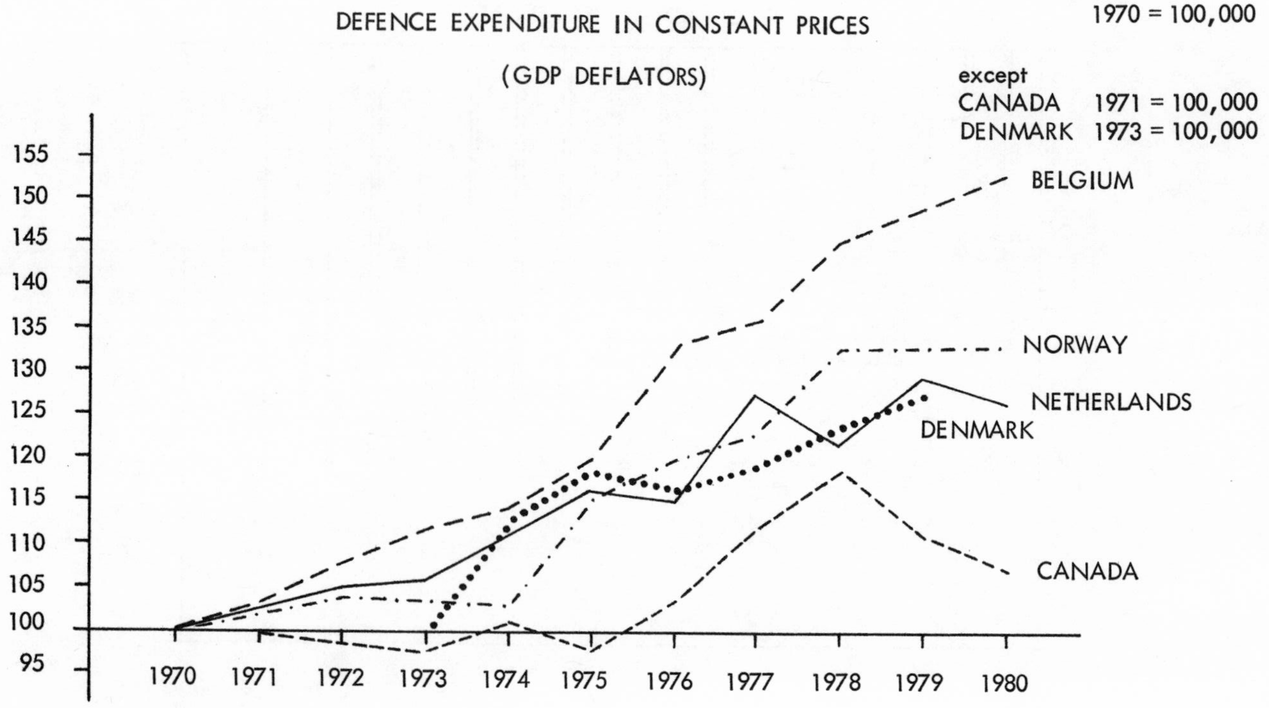

1970 = 100,000

except
CANADA 1971 = 100,000
DENMARK 1973 = 100,000

BELGIUM
NORWAY
NETHERLANDS
DENMARK
CANADA

155
150
145
140
135
130
125
120
115
110
105
100
95

1970 1971 1972 1973 1974 1975 1976 1977 1978 1979 1980

TABLE 12.12

DEFENCE EXPENDITURE IN CONSTANT PRICES
(GDP DEFLATORS)

1970 = 100,000

230
220
210
200
190
180
170
160
150
140
130
120
110
100
90
80
70

1970 1971 1972 1973 1974 19 75 1976 1977 1978 1979 1980

TURKEY
LUXEMBOURG
GREECE
PORTUGAL

TABLE 12.13

DEFENCE EXPENDITURE IN CONSTANT PRICES

(GDP DEFLATORS)

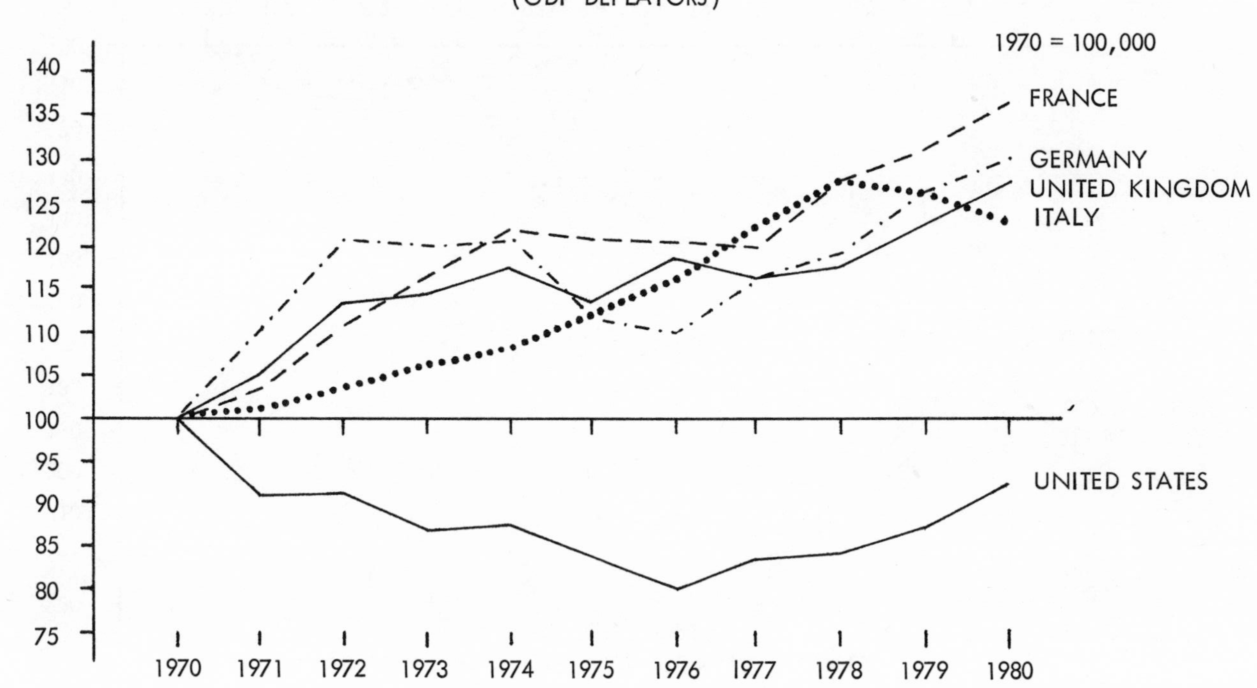

equal to 100. It is noteworthy that especially the smaller NATO countries have substantially increased defence spending in real terms over the past ten years (See Table 12.11). The only exception is Canada. Two developing countries of the Alliance (Turkey and Greece) have also greatly increased defence expenditures. A much more stunning picture emerges with regard to the larger countries--France, Germany, the United Kingdom, Italy and the United States (Table 12.13). Admittedly, the United States has greatly increased its military appropriations in the past eighteen months, but the European efforts have been growing consistently over the past ten years.

What should be clear from this series of graphs is 1) that no perfect, single indicator exists for comparing national defence expenditures and 2) that the indicator or indicators selected by any given group almost always reflect a political bias of one sort or another.

In his recent report to Congress the U.S. Secretary of Defence Caspar Weinberger takes ample account of the problems and complexities of the burden sharing measurements, particularly as "some indicators can be misleading if considered in isolation" while other "allied contributions are not readily quantifiable".[22] For instance, "if allied defence manpower costs reflected their true civil-sector opportunity costs, the value of non-U.S. NATO defence contributions would be larger than they appear with conscription costs". Furthermore, "since Western Europe and the Western Pacific are the potential battlefields, our allies contribute the entirety of their civil infrastructure to the potential war effort". Finally there is the non-military economic assistance to the developing countries which is considered by a number of European allies and Japan "as an important share of their contribution to world security and stability". These considerations as well as the graphs reviewed above illustrate the complexity of the burden sharing problem and the resulting difficulties in determining what a fair share of that burden should be. Therefore Dr. Luns, Secretary General of NATO, wisely called for an end to the "unprofitable transatlantic debate over the question of who provides what for Allied defence"[23]

There is, however, something far more profound behind Europe's resistance to increased defence spending than this sterile debate on who spends how much. Differing American and European perceptions of the Soviet threat and of Soviet efforts to expand influence in the Third World are responsible for transatlantic dissonance. For the Americans, curtailing the debate over arms control and rejecting SALT are part of a new determination to deal forcefully with the Soviet Union; whereas for the Europeans, forceful policies are right and acceptable only if accompanied by persistent determination to abate the arms race and to avoid a new cold war.[24]

Of course, Europe recognises the need to restore an East-West military balance, particularly with regard to the long-range theater nuclear force (LRTNF); but arms control is a major objective and Europeans expect less rearmament than the U.S. The Chancellor of the Federal Republic of Germany, Mr. Schmidt, in a luncheon address to visiting NATO Defence Ministers, clarified the German position by saying that "equilibrium or balance of military capabilities is a must, but it is not in itself sufficient to stabilise peace... One must talk and listen to the other side" and "compromises are to be sought".[25] The German position reflects that of most other European governments; and, in a recent speech before the Atlantic Institute in Paris, Mr. Corterier, the parliamentary spokesman on foreign affairs of the German Social Democratic Party, warned that U.S. disregard of European objectives and U.S. failure to consult would create more problems for the Alliance than for the Soviet Union.[26]

These divergencies of opinion and assessments have far-reaching implications for the cohesiveness of the Alliance and its joint capacity to mobilise sufficient resources to counter the Soviet military effort. As the Europeans must not be seen in Washington as insuffuciently interested in defending themselves, so also the Americans must not be seen in Europe as inadequately attuned to opportunities for treating security problems through negotiations.

SUMMING UP

Although economic difficulties could give the Soviets added incentive to seek arms control negotiations, a continued expansion of Soviet military capabilities can be expected, at least until 1985. Given this momentum, the shift in balance of power continues to move in favour of the Soviet Union and, if appropriate steps are not taken, could result in a possible inferiority of the Western position. NATO countries must allocate more for defence, although, given the likely medium-term economic outlook, proposals for increased defence spending will present Western welfare societies with divisive and difficult choices. Nevertheless, the West has the potential to check Soviet advances without risking intolerable economic strains, even though social and political strains are more difficult to calculate. The Western potential can only be successfully mobilised if all nations share the same strategic objective and assume a defence burden commensurate with their economic wealth. Although Western European societies recognise the necessity of maintaining the balance of power, and are prepared to make sacrifices, they are also worried that too much emphasis on the military balance could result in a new, more intensive arms race. The European objective constitutes, in fact, a constructive challenge to the Soviets through the dual approach successfully pursued for many years. Any prolonged deviation from this policy by one nation emphasizing only the deterrence part of the dual approach will seriously undermine allied cohesiveness and will result in damaging Western credibility that it can respond effectively to the Soviet challenge.

Challenging the Soviets constructively, however, means that increased defence spending is necessary to keep pace with the massive Soviet arms procurement of the last fifteen years. It is also in NATO's interest to achieve agreements with the East on the limitation of strategic and tactical nuclear weapons, on force reductions, and on confidence building measures--with the aim of securing peace not only with military means, but with political ones as well.

The United States is now taking appropriate steps to redress the military imbalance, but the American people do not want to bear the burden of defence alone. Given the reality of Western European interests in a good working relationship with Eastern Europe and the Soviet Union, and given Europe's very real fear of a new arms race, allied cohesiveness now depends importantly on American ability to manage its relations with the Soviet Union constructively.

FOOTNOTES

1. John M. Collins, U.S./Soviet Military Balance: Concepts and Capabilities, 1960/1980, Congressional Research Service, Library of Congress.

2. International Herald Tribune (12 January 1981).

3. See U.S. Wireless File, 20 March 1981, for Senator Percy's comments; Newsweek (25 April 1980) for an interview of Margaret Thatcher.

4. IHT (16 September 1980), p. 5. Comments by Ret. Gen. Maxwell D. Taylor.

5. Atlantic News (31 October 1981). See speech given by Dr. Josef Luns, Secretary General of NATO, given to the European Atlantic Group in London on 27 October 1980.

6. This feeling is probably best reflected in a recent letter to the New York Times from one of the U.S. founding fathers of the Alliance, Ambassador Theodore Achilles, in which he deplores the "decline in our pre-eminent leadership position, economically, militarily, morally and politically--in our own eyes and in those of our friends and of our adversaries." See Soviet and U.S. Defence Activities, 1970-1979: A Dollar Cost Comparison, National Foreign Assessment Center, SR80-10005, January 1980.

7. Michael Harrington, The Crisis of the American System (New York: Simon and Schuster, 1980), quoted in The New York Times, 1 May 1981.

8. U.S. Wireless File, 23 March 1981.

9. A popular expression current in Germany says: "Our security is also the security of the other side," meaning that only an equilibrium that is perceived by both sides as such, is a genuine guarantee for security.

10. The Guardian (17 March 1981). Speech by Dimitry Ustinov, Soviet Minister for Defence, given in Moscow on 16 March 1981.

11. Deutsches Fernsehprogramm (ARD), 16 March 1981.

12. The Financial Times (21 August 1980). Report on a doctoral thesis prepared by Dr. Bruno Koepple, Defence Engineer.

13. Imogene Edwards, Margaret Hughes, and James Noren, The Soviet Economy in a Time of Change, U.S. Congress, International Economic Committee, 10 October 1979, pp. 369-401.

14. The International Herald Tribune (19 June 1980). Comments by Frank A. Weil, former U.S. Assistant Secretary of Commerce.

15. Edwards, Hughes and Noren, Soviet Economy, p. 371.

16. Collins, US/Soviet Military Balance.

17. See my article, "Soviet Defence Expenditure," NATO Review (October 1981).

18. See comments by Mr. Robert Huffstutler, Director of Strategic Research, CIA, in testimony before Congress: "Whatever choices they (the Soviets) make with regard to defence spending, we think it highly unlikely that, even in the longer term, economic difficulties will force a reversal of the Soviet leaders' long-standing policy of continuing to improve their military capabilities." NATO Press Service, "Latest News," September 3, 1980.

19. U.S. Wireless File, 8 April 1981

20. Ibid.

21. Vorwärts (13 April 1981). See article by Mr. Egon Bahr.

22. U.S. Secretary of Defense, Report on Allied Commitments to Defense Spending (U.S. Government Printing Office, March 1981), pp. 1-3.

23. International Herald Tribune (23 February 1981). Speech given by Dr. Josef Luns at the "Wehrkunde Tagung" in Munich.

24. Peter Calvocoressi, London Sunday Times (8 February 1981); see also the different statements made at the recent "Wehrkunde Tagung" in Munich by U.S. Undersecretary for Defence, Mr. Frank Carlucci and by the German Minister for Defence, Mr. Hans Apel. Whilst Mr. Carlucci deplored the fact that "the U.S. no longer enjoys the strategic edge on the Soviet Union", Mr. Apel emphasised that "establishing and maintaining political stability on the basis of military equilibrium has top political priority". He added that Germany will "continue to pursue the policy of detente with patience when things seen to

stagnate" and will do so "with a proper sense of proportion for what is feasible." International Herald Tribune (23 February 1981).

25. Atlantic News (9 April 1981)

26. Ibid. (6 February 1981). Speech given by Mr. Peter Corterier, Parliamentary spokesman on foreign affairs of the German Social Democratic Party. He has since become a state minister in the Ministry of Foreign Affairs, Bonn.

Contributors

Derek C. Arnould	Canada. Director of External Information of the Canadian Department of External Affairs. Formerly head of General Political Affairs, North Atlantic Treaty Organization, Brussels.
Arlene Idol Broadhurst	United States. Formerly Assistant Professor, University of Southern California, Germany Program, Munich. Currently conducting research in Montreal, Canada.
Hedley Bull	Australia. Professor of International Relations, Oxford University, and Fellow of Balliol College. Author of _The Control of the Arms Race_ and _The Anarchical Society: A Study of Order in World Politics_.
Martin Edmonds	United Kingdom. Professor at Fylde College, Department of Politics, Fylde College, University of Lancaster. Editor of _International Arms Procurement: New Directives_.
Brigadier Kenneth Hunt	United Kingdom. Director of the British Atlantic Committee and formerly assistant director of the International Institute for Strategic Studies, London. Author of _Requirements of Military Strategy in the 1970s_; _Defense with Fewer Men_.

Richard Ned Lebow	United States. Professor of International Affairs at Johns Hopkins University, Bologna, Italy. Author of *Between Peace and War: The Nature of International Crisis* and co-author of *Divided Nations in a Divided World* (with Gregory Henderson and John Stoessinger).
Pierre Lellouche	France. Research Fellow at the Institut Français des Relations International. Most recent work, *Internationalization of the Nuclear Fuel Cycle and Non-Proliferation Strategy*. Contributor to *Foreign Affairs*.
Malcolm Mackintosh	United Kingdom. Consultant to the International Institute for Strategic Studies, London. Specialist in military affairs of the Soviet Union and Eastern Europe. Author of *Strategy and Tactics of Soviet Foreign Policy*; *The Evolution of the Warsaw Pact*.
Rainer Rupp	Federal Republic of Germany. Member of the Economics Directorate of the North Atlantic Treaty Organization. Specialist in economics and defense. Contributor to the *NATO Review*.
Marten van Heuven	United States. Counselor for Political Affairs at the United States Embassy in Bonn, West Germany. Articles published in the *Digest of International Law* and *International Lawyer*.
Ivan Volgyes	United States. Professor of Political Science, Graduate College, University of Nebraska. Author of numerous books and articles on Eastern Europe; most recently, *Civil-Military Relations in Communist States* with Dale Herspring.
Lawrence L. Whetten	United States. Director of Studies, University of Southern

California, Germany Program. Extensive publication of books, articles, and monographs. Most recently, *The Future of Soviet Military Power*, *Germany East and West: Collaboration and Confrontation*, and *New International Communism* (forthcoming).

Index